Leviticus as Discourse

Leviticus as Discourse

Difficulty and Generativity

Allison K. Hamm

☙PICKWICK *Publications* • Eugene, Oregon

LEVITICUS AS DISCOURSE
Difficulty and Generativity

Copyright © 2025 Allison K. Hamm. All rights reserved. Except for brief quotations in critical publications or reviews, no part of this book may be reproduced in any manner without prior written permission from the publisher. Write: Permissions, Wipf and Stock Publishers, 199 W. 8th Ave., Suite 3, Eugene, OR 97401.

Pickwick Publications
An Imprint of Wipf and Stock Publishers
199 W. 8th Ave., Suite 3
Eugene, OR 97401

www.wipfandstock.com

PAPERBACK ISBN: 979-8-3852-2005-2
HARDCOVER ISBN: 979-8-3852-2006-9
EBOOK ISBN: 979-8-3852-2007-6

Cataloguing-in-Publication data:

Names: Hamm, Allison K., author.

Title: Leviticus as discourse : difficulty and generativity / Allison K. Hamm.

Description: Eugene, OR: Pickwick Publications, 2025. | Includes bibliographical references and index.

Identifiers: ISBN 979-8-3852-2005-2 (paperback). | ISBN 979-8-3852-2006-9 (hardcover). | ISBN 979-8-3852-2007-6 (ebook).

Subjects: LSCH: Bible.—Leviticus—Criticism, interpretation, etc. | Sacrifice—Biblical teaching.

Classification: BS1255.2 2025 (print) | BS1255.2 (ebook)

VERSION NUMBER 02/21/25

Where noted, scripture quotations are taken from *The New Revised Standard Version of the Bible,* © 1989 by the Division of Christian Education of the National Council of the Churches of Christ in the United States of America. Used by permission. All rights reserved.

"Hamm writes not just about one difficult book in the Bible but about what a curious and profoundly humanizing thing it is to try to make sense of difficult books at all. Thus, she demonstrates how patient and persistent practices of interpretation shaped ancient Israel as a community. Lucidly argued, this is a book for a wide range of serious readers, even those who are not disposed to find the Bible interesting."

—**ELLEN F. DAVIS**, Amos Ragan Kearns Distinguished Professor of Bible and Practical Theology, Duke Divinity School

"*Leviticus as Discourse* beckons scholars and lay readers, 'Don't skip Leviticus!' Allison Hamm is a patient and clear guide, re-introducing Leviticus not just as an instruction manual for ancient priests, but as a loving invitation to modern readers to grow and see beyond our lived experience. Reading *Leviticus as Discourse* reminds us that speech creates and destroys life, and it sketches the masterful weaving of law and narrative in this ancient book as a powerful antidote to the corroded public discourse that plagues our society. As a congregational rabbi, I know this book will be a great help for those ten weeks each year that our community reads Leviticus and struggles to translate its lessons for our modern world."

—**DANIEL GREYBER**, rabbi, Beth El Synagogue

"Engaging both the best biblical scholars (Douglas, Milgrom) and the best literary theorists (Steiner, Ricoeur), Allison Hamm takes up the real difficulty posed by the book of Leviticus. Combining deep theoretical insight with deft exegetical probes—all written with a beautiful pen—Hamm moves us from the book's difficulty to its profound generativity for reading communities today. Leviticus moves from back then to here and now, with wide-ranging and life-giving consequences, even in the public square, for all who have ears to attend to this discourse. Hamm's book is a most promising development in Leviticus studies but also has serious ramifications for the study of every book of the Bible."

—**BRENT A. STRAWN**, D. Moody Smith Distinguished Professor of Old Testament, Duke University

"Distilling the insights of earlier writers such as Mary Douglas and Jacob Milgrom, Allison Hamm offers an entry into Leviticus that is deeply learned and vitally alert to contemporary significance. With discernment and clarity, Hamm guides the reader to engage Leviticus anew, opening a world at once strange, delightful, and transformative. Her finely-honed scholarly judgment leads us through difficult concepts and dense passages with suppleness and grace. Hamm's offering shows how painstaking scholarship, pedagogic generosity, and spiritual sensitivity can yield a sparkling work that addresses readers on every level. She convincingly demonstrates that Leviticus is a worthy and enriching conversation partner and invites us to partake of its wisdom for our day."

—**NEHEMIA POLEN**, professor of Jewish thought, Hebrew College, Newton, Massachusetts

For my teachers

Contents

Preface | ix
Introduction | xi

Part I

1. Leviticus as Discourse | 3
2. Interpreting Discourse | 38
3. On Difficulty | 59

Part II

4. The Discourse of Sacrifice: Cultivating Communication | 93
5. Dangerous Discourse, Divine Discernment: Leviticus 24:10–31 | 120
6. Developmental Discourse: Leviticus 10 | 153

Conclusion | 186
Bibliography | 191
Index | 205

Preface

THIS BOOK BEGAN THE first time I read Leviticus.
   That is, the first time I read the whole book, straight through, from beginning to end. Although I had grown up in a faith community for whom Scripture occupied a central role in education and formation, I had read only bits and pieces of Leviticus and retained only a cursory knowledge of its contents. It was not until my first term as a graduate student—on a trajectory of liturgical studies, I thought—that I encountered the book in its integrity as a complete literary unit. Scrambling to finish the assigned reading for the next morning's class, my eyes filled with tears late one night as the vision of Leviticus 26 seemed to come to life before me. I was stunned. There, almost at the end of pages and pages of obscure sacrificial and purity laws (were they laws? Instructions? Or something else?), was a vision of life that was timeless in its appeal—a vision of peace and abundance, of flourishing and shalom. I had no idea that *this* was in Leviticus, coexisting with so much else that seemed indecipherable and irrelevant. And I had no idea what it meant. What was the relationship between this vision and these laws? What was the logic of the book? Why was it written like this, and for whom? How was I to make sense of the fact that a vision of life that has resonated with readers for millennia was apparently inseparable from and contingent upon a *way* of life that has likely never been wholly observed? Above all, why was it so difficult to understand?
   So began ten years of fascination with this strange and beautiful text. The questions it evoked came to shape the course of my graduate work, first with a shift of emphasis from liturgical studies to Hebrew Bible, literary and theological interpretation, and the history of Jewish and Christian interpretation. I am indebted to all who made it possible for me to pursue

these questions: to Duke Divinity School for their generous funding; to Craig Dykstra and Thomas Long for facilitating an independent study on hermeneutics and the biblical imagination when I was just beginning to feel my way toward a thesis; to the faculty of Duke Divinity School for responding to my continual requests for seminars on Leviticus, the Pentateuch, the Deuteronomistic history, and the priestly literature, and for humoring me when I made every course and term paper an opportunity to explore my questions about Leviticus; to Marc Brettler for reading Hebrew with me on his lunch break for multiple semesters; to Stephen Chapman, Laura Lieber, and Nehemia Polen for sharing so generously of their time, encouragement, and bibliographic expertise; and above all to Ellen Davis for her steadfast support and for seeing a "there" there when I could not.

The questions have evolved over the course of these ten years, of course; some answered, and some abandoned. Others have changed the way I understand what it is to ask a question—what it means, and what is at stake, when we encounter something we do not understand. What follows in these pages is a little bit of what I have learned about that encounter.

Technical words and terms appearing in Hebrew are transliterated in parentheses upon first appearance to aid those who do not read Hebrew. When a word, verse, or phrase is quoted or paraphrased in English in the main text, Hebrew is often provided parenthetically without transliteration for the reference of more advanced readers of Hebrew. In grammatical discussions where the appropriate translation is itself the object of discussion and comprehension would be muddled rather than clarified by English, Hebrew words or short phrases sometimes appear without translation. Unless otherwise noted, all translations are my own.

Introduction

"To interpret meaning is . . . to arrive in the middle of an exchange which has already begun and in which we seek to orient ourselves."
—RICHARD KEARNEY[1]

THIS BOOK IS ABOUT interpretation as an activity of self-orientation. It is about what we do when we encounter something we don't understand, why we do it, and what happens in the process. It is also about Leviticus.

The first reason that this book is about both interpretation and Leviticus is that for most readers, Leviticus is the book most associated with bringing aspirations of reading the Bible cover-to-cover to a screeching halt, and so presents itself as an ideal test case for exploring what to do when we encounter something that is difficult to understand and relate to. As Shai Held has observed, "Leviticus seems so utterly foreign, the rituals and practices it describes so alien, the religious vision underlying them so obscure, that connecting to it seems impossible."[2] If we can find a way to overcome the obstacles that Leviticus puts in its readers' paths, perhaps we can find a way to overcome other seemingly impossible things, like relating to people and ideas and ways of being in the world that seem fundamentally opposed to our own. The emphasis here is less about interpreting *Leviticus*, per se, than it is about the activity of interpretation itself; the skills it requires and dispositions it produces in

1. Kearney, *On Paul Ricoeur*, 5.
2. Held, *Heart of Torah*, 3.

us, as readers, and how learning to be good readers—patient, hospitable, curious readers—may help us learn to be better humans.

A second, less lofty, reason that this book approaches questions of interpretation as they arise in relation to Leviticus is that it a response to a specific conversation occurring in biblical studies. Since Jacob Milgrom and Mary Douglas began writing about the book's capacity to speak meaningfully in contemporary moral and ethical discourse a rapidly growing literature has emerged, expanding the field beyond traditional source-critical methods to include anthropological, literary, and rhetorical readings, along with insightful interdisciplinary approaches. Breathing new life into what was once a neglected and often disparaged corner of biblical studies, this renewed interest among students and scholars alike has sprung in large part from the notion, so cogently demonstrated by Milgrom and Douglas, that the vision of life projected in Leviticus may have more in common with the concerns of contemporary life than was once thought. If this strange and ancient text can be properly understood, it may have something meaningful to contribute to contemporary discourse.

Curiously, the scholarly conversation tends to trail off when it turns toward what those contributions actually are, and how they make a difference. At some point between identifying the significance of what Leviticus may have meant in historical contexts and what it means for readers today, the difficulty of bridging the gap seems to nudge readers back toward the familiar shores of the historical critical project. This raises several intriguing hermeneutical questions about the task and aim of interpretation, and the nature of texts and the text/reader relationship. What do we hope to accomplish in "interpretation"—that is, what kind of understanding do we have in mind, and how do we know when we have attained it? What is the locus, or loci, of interpretation? Are some texts too distant, conceptually and chronologically, to spark new conversations? In short: is it possible to bridge the gap between what Leviticus *meant* in past socio-historical contexts, and what it *means* for readers today—and how?

To a certain extent, much of what is discussed here may be transferred to other texts, in other interpretive ventures, insofar as one of the major focal points is the question of what a text is and what happens in the process of reading. In other ways, however, the study is distinctly shaped by the unique character of Leviticus, and the questions that arise directly from its particular strangeness and difficulty: What can we reasonably expect from our encounter with *this* book? What is the place of Leviticus in contemporary discourse, if any?

Arriving in the middle of several conversations as we are, our work will proceed as a series of orientations.

The first of these will be to the scholarly conversation about Leviticus, where we'll listen especially for how biblical scholars have approached the question of the text's capacity to speak in the text/reader relationship. Our aim is to gain a sense of where there have been gaps through which new directions of thought might emerge. In tandem with this will be a fresh orientation to the biblical text. The literary presentation of Leviticus as an event of discourse is the first, most obvious, clue about the kind of text that it is and how it communicates in the text/reader relationship. Surprisingly, the character of the book as discourse has received remarkably little attention, which suggests a promising point of entry for our project of moving the scholarly conversation beyond what Leviticus "said" in historical contexts to what it might "say" in new encounters between the text and its readers. For help on this point, we will turn to the hermeneutic philosopher Paul Ricoeur as an interlocutor, who clarifies discourse as a "creative process of giving form to both the human mind and the world."[3] Ricoeur viewed the task of interpretation as "the art of discerning the discourse in the work" so that reading is an activity with the potential to be a creative, generative encounter between the reader and the kind of world displayed in a certain kind of text.[4]

But what happens when the world that the text displays appears either indistinguishable or uninhabitable? This is the precise point at which the conversation has trailed off, suggesting that a clear articulation of the aim of interpretation may not be sufficient for ensuring a productive encounter with Leviticus. For that, George Steiner's insightful query into difficulty as an aspect of interpretation comes to our aid. Steiner wonders what it means to say that something is hard to understand, which leads him through an exploration of various kinds of difficulty and the interpretive skills that each requires. While the fit is not exact, Steiner's taxonomy helps to elucidate the challenges encountered in Leviticus and give us a better sense of *how*, exactly, to navigate them.

With this orientation to reading as a potentially creative—and unavoidably difficult—encounter between text and reader, we will put this

---

3. Ricoeur, *A Ricoeur Reader*, 69.

4. Ricoeur, *Hermeneutics and the Human Sciences*, 101; and Ricoeur, "Biblical Hermeneutics," 34.

hermeneutic of discourse to the test in Part II by asking how specific aspects of the priestly vision of life that Leviticus projects may spark new directions of thought for contemporary readers. In light of the central role that speech plays in the priestly conception of how new forms of life are brought into existence—the creation account of Gen 1:1—2:4 being the paradigmatic statement of the constitutive power of language—we will examine how speech functions in the priestly writers' portrayal of life in the wilderness community. While this is not the only entry point we could take to test the possibility of engaging the discourse of the text in contemporary conversations, it does recommend itself in light of the book's literary portrayal as an event of discourse, in which YHWH's address to Israel generates new forms of life for the nascent wilderness community. If one of our guiding questions is whether the present-day encounter between text and reader may be similarly generative, then a better understanding of what the priestly writers understood speech to accomplish will surely further our attempt to understand the kind of book that Leviticus is and how it communicates.

Following the cues of the book's literary structure in which the first seven chapters detail the sacrificial regulations, chapter 4 begins with an examination of the role of the sacrificial system in structuring the community in patterns of good communication. The almost total absence of speech in the portrayal of the sacrificial instructions makes this a counter-intuitive probe of the role of language in the wilderness community. In fact, one of the most important studies of the priestly traditions in recent decades, Israel Knohl's *The Sanctuary of Silence: The Priestly Torah and the Holiness School*, comes immediately to mind as a check on the wisdom of such an endeavor. As part of his larger project of demonstrating that the Priestly Torah (PT) and Holiness School (HS) reflect two separate and independent sources within the priestly material, Knohl adopted Yehezkel Kaufmann's phrase "the Sanctuary of Silence" to characterize the cult of PT.[5] Knohl observed that although "PT does provide speeches that accompany the ritual and thus explain cultic actions [i.e., Lev 16:21; Num 5:19–22] . . . Prayer and song are completely absent from PT's cultic system."[6] This "unique phenomenon of the silence of the Priestly cult" was a significant datum in Knohl's quest to clarify the redaction of the priestly material and the Pentateuch more broadly, but

---

5. Knohl's discussion of the silence of the cult appears in *Sanctuary of Silence*, 148–52; see also Kaufmann, *The Religion of Israel*.

6. Knohl, *Sanctuary of Silence*, 148.

the focus of this study is of an entirely different nature.[7] Whereas Knohl was interested in the presence or absence of liturgical language—prayer, songs, or speech—in the historical operation of the cult, to the extent that this can be determined from its textual representation, this study takes a different approach in probing the communicative function of the sacrificial system and its role in structuring the broader speech-patterns of the community. My approach is synchronic and literary, considering the distinction between the sources to the extent that it informs a reading of the text in its final form, but concerned primarily with identifying the direction of thought that the priestly portrayal of the sacrificial system opens up in the present encounter between text and reader. As such, I see no conflict between Knohl's depiction of the virtual silence of the cult in its historical context and our present attempt to discern the role of the sacrificial system in structuring Israel's patterns of discourse. Chapter 4 will thus argue that the relative lack of speech in the literary portrayal of the sacrificial system is not an indication of a lack of discourse, but of a significant shift taking place in how discourse is to be enacted within the wilderness community. Careful attention to the communicative function of sacrifice and the way that human speech does surface within the sacrificial instructions reveals that discourse, broadly conceived, is a constitutive force in structuring and sustaining the Israelite community.

Chapter 5 will examine the most explicit treatment of human speech in the book of Leviticus, the so-called narrative of the blasphemer that appears in 24:10–23. The narrative distills some of the most important themes of Leviticus, expanding and elaborating on the view of speech that emerges from its treatment in the sacrificial regulations, namely, that it is a powerful force capable of altering reality. The story explores the potential consequences of destructive speech and the responsibility of the community to limit its effects, homing in on this central aspect of the priestly vision of life that the whole book projects. Finally, chapter 6 will explore how Leviticus 10 opens up a substantive reflection on the challenges and requirements of interpretation. This chapter directly engages the difficulties of interpretation through its literary portrayal of Aaron in the aftermath of the deaths of his sons, Nadav and Avihu, revealing a priestly understanding of interpretation as situational, unavoidable, and potentially dangerous. At the same time, the narrative underscores the necessity of interpretation to maintaining a life of human flourishing.

7. Knohl, *Sanctuary of Silence*, 148.

Simply put, the priestly writers reflect an awareness that to be human is to be engaged in the ongoing work of interpretation: of orienting oneself in relation to YHWH, to one another, and to the life possibilities that emerge from those encounters.

Through these exegetical probes, we will be seeking to orient ourselves to the vision of life that the priestly writers project in the book of Leviticus, and to see whether there are points of contact between that world and our own—to see, as Ricoeur writes, if it is a world "which I could inhabit and wherein I could project one of my ownmost possibilities."[8]

---

8. Ricoeur, *Hermeneutics and the Human Sciences*, 104.

PART I

1

Leviticus as Discourse

וַיִּקְרָא אֶל־מֹשֶׁה וַיְדַבֵּר יְהוָה אֵלָיו מֵאֹהֶל מוֹעֵד לֵאמֹר: דַּבֵּר אֶל־בְּנֵי יִשְׂרָאֵל וְאָמַרְתָּ אֲלֵהֶם

And He called to Moses and spoke to him from the Tent of Meeting, saying: Speak to the Israelite people, and say to them . . .

—LEV 1:1–2A

אֵלֶּה הַמִּצְוֹת אֲשֶׁר צִוָּה יְהוָה אֶת־מֹשֶׁה אֶל־בְּנֵי יִשְׂרָאֵל בְּהַר סִינָי

These are the commandments that the LORD gave Moses for the Israelite people on Mount Sinai.

—LEV 27:34

LEVITICUS BEGINS AND ENDS as an event of discourse. YHWH speaks to Moses and through him to Israel, instructing them in the requirements for maintaining the tabernacle and, through it, their relationship to the divine presence. YHWH's instructions to Moses thus become the blueprint for Israel's new way of life in the land, forming them as a community centered around the divine presence in their post-Egypt reality.

YHWH speaks, and something happens: new forms of life are generated, taking shape in the daily rhythms of Israel's cultic and communal life in the wilderness.

For Israel, this event of YHWH's discourse at Sinai generates new ways of thinking and being in at least three major ways. First, Israel learns the symbolic language of sacrifice that will enable them to maintain an open line of communication with the divine. Just as the divine speech is mediated to Israel through Moses, the people cannot directly respond to YHWH; instead, the sacrificial system mediates Israel's range of responses as an alternative form of discourse, simultaneously shaping the community in patterns of communication that can sustain their life together. Second, Israel learns that it is not only the divine word that is a powerful force in either maintaining or threatening the social order. Created in the image of the divine and tasked with reflecting YHWH's holiness (Gen 1:27; Lev 19:2), everyone within the community is held responsible to enact speech in ways that cultivate life rather than death. Third, Israel learns that even these major structuring parameters that enable the community to live in proximity to the divine do not reduce their relationship with YHWH to a system of mechanical formulas. An inevitable ambiguity and provisionality inheres even in divine discourse, necessitating an ongoing process of discerning the forms of life that lead to safety and flourishing. In these three important ways, YHWH's instructions to Moses initiate and involve Israel in a dynamic experience of living in proximity to the divine presence. The event of discourse does something, in and among the people of Israel.

For readers of Leviticus, there are two aspects to the literary shape of this divine discourse. On one hand, the narrative frame of the book presents YHWH's instructions to Israel as taking place in a specific moment in Israel's past. The community stands poised outside the newly constructed Tent of Meeting—in the wilderness, at Sinai, continuing the narrative of Exod 40:33—to receive the instructions for its initiation and ongoing maintenance. On the other hand, this historical narrative almost immediately gives way to a literary style that evokes a sense of timelessness and immediacy. The narrative flow of *vayyiqtol* forms in Lev 1:1 (וַיִּקְרָא . . . וַיְדַבֵּר) transitions seamlessly into conditional statements (תַּקְרִיבוּ . . . כִּי־יַקְרִיב, Lev 1:2) and imperfective verbal forms (וְסָמַךְ . . . שָׁחַט, Lev 1:4, 5), destabilizing any clear sense of grammatical tense or narrative time. Analyzing "The Language of Leviticus," John Sawyer observes, for example, that "no prose work [in the Bible] (with the exception of Qohelet) has fewer *vayyiqtol* forms per 10,000 words than Leviticus. Conversely, *veqatal* forms are almost three times as frequent in Leviticus . . . as they are anywhere else."[1] The effect of this unusual literary style, situated as it is in its historical-narrative frame, is that the event of discourse is portrayed as at once past, present, and future. Witnessing Israel's experience of encountering YHWH in the discourse at the Tent of Meeting, the reader of Leviticus thus feels herself to be somehow included in the vision of life that is generated, invited to imagine the kind of world that the discourse creates. While readers are aware that Leviticus relates an aspect of Israel's story, and that Moses's divine instructions are not directly addressed to the twenty-first century reader, the grammar of the book nevertheless creates an indeterminacy that suggests the potential of the discourse of Leviticus—mediated to Israel through Moses, and to the reader through the text—to generate new forms of life beyond a single historical locus.

From this observation, questions arise: Could there be an analogy between reading Leviticus—"reading" here maximally understood as everything involved in the process of interpretation—and Israel's encounter with YHWH at Sinai? Is the immediacy of YHWH's creative, life-generating speech at the Tent of Meeting lost to the twenty-first century reader, or might it be mediated through literary representation? Is there latent generative potential in the text/reader relationship? In short, can something happen when we read Leviticus—and how?[2]

To pose these questions is to join a larger conversation about the meaning and significance of Leviticus for contemporary readers. In many ways, this conversation has been shaped by the work of Jacob Milgrom and Mary Douglas, who were themselves responding to the dominant

---

1. Sawyer, "Language of Leviticus," in *Reading Leviticus*, 16–17.

2. The notion of sacred texts mediating an encounter with the divine word finds precedent in many religious traditions, of course. Notably, Ruth Langer has traced the development of ritualized Torah reading within the synagogue in her article, "From Study of Scripture to a Reenactment of Sinai." Langer observes that in the period following the destruction of the Second Temple, the Torah scroll itself comes to be seen as "the single object best connecting the community with God's revelatory voice" (Langer, 49). The ritual reading of the scroll is thus seen as more than mere study, but the "embodiment of the Sinai revelation" and "a reenactment of Sinai itself" (Langer, 51–52). The analogy that we will be probing in subsequent chapters similarly emphasizes the possibility of encountering the divine word through the text. In contrast to Langer's focus, however, my interest is in the ways that this encounter is mediated through the *language* of the text and the interpretive process that the reader engages, rather than in the ritualized reenactment of Sinai in synagogue reading.

perspectives of Leviticus that had shaped critical scholarship prior to the mid-twentieth century. Before turning to our questions in earnest, then, we begin by orienting ourselves to these earlier conversations.

The Muted Text: An Unlikely Conversation Partner?

In the preface to his Continental Commentary, Jacob Milgrom observed that when he began his research in the early nineteen-sixties Leviticus had been largely overlooked and undervalued as a topic of critical study by both Jews and Christians, as evidenced by the publication of only one comprehensive commentary over the course of the past century.[3] Indeed, Leviticus has long presented a unique challenge to both Jews and Christians as the book of the Bible most heavily laden with instructions for practices that have been obsolete for centuries. Rabbi Jonathan Sacks, for example, considers Leviticus to be the most difficult of the Mosaic books for contemporary readers to relate to, while Erhard Gerstenberger opened his 1996 commentary with the observation that Leviticus had been largely ignored in the Christian teaching, preaching, and study of his generation.[4] While accurate in certain respects, these comments belie the fact that Leviticus has also been a central text for both Jewish and Christian communities for over two millennia, if in varying ways. A brief orientation to the field of Leviticus studies prior to the nineteen sixties will thus help clarify the significance of what Milgrom and Douglas brought to the conversation.

Milgrom identified two main factors in treatments of Leviticus that eventually led to the interpretive desert—the "tabula rasa," as he called it—of the mid-twentieth century: bias and atomization.[5] Among

---

3. It is not quite clear what Milgrom meant by "comprehensive commentary," since several works had been published in the century preceding the 1990s in both English and German. These included Martin Noth's Old Testament Library commentary (1977), Gordon Wenham's New International commentary (1979), and Baruch Levine's JPS Torah Commentary (1989). Milgrom's comment in the introduction to *Leviticus 1–16* provides a clue in that he distinguishes between commentaries that were verse-by-verse or of a more popular nature (p. 66), but he still does not satisfactorily explain his characterization of Leviticus's neglect. The most plausible solution I might suggest is that by "comprehensive," Milgrom intended to designate verse-by-verse commentaries that exhaustively addressed all difficulties of Leviticus, both critical and theological, which was his aim in the Anchor Bible commentary. See Milgrom, *Leviticus: A Continental Commentary*, xi.

4. Sacks, *Leviticus*, 1; Gerstenberger, *Leviticus*, 2.

5. Milgrom, *Leviticus: A Continental Commentary*, xii.

Christian interpreters, two representative texts serve to illustrate the long history of bias toward Leviticus. In the modern era, the influence of Julius Wellhausen's legacy on studies of Leviticus, both critical and theological, cannot be overstated. His personal introduction to the Old Testament, in which his "enjoyment of the [prophetic books] was marred by the Law ... intrud[ing] itself uneasily, like a ghost that makes a noise," formed the foundation of his strong bias against the priestly material and the corresponding view that it was a late accretion in the formation of the Hebrew Bible.[6] In this formulation, Wellhausen's view of the Priestly Code as the final stage of the transformation from the "green tree" of authentic, heartfelt Israelite worship to the "dry wood" of rote, cultic legislation became a widely accepted historical narrative of spiritual decline.[7] This narrative relied explicitly on the notion, particularly familiar to Protestants, of a firm distinction between the spirit and the letter, as Wellhausen writes:

> The worshipper no longer thinks that in his gift he is doing God a pleasure, providing Him with an enjoyment: what pleases Him and is effectual is only the strict observance of the rite. The sacrifices must be offered exactly according to prescription: at the right place, at the right time, by the right individuals, in the right way. They are not based on the inner value of what is done, on the impulse arising out of fresh occasions, but on the positive command of a will outside the worshipper, which is not explained, and which prescribes every particular ... Worship no longer springs from an inner impulse, it has come to be an exercise of religiosity.[8]

This narrative of spiritual decline that Wellhausen saw in the formation of the Pentateuch and buttressed with his scholarly writing bore a striking resemblance to the long history of Christian supersessionism stretching all the way back to another seminal text in Christian interpretation of Leviticus: The Letter to the Hebrews.

While re-interpreting the Hebrew Scriptures in light of the Christ event is an anchoring thread that runs throughout the New Testament, questions surrounding the cult come most clearly into focus in the Letter to the Hebrews. In the process of reconsidering the role of the levitical priesthood (Heb 7:11), the purpose of the covenant (Heb 8:6–7), and the

6. Wellhausen, *Prolegomena*, 3.
7. Wellhausen, *Prolegomena*, 361.
8. Wellhausen, *Prolegomena*, 424.

efficacy of the sacrificial system (Heb 10:1, 4), the rhetoric of Hebrews draws a series of contrasts pitting "old" against "new" in a probing reconsideration of the tradition. Unfortunately for Leviticus, this rhetoric has often been construed as a systematic rejection of the cult and its logic as "obsolete" (Heb 8:13, NRSV) and irrelevant. As more recent work has demonstrated, however, this reading of Hebrews as a polemic against Levitical sacrifice is a distorting oversimplification of the nuanced and reasoned argument of the Letter.[9] Indeed, in some ways the history of interpretation of Hebrews can be read as a capsule of the history of Christian supersessionism—a history that has grounded bias against and marginalization of Leviticus even among scholars of the Old Testament.[10]

Without minimizing the grave social and historical consequences that have resulted from Christian supersessionism, bias against the cultic legislation that forms the backbone of Leviticus has not been the exclusive domain of Christian readers. Running parallel to Christian views of the priestly legislation as superseded by the New Covenant, a Jewish counterpart exists in what Jonathan Klawans has termed an "evolutionary" or "developmental" perspective of religion. Klawans cites an early expression of this view in Maimonides's comparison of the sacrificial laws to mother's milk that is naturally outgrown, and sees this view resurfacing throughout a history of synagogue reform and Jewish scholarship that "operates on the assumption that sacrifice is hopelessly outmoded and meaningless."[11] This view of sacrifice as a historically necessary and yet inferior precursor to better understandings and ways of relating to the

---

9. In my view, the open-endedness of the argument set forth in Hebrews actually leaves room for the possibility that some aspects of ritual law could continue to be observed within the ongoing practices of the faith community. For example, the critique of the law that is mounted in Hebrews is carefully circumscribed to appraise only specific aspects of ritual law as it intersects with the author's understanding of the significance of Jesus's work, and is not a general denunciation of "the law" as such, as Hebrews is frequently read. For some of the key voices that support this view of the logic of Hebrews as a positive engagement with the priestly material, begin with: Moffitt, *Atonement*; and Hays, "'No Lasting City'" in *Epistle to the Hebrews*, ed. Bauckham, et al., 151–73; followed by Skarsaune's response to Hays in the same volume, pp. 174–82; and Nanos's follow-up, pp. 183–88. For a Jewish perspective that positively engages the resonances between Hebrews and Leviticus, see Polen, "Leviticus," 213–25. Finally, for a provocative argument that the logic informing Hebrews is ultimately self-defeating if read as a full-scale critique of Old Testament law, see Wedderburn, "Sawing off the Branches."

10. For further bibliography and a framing of this discussion as bias more specifically in regard to the temple and cult rather than Leviticus, per se, see Klawans, *Purity*, particularly pp. 3–8, and 213–45.

11. Klawans, *Purity*, 8–9.

divine, such as prayer, relies on an anachronistic dissection of moral and ritual categories similar to the logic that grounded Wellhausen's low view of the priestly tradition. "In both cases," Klawans argues, "what becomes important in subsequent religious developments is also seen as inherently superior, of greater spiritual and even symbolic value."[12]

Ironically, these two major interpretative streams construe Leviticus in completely opposite ways. In Wellhausen's formulation, the book is the pinnacle of a late accretion that corrupted earlier, purer forms of spirituality, while claims of supersessionism and developmentalism would frame it as a primitive, outmoded expression of worship destined to be reformed. In either case, Leviticus loses: the text's ability to speak is muted by the bias that has shaped both religious and scholarly reading communities.

A second major factor that has contributed to the neglect of comprehensive study of Leviticus in the twentieth century is a tendency toward fragmentation. Milgrom critiqued the atomized nature of traditional Jewish study of the book, observing that "even in advanced schools of Torah studies Leviticus is not studied in its entirety, but only in a verse here, a verse there."[13] While this method of study could generously be understood as a necessary approach to the challenges of applying Leviticus holistically in the absence of a functioning sacrificial system, the lack of systematic or comprehensive treatment of the book as a whole is in fact characteristic of traditional Jewish commentary more broadly. In an influential study, James Kugel describes rabbinic literature as "atomistic," noting that treatments of a single verse or phrase may be so "interchangeable, modifiable, [or] combinable" that grounding a particular verse in its immediate surrounding context—in this case, Leviticus as a discrete book—is deprioritized in favor of weaving a web of broader connections, with the result that not only Torah, but the Hebrew Bible and Jewish traditions may be included within the interpretive context.[14]

Responsibility for the fragmentation of Leviticus does not rest solely with traditional Jewish scholarship and commentary, however. Mary Douglas also noted that in biblical scholarship more broadly Leviticus had largely "been read in an itemized way, items of law corresponding to elements of morality, or to elements of narrative, or to elements of

---

12. Klawans, *Purity*, 9.
13. Milgrom, *Leviticus: A Continental Commentary*, xii.
14. Kugel, "Two Introductions," 147.

hygiene, but not to their place in an integral composition."[15] As we will later examine more closely, the problem with this approach is that breaking Leviticus down into its constituent parts obscures an underlying logic that makes the book a meaningful whole. As a result, these atomized parts of the text appear as an odd collection of "esoteric and irrelevant" rules, unmoored from any unifying literary structures within which they are intelligible and logical.[16]

While we have framed the factors of bias and atomization from the perspective of the mid-twentieth century, it is important to underscore that these approaches to Leviticus did not originate in the modern era but sprang from deep roots in both Jewish and Christian interpretive traditions. With the developments of modern critical scholarship, however, other factors contributed to the already bleak outlook for Leviticus in the minds of modern readers. Two of these factors are particularly significant for our interest in Leviticus as discourse: first, a shift toward prioritizing the text's history, and second, the separation of theological from historical study in mainstream academic scholarship.

From the end of the Enlightenment through the twentieth century, biblical scholarship has, with a few notable exceptions, been characterized by its interest in the world that shaped and produced the biblical text, and study of Leviticus has not been exempt from these broader trends. In the modern era, questions of critical scholarship came to revolve around P, its relationship to H, and their mutual significance for determining the composition and redaction history of the Pentateuch. Furthermore, the significance of these text- and redaction-critical probes were of interest primarily for what they might reveal about the history of Israelite religion and the transmission of its traditions—specifically, about the world that gave rise to the biblical text.[17] More importantly for the purpose of this study, in spite of an expansion of knowledge about Leviticus and its provenance, the text became no more accessible to modern-day readers interested in its contemporary significance. In fact, the new emphasis of modern critical scholars on the historical and social world that lay behind the received form of the text had the unintended effect of amplifying its foreign and alien character for modern readers.

---

15. Douglas, *Leviticus as Literature*, 86.

16. Milgrom, *Leviticus: A Continental Commentary*, xiii.

17. For useful summaries of the shape of historical-critical interest in Leviticus, see Bibb et al., *Text, Time, and Temple*, 1–15; and Elliott, *Engaging Leviticus*, xi–xxi.

A major reason for this scholarly prioritization of the text's history was the occurrence of a growing divide among mainstream, largely Protestant, scholars between what was considered objective, historical study of the biblical text and the consideration of its theological and practical meaning. Positively, this separation meant the possibility of a new autonomy for scholars from the ecclesiastical authorities of received tradition that shaped interpretation of Scripture according to doctrine and creed.[18] Yet this new autonomy also "freed" scholars from consideration of how study of the history of a text might come to bear upon the moral vision of its readers, a role traditionally filled through theological interpretation. Moreover, Ellen Davis has observed that to engage in such consideration was seen as a category error in light of an assumption on the part of modern critical scholars that "the social world informing the text does not include us in any way."[19] With these two forces at play—a new scholarly awareness of the extent to which the historical location of the text was not contiguous with that of its readers, and an increasingly tenuous connection between historical and theological interpretation in mainstream biblical scholarship—Leviticus seemed to drift further into irrelevance.

When Milgrom and Douglas began their work with Leviticus in the middle of the twentieth century, then, the book had largely been relegated to the margins of biblical study. To the extent that it was read and studied at all, it was of value to Christian scholars primarily as a source of information about the formation of the Pentateuch and development of Israelite religion, and to Jewish scholars for its halakhic implications.[20] Douglas rightly perceived that among scholars and lay readers alike, "Leviticus is usually put into a kind of glass cabinet: it can be looked at, respected, and wondered at, but the real heart of religion is presumed to be found in other parts of the Bible."[21]

Speaking of Leviticus: Recent Developments

Bias and neglect are no longer the defining characteristics of Leviticus studies, however. The past fifty years have seen a resurgence of interest

18. For an incisive and well-balanced summary of the values that shaped the diverse field of historical critical studies, see Collins, *The Bible after Babel*, 4–5.
19. Davis, "Prophecy and the Power of Life" in Paddison and Messer, *The Bible: Culture, Community, Society*, 51.
20. Milgrom, *Leviticus: A Continental Commentary*, xii.
21. Douglas, *Leviticus as Literature*, 1.

in Leviticus on a variety of fronts, including an optimistic gesture toward the text's ability to speak beyond its originating context. This section will sketch the current shape of the field as it informs our interest in the discourse of Leviticus in two parts. First we will consider the groundbreaking work of Jacob Milgrom and Mary Douglas, who changed the tone of the interpretive conversation by countering the two main factors identified above as driving forces in the marginalization and neglect of serious study of Leviticus, namely, an atomized focus on individual elements of the text that obscured a view of the book as a coherent, logical whole, and bias against ritual and priestly matters that led to the dismissal of those aspects of Leviticus considered irrelevant or obsolete. By forging a path through these impasses, Douglas and Milgrom showed that it was not only possible to understand the book, but perhaps even desirable; Leviticus may have something valuable to contribute to contemporary conversations. While critical scholarship has in many ways metabolized and moved beyond Milgrom and Douglas, the primary motivation driving their work—namely, to articulate the book's timeless moral and ethical significance in a way that has real bearing on people's lives—has been curiously sidelined. Because of this, revisiting their contributions to the field is important not only as background for the current conversation, but also because the interpretive approach taken in the following chapters builds on this particular facet of their work.

Second, we will take stock of some key aspects of scholarship as it has developed since Milgrom and Douglas in response to the question of how Leviticus may—or may not—speak. We will briefly sketch the scholarly conversation surrounding the kind of text that it is and how it communicates, concluding with a case study of James Watts's rhetorical analysis of Leviticus as representative of how the question of discourse has generally been approached.

Redirecting the Conversation: Mary Douglas and Jacob Milgrom

Mary Douglas's interest in Leviticus began with her study of the dietary laws of Leviticus and Deuteronomy. Confronted with the local rules about food that she experienced during her field study in Congo, Douglas turned to the Bible for parallel examples of food laws functioning as a classification system of purity in primitive societies. This appeal to the Bible for comparative data was common among anthropologists of

Douglas's time, following a precedent set by William Robertson Smith and transmitted to Douglas through the influence of Émile Durkheim and E. E. Evans-Pritchard.[22] But while her initial interest in the Old Testament may have been as a proof-text for examples to support other research, Douglas became increasingly fascinated with the biblical text itself as a primary ethnographic source.[23] The first iteration of her theories on defilement and ritual pollution appeared in *Purity and Danger* in 1966, with an entire chapter devoted to "The Abominations of Leviticus." This study would eventually come to be considered one of the most influential treatments of purity and defilement in any discipline, "stimulat[ing] a vivid discourse in Hebrew Bible studies" and becoming "the theoretical work that still dominates the discussion" of purity.[24]

A crucial plank in Douglas's analysis of pollution rules was the theory that defilement only makes sense when viewed within the total structure of a society's thought. "No particular set of classifying symbols can be understood in isolation," she wrote.[25] To illustrate this, Douglas turned to the example of dirt, pointing to how different societies and cultures define what is considered "dirty." All cultures have certain avoidance behaviors that express ideas of defilement, Douglas explained, but the specific behaviors can, and often do, vary from culture to culture. Furthermore, dirtiness is a dynamic concept, meaning that what is dirty is often a matter of appropriateness within a given place or time. Shoes on one's feet or on the floor are acceptable; shoes on the kitchen counter are not. Food on the plate is clean; food on your shirt is dirty. The concept of defilement, in short, depends on an ordered system of classification. "No single item is dirty apart from a particular system of classification in which it does not fit," she perceived; this is why the individual purity rules of Leviticus, when considered in isolation, have no meaning.[26]

---

22. Richard Fardon provides an incisive commentary on the place of the Old Testament in Douglas's intellectual formation in *Mary Douglas*. See especially pp. 41–45, and 185–205.

23. As Fardon observes, Douglas's fascination with the Bible continued throughout her life, culminating in her resolve to take up the study of Hebrew when she was well into her eighties. See Fardon, *Mary Douglas*, 190. Douglas herself reflects on this undertaking in her delightful essay, "Why I Have to Learn Hebrew," 147–65.

24. Schmitt, "Leviticus 14.33–57 as Intellectual Ritual" in Bibb et al., *Text, Time, and Temple*, 197; Klawans, *Purity*, 17.

25. Douglas, *Purity and Danger*, vii.

26. Douglas, *Purity and Danger*, xvii.

While her work in *Purity and Danger* had already generated a transformation in how the purity systems of the Bible were understood, Douglas's interest in the Bible was still gaining momentum. After writing a series of articles and a book on defilement in the book of Numbers in the early 1990s, Douglas turned to a full-scale treatment of Leviticus in which she maintained the structuralist approach that informed her study of pollution and avoidance behaviors more broadly.[27] In *Leviticus as Literature* Douglas embarked on a re-reading of the purity structures of Leviticus, rethinking and reworking how she understood them to function in the priestly worldview. At the same time, she also expanded her investigation to include the larger purity and sacrificial systems of the book, taking them into account as part of a broader structure of meaning. Douglas was intrigued to discover that there had been hardly any agreement on the meaning of the dietary laws among biblical commentators, summarizing previous interpretations as taking one of two tacks: either the rules were deemed to be essentially "arbitrary and meaningless," or they were read allegorically, in search of a deeper (and not necessarily inherent) spiritual meaning. "Which is to say," Douglas concludes, that such treatments were "not interpretations at all, since they deny any significance to the rules. They express bafflement in a learned way."[28] Her analysis, as we have seen, was that scholars had attempted to decipher the meaning of individual elements of the purity system rather than taking them together as a systematic whole. As she had consistently argued, the rules of Leviticus make no sense apart from the total structure of thought that grounds their meaning. Consequently, "any interpretations will fail which take the Do-nots of the Old Testament in a piecemeal fashion. The only sound approach is to forget hygiene, aesthetics, morals and instinctive revulsion . . . and start with the texts."[29]

Douglas was not advocating an a-historical approach, blindly ignorant of any socio-historical context; instead, she was making a forceful argument for prioritizing the logic of the biblical text as its own best interpreter. This prioritization of the text and its literary context was

---

27. Douglas's series of articles leading up to her full-length work on Leviticus include, "The Forbidden Animals in Leviticus" (1993); "Atonement in Leviticus" (1993); "The Glorious Book of Numbers" (1994); "Holy Joy" (1994); and "The Stranger in the Bible" (1994). For the most complete bibliography of Douglas's publications of which I am aware, see Fardon, *Mary Douglas*, 269–92.

28. Douglas, *Leviticus as Literature*, vi; *Purity and Danger*, 54–57.

29. Douglas, *Purity and Danger*, 62.

Douglas's conscious response to the problem of the lack of comparative material for the purity systems of Leviticus, as she relates in the first chapter of *Leviticus as Literature*:

> The first task of the anthropologist in studying religions is to locate the religion in some community of worshippers in some known historical time and space, and there is no shortage of information about common religions in the Near East. But the Bible itself made a clean sweep of its regional connections ... the religion of the Pentateuch claims to have nothing in common with the neighbouring religions.[30]

The logic of Douglas's argument was that in the absence of comparative data from the ancient Near East, the best source of insight into the logic of the text is the text itself. The meaning of the individual purity rules comes into focus in relationship to the other rules, and together they express an entire system of thought.

One of the main influences shaping Douglas's structuralist approach was Émile Durkheim's insight that a society's values are ensconced in their rituals. Douglas's work became so influential in the study of Leviticus first because she was a pioneer in applying a Durkheimian perspective to the biblical purity laws, and also because of the influence of this anthropological school on the contemporaneous work of Jacob Milgrom. Douglas's insistence that the dietary rules of Leviticus 11 form a logical system that reflects the broader values of a society found a ready hearing with Milgrom, who three years prior to the publication of *Purity and Danger* had argued that the dietary laws formed and expressed an "ethical system" with an overarching rationale of holiness.[31] While Milgrom had already begun to develop his view that the purity rules formed their own internal logic, he acknowledged that he had reached something of an impasse regarding what that logic was. "Frankly, this sleuthing assignment cannot be fulfilled," he wrote; "the tracks lose themselves in the sands of unrecorded time."[32] At the time, he offered some provisional explanations of the animal classifications on linguistic and archaeological grounds, but his later work would benefit greatly from Douglas's Durkheimian insight

---

30. Douglas, *Leviticus as Literature*, 2. Milgrom's discussion of Leviticus 11 in *Leviticus 1–16*, 718–36, and his treatment of the "Antiquity of P" on pp. 3–13 provides support on this point, clarifying the lack of comparative evidence for the purity systems of Leviticus.

31. Milgrom, "Biblical Diet Laws," 291.

32. Milgrom, "Biblical Diet Laws," 294.

that the logic of the dietary laws could not be understood in isolation from other aspects of the ritual system and must also take into account the logic grounding the purity and sacrificial systems. On many points Milgrom would take issue with Douglas's treatment of Leviticus 11 as it was formulated in *Purity and Danger*, as she herself later would do, but on this they were in accord: Israel's animal taxonomy had to be viewed in light of the other classification systems of the priestly rationale.[33]

When Milgrom published the first volume of his Anchor Bible commentary on Leviticus he followed an explicitly synchronic approach, in an implicit counterpoint to the form- and source-critical methods that had dominated previous studies of the priestly material. Rather than "dissecting the whole into its parts," Milgrom's approach took "each literary unit as a whole and attempt[ed] first to demonstrate the interaction of its parts."[34] At the macro level he examined three systems: sources of impurity, which "form a system governed by the priestly rationale"; dietary laws, which were "contiguous to and form a continuum with the bodily impurities"; and the sacrificial system, which was "intimately connected with the impurity system."[35] Underscoring the need to read these systems as mutually informative and constructive of meaning, Milgrom reiterated his earlier view that the specific details of the rules, when abstracted from the context that gave them significance, appear to be "arbitrary and meaningless in themselves." However, they "serve a larger, extrinsic purpose" when taken as a whole, namely that together they articulate the broader priestly vision of a holy and ethical life.[36]

Once it had been demonstrated that a coherent and rational logic grounds the priestly systems, countering the negative bias that permeated attitudes about Leviticus was only a matter of course. For Douglas, Leviticus was a casualty of two popular misperceptions that had distorted views of early forms of religion more broadly: the idea that ancient cultures reflected a primitive mentality, and a widespread resistance to ritualism of any sort. Douglas located both of these misperceptions in "the confused nineteenth-century dialogue between anthropology and theology" that allowed scholars to discuss topics such as "the natives' intellectual problems," disparaging rituals as illogical superstition and

---

33. Milgrom, *Leviticus 1–16*, see esp. 719–26.
34. Milgrom, *Leviticus 1–16*, 2.
35. Milgrom, *Leviticus 1–16*, 46–49.
36. Milgrom, *Leviticus 1–16*, 46.

explaining them in terms of moral evolutionism.[37] In contrast, Douglas identified with the generation of Oxford anthropologists who, following Evans-Pritchard, believed that "however peculiar they might seem to us, the strange beliefs of a foreign tradition make sense."[38] Douglas's analogy between the concept of dirt and avoidance behaviors is perhaps the clearest demonstration of applying her anthropological training to the work of dismantling the misperception of biblical purity rules as primitive and illogical. "The concept of dirt," she wrote, "makes a bridge between our own contemporary culture and those other cultures."[39] For contemporary readers struggling to relate to the logic of ritual purity the concept of dirt establishes common ground, showing that both concepts are grounded in a logic of classification that determines what is "dirty" or "clean." While the biblical notion of purity is more complex than a simple matter of being clean or dirty, Douglas used the analogy of dirt to show that impurity is grounded in a logical system of thought. The concept of dirt casts the logic of purity in terms we can more readily understand, laying the groundwork for a more nuanced understanding of biblical purity rules on their own terms.

In response to the unexamined antiritualism that characterized much of the study of religion in her generation, Douglas worked to demonstrate continuity between Leviticus and the rest of the Bible. As an anthropologist interested in the unifying experiences of humanity, Douglas was intrigued by the fact that of all the books in the Bible, Leviticus and Numbers remained "obdurately opaque" while the rest of the Bible "seems to stand as a beacon of clarity and light in spite of radical changes of emphasis" and reinterpretations through succeeding generations.[40] Observing that "a negative bias runs throughout source criticism, a prejudice against the priestly editors," Douglas was skeptical of the source-critical distinction set forth by Israel Knohl and others that characterized the view of holiness expressed in P as technical and narrow, in contrast to a more holistic, expansive holiness of H.[41] In this distinction between the sources, P is understood to frame holiness as a cultic

37. See Douglas's discussion in *Purity and Danger*, 1–35; and *Leviticus as Literature*, v–viii.
38. Douglas, *Leviticus as Literature*, v–vi.
39. Douglas, *Purity and Danger*, xi.
40. Douglas, *Leviticus as Literature*, 12.
41. Douglas, *Leviticus as Literature*, 33. Douglas was referring to Knohl's argument as articulated in *The Sanctuary of Silence*.

concern limited to the operations of the sanctuary, while H advances the concept of holiness to include the entire land of Israel and the social-ethical morality that Israel is called to embody as YHWH's covenant people.[42] Citing Knohl's comment on Lev 6:2–6 (a P text) in which he claims that "the ritual experience is detached from the sphere of social morality," Douglas expressed frustration with Knohl's "mild sarcasm" that "conforms with a long tradition of P-baiting."[43] This distinction between P and H, Douglas thought, "sounds suspiciously like a denominational preference, [resulting in] literary interpretation driven by theology."[44] She read this source-critical parsing as a criticism of priestly concerns based on an anachronistic, "modern, dilute idea of holiness" which elevated the so-called ethical morality of H over the "old power and terror" of P's cultic holiness.[45] Douglas's underlying point was that Leviticus is not an obscure anomaly among the books of the Torah, the black sheep of the flock. Properly understood, it enriches and expands themes that are woven throughout the Bible as a multi-faceted whole. By drawing out the ways that the symbol systems of Leviticus reflect values consistent with themes that run throughout the Bible, particularly the covenantal justice that she saw uniquely expressed through the dietary and purity laws, Douglas mounted a vigorous challenge to antiritualism as it was expressed in bias against the priestly writers.[46]

Milgrom's approach to countering the priestly bias that had previously marginalized Leviticus was more subtle than Douglas's explicit resistance to the moral evolutionism and antiritualism of previous scholarship. Rather than mounting a direct defense, Milgrom rehabilitated views of Leviticus through an exegetical practice that probed for the underlying values grounding the logic of the purity and sacrificial systems, thus illumining the larger ethical principles that the rituals expressed. Milgrom argued that the values embodied in the priestly vision of life offer timeless moral and ethical insight that "can help us resolve the vexing moral and social issues confronting humanity in our time."[47] In the sacrificial system, for example, he saw a practice of recognizing and honoring the sanctity of all life through the regulations that apply to the taking of

---

42. Milgrom, *Leviticus 1–16*, 48–49.
43. Douglas, *Leviticus as Literature*, 129.
44. Douglas, *Leviticus as Literature*, 34.
45. Douglas, *Leviticus as Literature*, 129.
46. Douglas, *Leviticus as Literature*, 2.
47. Milgrom, *Leviticus: A Continental Commentary*, 50.

animal life. Sacrifice is restricted to only three types of domestic animals (Lev 1:1–17; 3:1–17), which can be offered only at a central altar (Lev 17:2–9), and violating either of these restrictions is equated with murder, as articulated in Lev 17:3–4:

> If anyone of the house of Israel slaughters an ox or a lamb or a goat in the camp, or slaughters it outside the camp and does not bring it to the entrance of the tent of meeting, to present it as an offering to YHWH before the tabernacle of YHWH, he shall be held guilty of bloodshed; he has shed blood, and he shall be cut off from the people (NRSV).

These restrictions articulate, in Milgrom's reading, a way of life that is an "ethical summit," complementing and illumining the seemingly odd animal classifications in the dietary regulations in Leviticus 11:

> If the long list of prohibited animals has as its aim the restriction of meat to three domestic quadrupeds, whose blood (according to H) must be offered up on the altar of the central sanctuary, what else could the compliant Israelite derive from this arduous discipline except that all life must be treated with reverence?[48]

Similarly, Milgrom pointed out that the graduated economic values of the purification offerings keep concern for the poor at the center of the worshipping life. Everyone in the community, regardless of economic position or means, is allowed to bring what he or she can afford as an acceptable offering to YHWH (Lev 5:1–13). And even the social structures of the Israelite community, rather than constituting a strict hierarchy of priestly control, can be understood to reveal an ordered, mutually dependent division of responsibility in which worshippers relied on the priest for facilitating the proper sacrificial practices in a "partnership of trust," while the priests, in turn, bore greater responsibility before YHWH on behalf of the community, as vividly portrayed in Leviticus 10.[49]

By countering the fragmentation and negative bias that had rendered studies of Leviticus (and the priestly material more broadly) tedious and arcane, Douglas and Milgrom shifted the course of biblical studies by showing that Leviticus was much more interesting than had once been thought. Instead of an arbitrarily assembled anthology of laws with no discernible logic or structure, it was now possible to see Leviticus as a meaningful literary work congruent with the rest of Torah. While their

48. Milgrom, *Leviticus 1–16*, 50.
49. Milgrom, *Leviticus 1–16*, 51, 56.

primary contribution was to make the logic of the priestly worldview intelligible to modern readers, both Milgrom and Douglas presented this as the first step of a larger interpretive process in which the resources of Leviticus could be brought into creative conversation with the concerns of modern life. Douglas, for her part, looked for points of connection in order to explain the priestly logic of the text in terms that would be comprehensible to a modern audience, while leaving to the discretion of the reader the question of what to do with this new-found understanding.

For Milgrom, connections to contemporary discourse often took the form of brief analogical excurses at the end of commentary sections. Bryan Bibb aptly observes that "Milgrom did not answer every question as much as provide a firm framework through which those questions may be addressed."[50] This exegetical method reflects Milgrom's belief that interpretation is an ongoing revelatory process in which men and women of every generation are responsible to discern the meaning of the Torah given at Sinai, participating as "active partner(s) of God in determining, as well as implementing, the divine will."[51] This active partnership in discerning the meaning and application of Torah compels readers to ask "questions about underlying principles and new applications more than specific intent."[52] What Milgrom sought to emphasize in this statement is the idea that the values and principles reflected in the text carry significance for new applications and need not be bound to the sociohistorical situation in which they originated. There is consequently a certain open-endedness in the connections that Milgrom drew between the biblical text and contemporary experience. For example, he pointed to aspects of the sacrificial and dietary rules as being grounded in the "sanctity and inviolability of life," but did not suggest what it may look like to honor this "sanctity of life" in the twenty-first century.[53] Similarly, he explained the rationale grounding the priestly distinctions between what is pure and impure as "the beginnings of an ecological doctrine."[54] But he did not develop this insight to suggest how the particularities of Israel's ecological doctrine might come to bear on the contemporary experience in which natural resources are simultaneously squandered

50. Bibb et al., *Text, Time, and Temple*, 2.

51. Milgrom, *Leviticus: A Continental Commentary*, 1–6, esp. 5; and *Leviticus 1–16*, 1370.

52. Milgrom, *Leviticus: A Continental Commentary*, 4–5.

53. Milgrom, *Leviticus: A Continental Commentary*, 18.

54. Milgrom, *Leviticus: A Continental Commentary*, 115.

and hoarded, global warming is intensifying at an alarming rate, and the weight of unrestrained human consumption is disproportionately borne by the animal world.

The two most fully developed connections that Milgrom drew between the Bible and contemporary concerns reflect this dual tendency toward emphasizing the Bible's ongoing relevance and gesturing toward possible applications, while leaving them undetermined and open-ended. In the first instance, Milgrom recounts his experience of participating in a forum on the Jubilee at the Ecumenical Institute in Bossey, Switzerland, in May of 1996. Hearing accounts of the pain and suffering in their countries expressed by representatives of the Third World nations, Milgrom observed:

> The jubilee has become the rallying cry for oppressed peoples today, as was the exodus theme for their counterparts in previous decades. This time, however, they are not enslaved politically... but shackled economically. The global market economy has generated unprecedented growth and prosperity, but not for them.

He went on to describe the rising wealth inequality and global pollution that implicates the rest of the world in the suffering of the Third World nations. These led representatives at the forum to present a proposal to "the creditor nations" for debt cancellation, restitution of land and natural resources and an end to the practices perpetuating their despoilment, and the raising of wages to a subsistence level worldwide. In this plan, Milgrom saw a practical demonstration that "the jubilee laws, mutatis mutandis, offer a realistic blueprint for bridging the economic gap between the have and have-not nations, which otherwise portends political uprisings that can engulf the entire world."[55] The legislation of Leviticus, in other words, carries real potential as a practical source of wisdom for the ongoing pursuit of constructing a just and flourishing society: "The book of Leviticus, so long thought to be esoteric and irrelevant, [is] an old-new guide toward achieving quality life."[56]

In the second instance, Milgrom addressed what is perhaps the most clichéd misuse of Leviticus in modern culture. Drawing a bright line around the Bible's prohibition of homosexuality in Leviticus 18:22

---

55. For Milgrom's full discussion of the Jubilee legislation, see 2241–71 of *Leviticus 23–27*; along with *A Continental Commentary*, 298–312.

56. Milgrom, *Leviticus: A Continental Commentary*, xiii.

and 20:13, Milgrom argued that the law applies only to men, and only to Jewish gay men living in Israel. His larger concern was to emphasize that there is no justification for using the biblical prohibition as a pretext for the oppression and abuse of LGBTQ individuals that has occurred throughout the history of civilization. Milgrom wrote that,

> I grieve for their plight—their pariah status and their discrimination in the workplace and the military. But when the Bible is distorted to make God their enemy, I must speak out to set the record straight. I return to my contention that there is only one deduction to be derived from Lev 18 and 20: The ban on homosexuality is limited to male Jews and inhabitants of the holy land. The basis for the ban, as I have submitted, is the need for procreation, which opposes, in biblical times, the wasting of seed.[57]

For those who do fit the categories addressed by the prohibition, Milgrom went on to suggest that perhaps an appropriate new application of the prohibition for the twenty-first century may be for Jewish gay men to fulfill the biblical mandate to "be fruitful and multiply" (Gen 1:28) by adopting children as compensation for the "loss of seed."[58] This offers a solution in keeping with the principle that motivates the ban, which is the need for procreation, but it is not clear whether Milgrom suggested it as a solution that would eliminate the necessity of the ban, thus honoring the biblical principle of procreation while allowing Jewish gay men to pursue homosexual relationships, or whether he meant to support the ongoing application of the ban while limiting the socially isolating effect of lifelong celibacy. In either case, Milgrom's treatment gestures toward interpretive possibilities without fully developing them, and thus necessitates ongoing discernment as the text is encountered in new applications.

It is hard to overstate the influence of the contributions that Douglas and Milgrom made on the ways we now read and understand Leviticus. Jonathan Klawans rightly observes that no serious study of Leviticus or of sacrifice and purity in the Hebrew Bible more broadly can fail to take their work into account, and a proliferation of studies has indeed emerged in the space they opened up, expanding the focus of interest in Leviticus beyond the form- and source-critical questions that had dominated modern critical scholarship and toward new applications of

---

57. Milgrom, *Leviticus 17–22*, 1789–90.
58. Milgrom, *Leviticus 17–22*, 1787.

social-scientific, literary, and narrative theory.[59] Our next task is examine how the scholarly conversation in this new milieu has engaged the notion that Leviticus may speak meaningfully within contemporary contexts.

Recent Discussion: Current Scholarship on How Leviticus Speaks

The question of how Leviticus speaks, framed explicitly in this way, has not been a primary focus of recent scholarship. However, a related question is implied in all literary study of the Bible as it has developed in the modern period: What kind of text *is* this? This starting point for analyzing the kind of text we have and therefore the norms or conventions through which it might communicate is, of course, the question of a text's genre.

Embedded within Hermann Gunkel's (1862–1932) study of literary types or classes (*Gattungsforschung*) of biblical material, the study of biblical genres formed against a backdrop of oral tradition from which written texts ostensibly developed.[60] After identifying what were thought to be the earliest independent units of oral tradition, Gunkel then classified their genres (*Gattungen*) on the basis of criteria such as content, mood, and linguistic form.[61] These two dimensions of form criticism—delineating the literary unit and analyzing its specific features—remain fundamental to the conversation surrounding the kind of text that Leviticus is and how best to understand it.

While canonical reading traditions have long accepted the book as a complete and distinct literary unit, determining the parameters for

---

59. Klawans, *Purity*, 18. For a recent introduction to current studies see Bibb in *Text, Time, and Temple*, 1–9, as well as *Ritual Words*, 5–33. Also of use is the older, but still important, collection of essays in Sawyer and Douglas, eds., *Reading Leviticus*, which reflects the range of studies that trace their influence to Douglas's work.

60. For more on the development of genre in biblical studies, see Boer's introduction to *Bakhtin and Genre Theory*, 1–7, especially p. 3; and Newsom, "Spying Out the Land" in the same volume, 19–30. For a lucid exploration of the processes through which texts may have come to exist in the ancient world, including a careful evaluation of the relationship between orality and literacy, see Carr, *Writing on the Tablet of the Heart*. An alternative view is expressed by Schniedewind in *How the Bible Became a Book*. In conversation, these two volumes provide a good introduction to the current state of scholarship surrounding the production of biblical literature.

61. Gunkel's original formulations of his method appeared in *Genesis* (1901); and *Die Psalmen* (1926). For useful and brief introductions to Gunkel that situate form criticism within the larger context of biblical studies, see Trible, *Rhetorical Criticism*, 21–23; and Ska, *Introduction*, 112–16. Berlin's essay, "Literary Approaches to the Bible," provides a clear and considered overview of how literary study of the Bible has developed up to now.

critical analysis has been less straightforward. Awareness of Leviticus's composite nature and reliance on the Pentateuchal material that surrounds it has led some modern critical scholars to question whether Leviticus should be treated as a separate book at all rather than a lengthy interpolation—a sort of addendum to Exodus that interrupts the narrative progress that is then resumed in Numbers. More recent scholarship has highlighted the literary artistry that sets Leviticus apart as a distinct unit, in keeping with the careful literary analysis supporting Milgrom and Douglas's insistence that the ritual instructions comprising the majority of the book only make sense when viewed holistically.[62]

Milgrom pointed especially to the literary techniques of parallelism and chiasm that span the book in its final form as evidence of the "structured sophistication of much of the books' content."[63] Intrigued by how these techniques may have been utilized in the conscious structuring of the book as a whole, Douglas suggested that Leviticus is a highly complex form of ring composition in which a series of interlocking chiastic structures, better conceived as literary rings, mapped out the spatial architecture of the desert tabernacle.[64] The strength of this proposal was that it was able to account for the progression of the book's content in a way that had proven impossible under the rubric of a straight, linear development from beginning to end. It also suggested that various non-adjacent chapters should be read in light of one another, thus illumining certain blocks of material through analogy to others. The sacrificial instructions of chapters 1–7 explain "how sins and defilement need atonement," for example, while chapters 11–15 "give examples of defilement," and chapter 16 "describes how atonement is made." Chapters 11–16 thus form the second half of the ring to expand and complete "the theme of the first half, 1–7."[65] Most importantly for our purposes, Douglas's structural proposal demonstrated a compelling argument that the final form of the

---

62. For the best introduction (with bibliography) to the question of Leviticus's status as a book, see Rendtorff, "Leviticus as a Separate Book?" in Sawyer and Douglas, eds., *Reading Leviticus*, 22–35.

63. Milgrom, *Leviticus 1–16*, 42; see also p. 2 for Milgrom's articulation of the methodology of his study as synchronic, in which "it studies each literary unit as a whole and attempts first to demonstrate the interaction of its parts" while also acknowledging the text's composite nature.

64. Douglas's earliest formulation of this theory appeared in "The Forbidden Animals in Leviticus" and was later refined and republished in *Leviticus as Literature*.

65. Douglas, *Leviticus as Literature*, 225.

book has been carefully structured as a *book*, so that the sum of the whole is greater than its parts.[66]

Christophe Nihan's meticulous reading of Leviticus within the framework of Pentateuchal redaction criticism offers perhaps the most thorough example of the recent shift toward interpreting Leviticus as a unified literary creation as it appears in its final form. Nihan points to the book's parallel introduction and conclusion (Lev 1:1; 27:34); its pride of place as the "center of five-fold Torah," with Exodus/Numbers and Genesis/Deuteronomy serving as a twofold frame; and a three-part structure within the book that articulates an overarching theme of "Israel's gradual initiation (by [YHWH] himself) into the requirements of the divine presence."[67] Other structural analyses have offered alternatives to Douglas's proposal of ring structure, but the broader development that these proposals reflect is the recognition that the literary qualities of Leviticus justify and compel a literary approach to the book as a discrete unit.[68] In the present study I follow these developments, recognizing that an awareness of the text's long history of composition and redaction provides an invaluable source of information in the process of interpretation. Yet in contrast to Nihan, I prioritize a synchronic reading of the Masoretic Text as it stands in order to probe the question of how Leviticus may speak when it is engaged by contemporary readers.

Taking the entire book as the literary unit to be investigated, what then of the specific themes, content, linguistic style(s), or other features that might point readers toward a generic designation? Leviticus is most

---

66. The basic notion of ring structure informing Douglas's proposal has largely been well received, finding support especially from Milgrom (for a succinct version of his response, see *Leviticus: A Continental Commentary* 6–8); along with Rendsburg, "The Two Screens"; and Rendtorff, "Leviticus as a Separate Book?", 22–35. Critics question the plausibility of Douglas's extension of the ring structure to an analogy with the wilderness tabernacle, but while Douglas does make much of this point, her basic structural argument does not stand or fall on accepting the connection. The explanatory power of ring composition to clarify the structure of the book is largely convincing, even without the tabernacle analogy.

67. This threefold frame consists of chs. 1–10 and 11–16, which articulate the "mediation of the divine presence in Israel in and through the sacrificial cult," and chs. 17–26, which complete "the restoration, in Israel, of the relationship between God and mand that existed before the Flood." See Nihan, *Priestly Torah*, 71, 106–9.

68. Notable structural analyses include Warning's suggestion that the extant text of Leviticus "has been artistically structured by means of thirty-seven distinct divine speeches," in *Literary Artistry*, 22; and Smith's proposal that seven major units, alternating between sections of law and narrative, structure the development of the book in "The Literary Structure of Leviticus."

commonly understood to be a legal text or law book, anthologized as a sort of instruction manual to assist the Jerusalem priesthood and/or worshippers in the observance of the sacrificial and purity regulations and to ensure their correct performance.[69] This is an apt designation for much of the book, which consists primarily of long blocks of ritual prescriptions that conclude with explicit statements of their status as Torah (i.e., 7:37–38; 8:4–5; 15:32–33; etc.) and culminate in the final phrase of the book: אֵלֶּה הַמִּצְוֹת אֲשֶׁר צִוָּה יְהוָה אֶת־מֹשֶׁה ("These are the commandments which YHWH commanded Moses," Lev 27:34).[70]

In a narrower approach to the text as legal instruction, others have emphasized the specific content of what Leviticus prescribes over its prescriptive nature. The fact that it primarily addresses and describes ritual processes has become an important point of distinction in the question of how Leviticus communicates, shifting interpretive emphasis away from text-as-prescription to text-as-*description*. This emphasis has characterized the approach of ritual studies, which suggests that the detailed literary portrayal of ritual systems inductively communicates something beyond mere mechanics of ritual procedure. Building on Milgrom's insistence that "the rituals in Leviticus contain fundamental values that in aggregate prescribe a holy and ethical life," Frank Gorman observed that traditional literary-, form-, and historical-critical methods of analysis had privileged narrative as the primary form of Israel's theological reflection.[71] As a result, general study of the Pentateuch had overlooked the way that the priestly ritual system portrays "the meaningful enactment of world in the context of creation theology."[72] Gorman drew heavily on insights from cultural anthropology to probe how the ritual system expresses the "conceptual, ideological, and theological framework of the Priestly cult."[73] As reflected in Gorman's work, the contribution of ritual studies to the question of how Leviticus speaks has been to show that the literary representation of ritual systems is a unique form of communication, symbolically conveying the priestly vision of life and portraying the kind of world that the priestly writers believed could be enacted and sustained through participation in the ritual systems.

69. See, for example, Douglas, *Leviticus as Literature*, 12; and Damrosch, *Narrative Covenant*, 263.
70. See also Lev 6:2—7:11; 11:46—15:32; and 26:3–46.
71. Milgrom, *Leviticus: A Continental Commentary*, xiii.
72. Gorman, *Ideology of Ritual*, 9.
73. Gorman, *Ideology of Ritual*, 7. See Gorman's notes on 8–9 for bibliography.

But if the literary unit to be analyzed is the book as a whole, other features stymie a simple generic designation of "legal text." The book also includes short narrative blocks in chapters 10 (or 8–10) and 24:10–23, masterfully woven into the ritual instructions and portrayal that constitute the majority of the text. Furthermore, these short vignettes are not "interruptions" to the laws or vice versa, as David Damrosch has observed. "Far from interrupting the narrative, the laws complete it," Damrosch writes, "and the story exists for the sake of the laws that it frames."[74] The result is a "complex but harmonious interplay between two *forms* of narrative" that Damrosch argues was "the most ambitious revolution in genre since the early Yahwistic merging of prose chronicle and poetic epic."[75] Damrosch has not been alone in the suggestion that this is a literary technique more complex than a simple splicing together of genres with similar thematic content. Frank Crüsemann also sees the reflexive contrast between law and narrative in Pentateuchal studies as an artificial explanatory construct that obscures the unique compositional artistry of the priestly writings. "Attempts to play one off against the other in form and content," Crüsemann writes, "sidestep both the clear literary evidence as well as the task itself, to understand this correlation—the unity of both."[76]

Furthermore, some odd features of the "laws" themselves emerge under close scrutiny, destabilizing even this seemingly obvious designation. As we will examine more closely in chapter 3, there is a curious absence of imperatives; only forty-one appear in the entire book, far fewer than most other biblical books.[77] And while a great deal of detail is devoted to certain procedures and processes, the instructions do not provide sufficient information to allow the reader to exactly reproduce them; either the text presumes a certain knowledge base of sacrificial procedures, or their exact reproduction is not the main point.[78] So Nihan suggests that the earliest blocks of legal material were oral "memory aids" within priestly circles that were eventually compiled but never understood to be a complete instructional manual.[79] Dale Patrick's suggestion that the legal texts of the

---

74. Damrosch, *Narrative Covenant*, 262.

75. Damrosch, *Narrative Covenant*, 262–63. Italics in the original.

76. Crüsemann, *Torah*, 282. Interestingly, Crüsemann does not interact with Damrosch's earlier study, though their arguments are congenial to one another.

77. See also Sawyer, "Language of Leviticus," 16.

78. Bibb, *Ritual Words*, 41.

79. Nihan, *Priestly Torah*, 219.

Hebrew Bible, including those of Leviticus, are "exercises in legal thinking" intended to stimulate "legal reasoning" offers a similar explanation for the selectively prescriptive character of the book.[80]

The conversation surrounding Leviticus's literary and generic character has illumined many unique features of the book, but its explanatory strength has been to highlight the text's complexity and multivocality. As we have seen, no single designation has emerged that adequately accounts for all the particularities of the actual text that we encounter on the page. This "problem" of the fluidity of real texts has been central to the development of modern genre theory, sparking a reevaluation of what genres are and how they function in critical analysis. While the notion of genre is a critical category extrinsic to texts themselves, it is nevertheless an indispensable tool for describing and making sense of the various kinds of communication we encounter. The intransigence of Leviticus to conform to any single genre as we might define them is no indication that the pursuit could or should be abandoned, but rather that our existing categories for thinking with and about the text are inadequate. As Carol Newsom puts it, "a sense of genre is such an integral element of the understanding of texts in general" that it is engaged implicitly or explicitly in any evaluative discussion.[81] Recent developments in cognitive or perceptive approaches to genre have underscored this idea that genre stems from innate cognitive processes of comparison and contrast through which meaning is constructed.[82] We come to understand what something is about through the "play of differences between its genres"; that is, through comparisons of features and an intuitive recognition of how certain types of communication differ from others.[83] The genre question is unavoidable.

---

80. Patrick, *Old Testament Law*, 198.

81. Newsom, "Pairing Research Questions," 258. This recognition stems in large part from Wellek and Warren's foundational exploration of genre in *Theory of Literature*, 235. Similarly, Beebee's theory of the "use-value" of discourse, namely that genres are "the way texts get used," makes a strong case for the inevitability of discursive mediation. See Beebee, *Ideology of Genre*.

82. For a general introduction to the "prototype theory" of genre, see Paltridge, *Genre*.

83. Beebee, *Ideology of Genre*, 249–50. Collins further clarifies the relationship between a text's meaning and the extent to which generic designations aid our comprehension of it in writing that "identification of a genre of a text does not tell us what the individual text means. It only provides a foil against which the meaning of the individual text may be seen." Collins, "Epilogue," 398.

But rather than being understood as templates or checklists of features constraining and defining texts and their production, genres are now considered in much more fluid and expansive terms that seek to describe the relationships between texts that make their differences meaningful.[84] So genres are "instruments of meaning" used in any number of configurations to communicate in specific ways with their audiences.[85] They might be thought of as "family resemblances,"[86] "prototypes," or "contracts between writers and readers, providing common expectations for what the text in question is intended to do and what means it is likely to use."[87] Genres give interpreters frameworks and vocabularies with which to explore the basic questions of what, and in what ways, a particular text communicates, but real texts move freely among these designations, dynamically mixing, blurring, blending, and expanding them.

These insights of modern genre theory resonate with studies of Leviticus that have endeavored to move generic analysis of Leviticus beyond the basic designations of law and narrative to form a more integrative grasp of how the book functions as communication. David Damrosch, as we have already seen, has suggested that law and narrative were so artfully blended as to constitute a revolution in genre, producing an entirely new way of telling the story of Israel's life with YHWH.[88] While not suggesting any particular label for it, Mary Douglas consistently urged that Leviticus must be read on its own terms rather than as an odd amalgamation of other more familiar literary forms. In molding its material

---

84. While the conversation between biblical studies and genre studies has lacked the kind of systematic or consistent engagement one might wish, several useful overviews of the major developments and considerations are available. For some starting points with biblical studies specifically in view, see Newsom, "Spying Out the Land" and "Pairing Research Questions and Theories of Genre"; Collins, "Epilogue"; and Zahn, "Genre and Rewritten Scripture." A useful overview of contemporary genre theories more broadly can be found in Duff, *Modern Genre Theory*.

85. Fowler, *Kinds of Literature,* 22. Fowler famously suggested that genres are better understood as pigeons than pigeonholes; particular texts within a genre might share obvious resemblances to one another, while also displaying their own unique characteristics.

86. The notion of "family resemblance" draws on Wittgenstein's analogy of a familial affinity between phenomena, taken up by genre theorists in the 1960s. See Newsom, "Pairing Research Questions," 241–44.

87. Newsom, "Rhetorical Criticism," 691. This notion of genre as a social contract is one that Newsom has consistently appealed to, drawing on Jonathan Culler's work on the intertextuality and communicative function of genre. See Culler, *Structuralist Poetics*; and Newsom, "Spying Out the Land," 23.

88. Damrosch, *Narrative Covenant*, 262–63.

to produce a unique internal structure, "Leviticus is a genre," she argued.[89] Focusing particularly on the ways that the "ritual-like qualities" of Leviticus—its "repetition, redundancy, formal language, idealized traditions, and a sense of continuity and direction"—create a text that mirrors the rituals it describes, Bryan Bibb suggests a generic designation of "narrativized ritual."[90] Reading Leviticus could thus be an "invitation into [a] ritualization process through which a person must develop his or her own appropriation of the shared values being communicated."[91]

Bibb's attention to the text's communicative function gestures toward an audience beyond that of the ancient world, but joins the majority of Leviticus studies in focusing primarily on the question of how and what the text may have communicated in its historical context(s). A notable exception has emerged in James Watts's 2007 collection of essays, *Ritual and Rhetoric in Leviticus: From Sacrifice to Scripture*. Watts is one of the few biblical scholars working closely with Leviticus to have taken up the exact question of how the text functions as communication.[92] This aspect of his work will be our particular focus, but we will also see that at a broader level the methodology informing his scholarship offers a useful case study to conclude our survey of recent scholarship on the question of how Leviticus may speak in the text/reader relationship. First, it seriously engages the knowledges produced by the past century of historical criticism while expanding beyond that framework to utilize nontraditional and interdisciplinary approaches. Specifically, Watts employs literary and rhetorical critical methods in his probe of the text's function as communication. Second, Watts's study is representative in that it also

---

89. Douglas, *Leviticus as Literature*, 197.

90. Bibb, *Ritual Words*, 62, 34.

91. Bibb, *Ritual Words*, 2.

92. Watts's approach to Leviticus is situated within a much larger field of rhetorical criticism of the Bible that has flourished since James Muilenburg's 1968 Presidential Address to the Society of Biblical Literature, which is widely recognized as a generative moment in contemporary interest in the Bible's literary artistry (Muilenburg, "Form Criticism and Beyond"; reprinted in House, ed., *Beyond Form Criticism*, 49–69). Within this broad and varied field, however, Leviticus had largely remained an afterthought. Prior to Watts's work in *Ritual and Rhetoric*, only three articles examined portions of Leviticus through a rhetorical lens: see Baker, "Division Markers"; Magonet, "The Structure and Meaning of Leviticus 19"; and Whitekettle, "Leviticus 15.18 Reconsidered: Chiasm, Spatial Structure and the Body." For broader context on Watts's rhetorical approach to the legal material of the Pentateuch, see also Watts, *Reading Law*. Watson and Hauser's, *Rhetorical Criticism of the Bible*, though now somewhat outdated, provides an excellent introduction to the field and reference point to the literature.

seriously engages Milgrom's and Douglas's work, critiquing and further developing some of the premises of Leviticus studies as they have taken shape in the past fifty years.

The primary point of connection between Watts's study and our interest in how Leviticus speaks to contemporary contexts is his suggestion that the communicative function of Leviticus may extend beyond a single historical locus. A key element of his argument is the observation that "rhetorical analysis calls attention to the text's function in transactions between people, both at the time of its composition *and in later social situations*."[93] He observes that author/reader relationships shift as readers change and reconceive the meaning of particular texts; in this way, a text can be understood to produce different rhetorical effects.[94] This seems to offer a promising way to ground the enterprise of bringing Leviticus into conversation with contemporary life, establishing an interpretive hermeneutic through the lens of rhetorical analysis. Indeed, Watts claims that his essays "build a cumulative case for using rhetorical analysis to interpret the significance of . . . the entire Jewish and Christian collections of scriptures and their function in ancient and contemporary religious communities."[95]

Watts also suggests that in calling attention to the function of texts as transactions between people, rhetorical analysis safeguards against anachronistically privileging contemporary values in interpretations of ancient texts. Evaluating the priestly rhetoric with an awareness of its effect in its original situation, to the extent that this can be known, would thus help circumvent scholarly bias against the priestly texts, for example. Watts thus calls for "new imaginative construals of the values in priestly rhetoric that consciously try to avoid the biases inherited from later religious and political commitments."[96]

Unfortunately, Watts's framing of the communicative function of Leviticus through the lens of rhetoric introduces a methodological limitation that ultimately undercuts his ability to make constructive proposals about the text's ongoing significance. In keeping with the general approach of rhetorical criticism as it has developed in continental biblical scholarship since the 1960s—and, more broadly, since the time of Aristotle—Watts employs an understanding of rhetoric as an art of

---

93. Watts, *Ritual and Rhetoric*, 35. Emphasis mine.
94. Watts, *Ritual and Rhetoric*, 102.
95. Watts, *Ritual and Rhetoric*, xvii.
96. Watts, *Ritual and Rhetoric*, 30. Italics in the original.

both persuasion and composition.⁹⁷ This leads him to construct his literary analysis around the question of "Who was trying to persuade whom of what by writing these texts?"⁹⁸ In framing the question in this way, the weight of inquiry falls on the individuals directly involved in the production and reception of the text at some moment of time in the past.⁹⁹ This creates an immediate complication, as Watts acknowledges, since identifying a plausible "original" author, audience, and rhetorical function in the case of Leviticus is unavoidably reconstructive. Another complication is that one of the key features of rhetoric is that it need not be explicit about its intentions to produce a certain effect on its readers. A rhetorical text "may use ambiguity and mystery as much as meaning and clarity to try to influence its audience," he writes. "A rhetorical analysis of ritual texts should therefore be alert to the possibility that some passages were intentionally written to be hard to understand and consider what persuasive purposes such deliberate obfuscation might have served."¹⁰⁰ So Watts acknowledges that rhetorical analysis is "necessarily speculative . . . for any text, because one cannot know an author's intentions with any certainty." Moreover,

> It is even more difficult when, as is the case with most biblical texts, we do not know who the authors and original addressees were, and we suspect that more than one person played a role in writing the texts. Nevertheless, because the text's persuasive function appears only in the context of that speaker/author and hearer/reader relationship, estimating their identities is essential

---

97. For the most comprehensive account of the rhetorical critical approach as it has taken shape in biblical studies, see Trible, *Rhetorical Criticism*, esp. pp. 5–106.

98. Watts, *Ritual and Rhetoric*, xv.

99. To be sure, an emphasis on authorial intent has been foundational to the rhetorical approach; as Trible has observed, "Muilenburg equated meaning with authorial intentionality. By 'author' he intended neither the implied nor the ideal but the flesh-and-blood individual(s) behind the words" (Trible, *Rhetorical Criticism*, 94). Indeed, Muilenburg's commitment to the inextricable relationship between form and content was motivated by his pursuit of the "thought and intention of the writer or speaker," a pursuit which he thought should be obvious to interpreters of a text's meaning: "a responsible and proper articulation of the words in their linguistic patterns and in their precise formulations will reveal to us the texture and fabric of the writer's thought, not only what it is that he thinks, but as he thinks it" (Muilenburg, "Form Criticism," 7). For further discussion of the place of authorial intent in rhetorical biblical criticism, see Trible, *Rhetorical Criticism*, 95–99; and Watson and Hauser, *Rhetorical Criticism*, 9–20.

100. Watts, *Ritual and Rhetoric*, 30.

and basic work in order to read any text as a *communication* between people, that is, as persuasive rhetoric.[101]

There is nothing inherently wrong with the provisional nature of historical reconstruction, if it is able to account for known data points to provide a plausible explanation of features of the text. What is troubling in this construal of a text's communicative function, though, is that Watts seems to equate the text with the person or persons who authored it, pursuing an interpretive locus not only in the original situation that produced the biblical text, but in the immediacy of a speaking/hearing relationship between people. The implication is that the text is a passive vehicle for relaying a fixed message. Because of his focus on its persuasive function, Watts concludes that what is to be interpreted in Leviticus is the original situation that resulted in something being written down: "To explain the unique form and contents of a particular text," Watts argues, "one must try to reconstruct what rhetorical relationship its *authors* intended for it: one needs to determine who they were, who [sic] they were trying to persuade, and of what, so as to figure out why they shaped the text in this way."[102] It is logical that if Watts understands a text to be a transaction between people, then rhetorical analysis must involve some approximation of an original author/audience relationship and an identifiable historical locus. But a text is not a person; as Phyllis Trible has rightly observed, "authorial intention constitutes a part, not the whole, of the meaning. Texts . . . may reveal more or less or other than their flesh-and-blood authors intend."[103] Watts's implicit equation of the text's mean-

---

101. Watts, *Ritual and Rhetoric*, 102. Italics in the original. The complication that Watts slips into here may well reflect a larger tension among rhetorical biblical critics surrounding the extent to which either authorial intentionality or a text's effect on its readers carries greater weight in determining a text's meaning. In emphasizing the text's persuasive function, Watts's approach departs somewhat from Muilenburg toward reader response, in an approach similar to that articulated by Dale Patrick and Allen Scult in their well-known survey, *Rhetoric and Biblical Interpretation*.

102. Watts, *Ritual and Rhetoric*, 102. Italics in the original.

103. Trible, *Rhetorical Criticism*, 97. Rhetorical approaches to genre theory have not overlooked the important distinction between rhetorical and literary genres, since rhetorical analysis of communication is centered on the action an utterance is intended to produce and thus necessarily includes attention to the situation and motive of the speaker. For more on this, see Amy J. Devitt, *Writing Genres*, which develops and expands Carolyn R. Miller's seminal work, "Genre as Social Action." For a useful example of rhetorical genre theory as it is engaged in biblical scholarship see again Molly Zahn, "Genre and Rewritten Scripture" as well as John Collins's critique of the usefulness of the approach in "Epilogue."

ing with its author's intent ironically results in a hermeneutic that Watts has strongly critiqued in Milgrom and Douglas's respective approaches to the interpretation of Leviticus.

Watts argues that the approaches that Milgrom and Douglas took to decode the meaning of the ritual systems of Leviticus blurs important lines between the interpretation of rituals and the interpretation of their literary representation. "Texts are not rituals and rituals are not texts," he writes.[104] The actual practice and performance of rituals in ancient Israel—along with any conclusions that might be drawn about their meaning or significance—are mediated through their textual representation, which may have been shaped for unacknowledged theological or political purposes. He argues that there is no direct access to the rituals themselves, in other words, and this limitation obliges interpreters to resist inferring historical conclusions about Israelite religion from the priestly texts.[105] Watts is thus wary of Milgrom's "effort to reconstruct the theological underpinnings of P's ritual system," arguing that the historical reality of ancient Israel may or may not be reflected accurately in the priestly texts. However, this is difficult to square with his own project of reconstructing an original author/reader relationship on the basis of the text's perceived persuasive function. It is also difficult to reconcile with his suggestion (noted above) that "new imaginative construals of the *values* in priestly rhetoric" are needed in order to move beyond the bias that has characterized scholarly treatments of priestly ideology.[106] Watts suggests that, instead of dismissing priestly rhetoric as the crabbed and controlling restrictions of a priestly ruling class, such construals would illumine the ways that priestly rhetoric conveys the larger religious and ethical ideals of the Hebrew Bible, such as fidelity to YHWH through adherence to the requirements of Torah. This seems to be a prescription for exactly the kind of work that Milgrom pursued in countering bias against the priestly literature by demonstrating the moral and ethical ideals that informed it, as we saw above.[107]

Watts also takes issue with Douglas for failing to "explain why Leviticus never makes its analogies explicit," for example, critiquing her argument that the meaning of the purity rules is conveyed implicitly

---

104. Watts, *Ritual and Rhetoric*, 29.

105. Watts, *Ritual and Rhetoric*, 27–36.

106. Watts, *Ritual and Rhetoric*, 11, 30. Italics in the original. Watts's larger discussion of Milgrom and his influence on Leviticus studies appears in pp. 3–10.

107. Watts, *Ritual and Rhetoric*, 164.

through sequences of analogies, "explaining one thing by presenting another that is analogous to it."[108] He maintains that "interpretation of these texts . . . must be guided by their explicit statements if it is to be defensible either on discursive or analogical grounds," but this argument conflicts with his claim that a rhetorical text "may use ambiguity and mystery as much as meaning and clarity to try to influence its audience," or that some texts may have been "intentionally written to be hard to understand."[109]

Watt thus seems to be caught between two conflicting interpretive priorities. On one hand, he maintains that if interpretations of ancient texts are to be more than speculative reconstructions, they must have some connection to historical data points. On the other hand, he questions the extent to which a text is a reliable reflection of a historical situation. Faced with these conflicting notions, Watts ultimately privileges authorial intent as determinative of the text's communicative function. Watts himself would likely reject this conclusion; he denies that the original author/audience relationship deserves privileged interpretive status since the rhetorical situation of a text changes as it is taken up by new audiences in changing socio-historical contexts.[110] But his construal of the rhetorical situation as discourse between people renders a distinction between literary and historical interpretation untenable. If a text is first and foremost a vehicle of authorial intent, with no creative or generative capacity of its own, then the interpretive locus is inextricably bound to its original context.

In sum, the conclusions that Watts draws about how parts of Leviticus may have functioned rhetorically in a historical setting around the time of its composition and redaction are well-argued and largely persuasive, but the study disappoints in its ability to offer constructive proposals to further our understanding of how Leviticus—*as a text*—communicates in changing interpretive contexts, as Watts had indicated it may. Although he appeals to the potential of rhetorical analysis to illumine the significance of Leviticus for contemporary religious communities, his understanding of what a text is (communication between people), and what is to be interpreted in it (the text's persuasive function) ultimately focuses his interpretive energy on reconstructing an "original" historical

---

108. Watts, *Ritual and Rhetoric*, 18–19. Douglas's articulation of this logic of analogy appears in *Leviticus as Literature*, 15–29.

109. Watts, *Ritual and Rhetoric*, 27, 30. For Watts's full critique of Douglas, see pp. 15–26.

110. Watts, *Ritual and Rhetoric*, 102, 153.

situation. We are left wondering whether Leviticus does actually have an ongoing communicative function—that is, whether the text is significant beyond the context of sixth-century Yehud.[111]

Conclusion

This chapter has observed promising movements in recent scholarship toward the notion that Leviticus may speak meaningfully in contemporary discourse, but the scholarly conversation has done much more to illumine how Leviticus may have "spoken" in past contexts than how it continues to "speak." With a few notable exceptions, which will be highlighted in the following chapter, scholars have largely utilized the recent breakthroughs in our understanding of the ritual systems and the priestly logic informing them to uncover the compositional, redactional, and socio-historical situations that produced the text, or to decode the logic that informs the rituals it describes. This has resulted in the implicit conclusion that Leviticus's primary interpretive value rests in what it discloses about history.

Curiously, the significance of Leviticus's self-presentation as discourse has largely been overlooked. Yet the book's basic character as discourse relativizes other generic designations, carrying the potential for a new hermeneutic that asks how the text may speak in the contemporary text/reader relationship. This idea is not without precedent in biblical studies more broadly. Martin Buss, for example, draws on Russian literary critic Mikhail Bakhtin's notion of "texts as utterances in dialogical relationship to one another" to develop a theory of genre based on the phenomenon of dialogue in the Hebrew Bible.[112] Buss builds his case on three claims: first, verbal structure, specifically address form, can be a basis for identifying genre. Biblical law, for example, consists most basically of pronouncements from an authoritative source to a generalized public. Further subtypes can be determined based on the type of address, style, content, or other distinctives.[113] Second, these dialogue structures tend to be arranged together in the Hebrew Bible, each representing a "dimension of life" engaged in metaphorical dialogue with one another.[114] The

---

111. Watts, *Ritual and Rhetoric*, xvii.
112. Bakhtin, *Dialogic Imagination* 281.
113. Buss, "Dialogue," 10–11.
114. Buss, "Dialogue," 13.

songs and prayers of the Psalms stand together in one place, for example, while Israel's origin stories appear almost entirely in Genesis and Exodus and the prophetic and priestly writings are similarly grouped together.[115] Third, dialogues take place metaphorically within these genres, "for genres are not internally homogenous."[116] Buss concludes that these dialogical relationships within the Hebrew Bible itself open up two further implications: first, that the Hebrew Bible can enter into dialogue with other literary complexes; and second, that "Biblical genres can also be placed in conversation with present-day life and speech."[117] This flings the door wide open to developing an interpretive hermeneutic that engages the discourse of Leviticus in contemporary conversation.

In the following chapter, we turn to an examination of Paul Ricoeur's interpretive theory to further develop the notion of discourse as a way to open up a new understanding of the kind of text Leviticus is and how it may communicate in situations beyond its originating context.

---

115. Buss, "Dialogue," 13–14. What Buss means by metaphorical dialogue is that the totality of life processes represented in the Hebrew Bible are not engaged simultaneously, nor even all within a single human life. "Nevertheless," he argues, "one can think of human life as metaphorically embodying a huge dialogue between these different aspects of life and thus between the genres in which they are expressed."

116. Buss, "Dialogue," 16.

117. Buss, "Dialogue," 17.

2

Interpreting Discourse

> "Language is a constant creation of alternative worlds."
> —George Steiner[1]

IF LEVITICUS IS DISCOURSE addressed simultaneously to the wilderness community and to the reading community, and if this discourse generates, for Israel, new forms of life and new ways of being in the world, can the discourse of the text also generate, for readers, new life possibilities? The argument of this study is that it can, and the task of this chapter is to demonstrate *how*. Paul Ricoeur's hermeneutic philosophy offers a way of conceiving of interpretation as just such a productive encounter between text and reader. Texts do things, and Ricoeur shows how the meaning of a text lies in what it makes possible in the world of the reader.

After establishing this theoretic framework, we will observe two examples of recent scholarship that have followed a similar approach to demonstrate that Leviticus can, in fact, generate new ways of thinking about contemporary issues, one pastoral and one ecological. But because these examples have been the exception rather than the norm, we will also consider some factors that pose real obstructions to seeing how the vision of life that Leviticus projects might take shape in the actual

---

1. Steiner, *After Babel*, 246.

world. With this clear-eyed view of the unique difficulties that Leviticus presents, we will be prepared to investigate the task of interpretation in greater detail in the chapter that follows.

What Is to Be Interpreted?

As one of the most influential philosophers of interpretation of the twentieth century, Paul Ricoeur has had an enormous influence on biblical studies for more than fifty years. Neither a theologian nor a biblical scholar, Ricoeur uniquely located his work at the nexus of phenomenology and hermeneutics. He was ultimately interested in the meaning of human existence, which he gradually came to understand as "always mediated through an endless process of interpretations—cultural, religious, political, historical, and scientific."[2] For Ricoeur, interpretation is fundamental to and inseparable from the human experience; although his approach was thoroughly grounded in the phenomenological tradition, Ricoeur rejected Heidegger's assertion of a direct route to ontology.[3] Conscious of the human limitations of finitude and fallibility, Ricoeur argued that a reflective understanding of human existence—its limits as well as its potential—can only be arrived at through a "long route" of detours through the symbolic works of culture.[4] We come to know ourselves, in other words, as we see ourselves reflected in the other; the meaning of human being is always mediated, always apprehended indirectly. Ricoeur's own long route of developing and testing this thesis culminated in his turn toward an inquiry into the role of language in mediating the development of the self—or, rather, one's understanding of self in relation to the world. As Kevin Vanhoozer has rightly observed, "Ricoeur's attention to language and literature ultimately serves his interest in understanding the meaning

2. Kearney, *On Paul Ricoeur*, 1. Ricoeur's intellectual trajectory has been extensively analyzed from a wide range of disciplinary perspectives, but for its masterful balance of range and concision there is none better than Kearney's account in this volume. See especially 1–33.

3. On Ricoeur's modification and development of Heidegger's project, see Vanhoozer, *Biblical Narrative*, 18–37.

4. For a wide-angle view of the cultural symbols that Ricoeur traversed in his hermeneutic trajectory, begin with Kearney, *On Paul Ricoeur*, 14–15. More specifically, Ricoeur's attention to biblical interpretation, as well as his larger projects of metaphor and narrative that have been of particular interest to biblical scholars, is usefully introduced in Ricoeur, *Essays on Biblical Interpretation* and *Figuring the Sacred*. For more complete bibliographies, see a series of bibliographies from Dornisch, "Paul Ricoeur" (1975), 23–26; "Paul Ricoeur" (1981), 23–29; and "Paul Ricoeur" (2003), 207–28.

of human being."⁵ Formulating a thoroughly phenomenological hermeneutic, Ricoeur was interested in what happens in the act of reading: What do texts *do*, and what is the relationship between text and reader?

Ricoeur takes as his starting point the "problem" of the polysemy of language, or rather the "problem of language as discourse" as he framed it in a series of lectures delivered at Texas Christian University in 1973 and published as *Interpretation Theory: Discourse and the Surplus of Meaning*. Put simply, the problem is that language—here meaning not "the particular structure of the particular linguistic system" but language as discourse, as "the general capacity to speak or the common competence of speaking"—can mean more or other than the sum of its individual parts.⁶ The ancient question is how it can be possible to say something which is not the case, and the answer lies at the level of the sentence, which is "an unlimited and indeterminate creation."⁷ Ricoeur thus understands language as discourse to be "an open process of mediation between mind and world . . . the creative process of giving form to both the human mind and the world, of forming (*Bildung*) man [sic] and reality at the same time."⁸ The surplus of meaning that arises in language is both problem and potential, then, opening a space for creativity and imagination as well as for misunderstanding and miscommunication. In either case, interpretation is key; the polysemy of language depends on it.

In face-to-face communication, the object of interpretation is the speaker's intent. Language functions to "exteriorize" the speaker's internal world as a fluid and flexible tool, filling in the gaps between speaker and hearer to expand, correct, or clarify until the speaker's intended

---

5. Vanhoozer, *Biblical Narrative*, 73, 86.

6. Individual words can carry multiple meanings, of course, but Ricoeur's primary focus was on what happens at the level of the sentence. A word might have multiple meanings, but "by itself is neither true nor false"; its meaning depends on the semantic relationships created in the formation of a sentence. Paul Ricoeur, *Interpretation Theory*, 1–8. Ricoeur's distinction here between semiotics and semantics, or *langue* as code vs. *parole* as a particular message, connotes a much larger inquiry that preceded his turn toward texts and literature. For more background on Ricoeur's encounter with semiotics and structuralism and bibliography of his writing on the topic, see Kearney, *On Paul Ricoeur*, 3, 19–20, 128–29; and John Thompson's cogent introduction in Ricoeur, *Hermeneutics and the Human Sciences*, xix–xxi.

7. Johnson's brief account of the distinction between word and sentence provides a particularly useful introduction to Ricoeur's thinking on this point. See *Hermeneutics and the Human Sciences*, xxi–xxiii.

8. Ricoeur, "Word, Polysemy, Metaphor," in *A Ricoeur Reader*, 69.

meaning has been conveyed and understood.[9] Ricoeur explains that the "reciprocity of intentions" in this situation of dialogue relies on three elements: a speaker, a hearer, and a context. Within a shared situation of dialogue, context is an interpretive screen helping to filter out all the meanings a conversation *could* have; it is the shared world of associations, connotations, and references that a speaker and hearer bring to dialogue as an exchange occurring in a specific nexus of time and space.[10] In dialogue, meaning emerges in the interplay of sense (what is said) and reference (what it is about), held together by the common situation of speaker and hearer as the outer limit of referential possibility.[11]

In the transfer from speaking to writing, however, these relationships undergo a fundamental transformation. Writing is not merely a fixation of the spoken word in which "the human voice, face, and gesture are replaced by material marks other than the speaker's own body," Ricoeur writes.[12] This was the limitation of the Romanticist tradition of hermeneutics insofar as it equated interpretation with identifying the author's intended meaning from the (presumed) point of view of the original audience.[13] What this model failed to take into account, Ricoeur argues, is that in the transfer from speaking to writing "the dialogical situation has been exploded. The relation writing-reading is no longer a particular case of the relation speaking-hearing."[14] No longer dependent on the human voice, the sentence attains a semantic autonomy from the speaker in its textual form. So freed, it is also "liberated from the narrowness of the face-to-face situation" which infinitely expands the range of potential addressees. A text can be picked up and read by almost anyone, with a chronological and geographic range far beyond the spoken word. And because it can go on existing in time and space indefinitely, the written word is also liberated from the immediacy of the original situation

---

9. "Language itself is the process by which private experience is made public," writes Ricoeur. "Language is the exteriorization thanks to which an impression is transcended and becomes an ex-pression . . . Exteriorization and communicability are one and the same thing for they are nothing other than this elevation of a part of our life into the *logos* of discourse. There the solitude of life is for a moment, anyway, illuminated by the common light of discourse." Ricoeur, *Interpretation Theory*, 19.

10. Ricoeur, *Interpretation Theory*, 16–19.

11. This is what Ricoeur refers to as the "dialectic of event and meaning"; see *Interpretation Theory*, 11–23.

12. Ricoeur, *Interpretation Theory*, 28.

13. Ricoeur, *Interpretation Theory*, 22.

14. Ricoeur, *Interpretation Theory*, 29.

in a distanciation of meaning from event. The context, or reference, of spoken discourse "is shattered by writing," not in a way that annihilates all reference—the text is still *about* something—but in a way that introduces a fundamental gap between the situations of the writer and reader, what Ricoeur describes as an "absence of a common situation."[15] Writing changes everything, in other words; it alters every aspect of discourse as an event in time and space.

In this construal of the relationship between writer and reader—or, more precisely, between a text and its reader, defined as anyone who can read—the task of interpretation becomes "the art of discerning the discourse in the work."[16] Ricoeur's use of the word "art" here gestures toward two themes that are central to his hermeneutical theory. First, interpretation is fundamentally an open process, a dynamic and ongoing activity that is never complete.[17] Meaning arises in the interplay of sense and reference, in the nexus of "the broadest historical and cultural connections" that cannot be encompassed by any single account.[18] Second, Ricoeur's articulation of interpretation as an *art* reflects and responds to the tension of the modern era between the explanation (*Erklären*) of scientific discourse and the notion of understanding (*Verstehen*) favored by hermeneutic philosophers.[19] While maintaining that explanation is not equivalent to interpretation, Ricoeur rejected the idea of a fundamental opposition in these two construals of how meaning is deciphered, underlining the distinction between sense and reference. To understand something is "to follow its movement from sense to reference: from what it says to what it talks about."[20] Interpretation is not complete when something has been explained, Ricoeur argued, but "it seems possible to situate explanation and interpretation along a unique *hermeneutical arc*

---

15. "In the same manner that the text frees its meaning from the tutelage of the mental intention, it frees its reference from the limits of situational reference," Ricoeur writes. *Interpretation Theory*, 31–36.

16. Ricoeur, *Hermeneutics*, 101.

17. "Between absolute knowledge and hermeneutics it is necessary to choose." Ricoeur, *Hermeneutics*, 156.

18. See Kearney, *On Paul Ricoeur*, 4–5.

19. Ricoeur writes that "the dialectic between explanation and understanding may be said to provide the ultimate reference of my remarks" in *Interpretation Theory*, where "what is at stake in this discussion is the correct definition of the hermeneutical task" (23). For discussion of the broader hermeneutical context, see Vanhoozer, *Biblical Narrative*, esp. 87–108, and Kearney, *On Paul Ricoeur*, 3–4.

20. Ricoeur, *Interpretation Theory*, 87–88.

and to integrate the opposed attitudes of explanation and understanding within an overall conception of reading as the recovery of meaning."[21]

But as we can now see, the recovery of meaning that Ricoeur has in mind is not the recovery of what an author may have meant to say, or how a text may have been understood by earlier audiences, or of any single, determinative "meaning" conceived as static and definitive. What is to be recovered is a relationship between text and reader, conceived as an event of discourse in which meaning may emerge, where discourse is realized as a creative process that gives form to both mind and world. What is to be interpreted, then, is the direction of thought that the text opens up within the reader's purview, the "type of being-in-the-world unfolded *in front of* the text" that Ricoeur articulated as "*a proposed world* which I could inhabit and wherein I could project one of my ownmost possibilities."[22] The world of the text that Ricoeur refers to is,

> the ensemble of references opened up by every kind of text, descriptive or poetic, that I have read understood, and loved. And to understand a text is to interpolate among the predicates of our situation all the significations that make a *Welt* out of our *Umwelt*. It is this enlarging of our horizon of existence that permits us to speak of the references opened up by the text or of the world opened up by the referential claims of most texts.[23]

21. Ricoeur, Hermeneutics, 123. Italics in the original.

22. Ricoeur, Hermeneutics, 104; see also Interpretation Theory, 36–37, 88–95. Italics in the original.

23. Ricoeur, Interpretation Theory, 37. A word of clarification on Ricoeur's language of "horizons" is necessary here, as it has been widely adopted and adapted in biblical studies and hermeneutics. The phrase originated in phenomenological philosophy to describe the way a person's perspective may be limited by his or her standpoint—that is, by the totality of her historical situation and knowledge—as well as gradually expanded through encounters with new ideas and experiences. Ricoeur's use of the word follows Gadamer's critique and refinement of the concept, which as it was used in historical inquiry had come to imply the notion of two different horizons, as if the historical situation and one's own present time were separate and distinct. Objective historical inquiry, the quest to understand the past on its own terms and not through the filter of "contemporary criteria and prejudices," had come to imply a sort of movement between worlds, a requisite "transposition" of ourselves from the present horizon into the historical horizon in order to understand it. For Gadamer, this was a theoretic framework that misconstrued "horizon" as a static, bounded conceptual world that does not exist in the reality of the human experience. There are not two horizons, closed to one another like the borders of geographic territory, but one horizon within which people freely move, as Gadamer explained: "The historical movement of human life consists in the fact that it is never absolutely bound to any one standpoint, and hence can never have a truly closed horizon. The horizon is, rather, something into which we move and that moves with us. Horizons change for a person who is moving. Thus the horizon of

Here Ricoeur's theory of interpretation can clearly be seen as a project thoroughly informed and guided by his overarching interest in the meaning of human existence. If the object of interpretation is the kind of world that a text discloses, and which the reader can imagine herself inhabiting, then interpretation is ultimately a process of orienting oneself in relation to this possible world. As Richard Kearney has put it, "to interpret meaning is, for Ricoeur, to arrive in the middle of an exchange which has already begun and in which we seek to orient ourselves in order to make some new sense of it."[24] The part of the conversation that took place prior to our arrival must be learned and explained, but interpretation, properly conceived, is the process of locating oneself within the conversation as it continues to unfold. So interpretation culminates in appropriation, "not to project oneself into the text," but "to receive an enlarged self from the apprehension of proposed worlds which are the genuine object of interpretation."[25] Interpretation thus comes to be seen as inseparable from ontology; to interpret is to involve oneself in a creative process that has the potential to transform one's sense of being in the world and the possibilities latent within it.

To be sure, Ricoeur's emphasis on the distanciation of the meaning of the text from authorial intent does not render the original situation of discourse irrelevant. What Ricoeur has shown is that the meaning of the text is not *limited* by or to the author's intention, in resistance to historicist claims that the primary meaning of a text is governed by the conditions of its production. Among literary theorists, a growing awareness of the limitations of historical study has drawn attention to the questions that context cannot answer. For example, Rita Felski has highlighted the ways that "conventional modes of historicizing and contextualizing prove deficient in accounting for the transtemporal movement and affective

---

the past, out of which all human life lives and which exists in the form of tradition, is always in motion" (Gadamer, *Truth and Method*, 304). Gadamer's "fusion of horizons" (*Horizonverschmelzung*) thus describes the expansion of one's viewpoint as it comes into contact with viewpoints and perspectives that were previously inaccessible or beyond one's frame of reference. It is not an abandonment or abdication of one's own world, neither is it the colonization of another's; rather, it is an expansion of the self to include the other in mutual understanding. "The concept of 'horizon' suggests itself," Gadamer explained, "because it expresses the superior breadth of vision that the person who is trying to understand must have. To acquire a horizon means that one learns to look beyond what is close at hand—not in order to look away from it but to see it better, within a larger whole and truer proportion" (Gadamer, *Truth and Method*, 305).

24. Kearney, *On Paul Ricoeur*, 5.
25. Ricoeur, *Hermeneutics*, 144–45.

resonance of particular texts."²⁶ Why do certain texts stand the test of time, appealing to multiple audiences across socio-historical locations? What is it about these texts that ensures their survival when contexts and readers change? Why do we keep reading them? Felski argues that these questions surrounding "how texts resonate across time" are just as important as questions about the historical environment and social forces that may have shaped a text's creation.²⁷ Context is simply not enough to explain the relationship between texts and readers.

So Felski calls for "postcritical reading," a phenomenology of reading that is attentive to questions of context and history, but also goes beyond them to ask what literature does and why such doing matters.²⁸ The hermeneutic that she proposes builds on Heidegger, Gadamer, and Ricoeur to emphasize the generative aspect of reading, while also weaving together Bruno Latour's "actor network theory" to highlight the agency of texts as non-human actors in the text-reader relationship, and the work of Marielle Macé and Yves Citton, whose "affective hermeneutics" attend to the ways that text and reader interact.²⁹ In Felski's model,

> Rather than looking behind the text—for its hidden causes, determining conditions, and noxious motives—we might place ourselves in front of the text, reflecting on what it unfurls, calls forth, makes possible. This is not idealism, aestheticism, or magical thinking but a recognition—long overdue—of the text's status as coactor: as something that makes a difference, that helps make things happen.³⁰

26. Felski first articulated her critique of over-attention to literary context in her provocative essay, "Context Stinks!," arguing that "history is not a box" and that critical appeals to the "clarifying power" of context "deprive the artwork of agency" (here 574, 582). Her critique is more fully refined and developed in *Limits of Critique*. One of the main pillars of Felski's argument is that a "hermeneutic of suspicion," a phrase coined by Ricoeur, has been received with such gusto that critics have forgotten that it is but one hermeneutic stance among many. On this point, Felski builds on Eve Sedgewick's early challenge to the "methodological centrality of suspicion" that she raised in her influential essay, "Paranoid Reading," in *Touching Feeling*. Sedgewick's aim in the essay was to "disentangle the question of truth value from the question of performative effect" (129); in other words, to ask what knowledge *does*. For Sedgewick, the interesting question of hermeneutics is not "is it true" but "so what?".

27. Felski, "Context," 575.

28. See especially Felski, *Limits of Critique*, 172–75.

29. Felski draws primarily on Latour, *Reassembling the Social*; Macé, "Ways of Reading," excerpted from *Façons de Lire*; and Citton, *Lire, Interpréter, Actualiser*. See esp. Felski's discussion in *Limits of Critique*, 151–85.

30. Felski, *Limits of Critique*, 12.

The point is not to discredit the value of historical studies as a vital aspect of interpretation. Rather, it is to recognize that the meaning of a text includes and *exceeds* what it has meant for other readers in other socio-historical locations. At its best, attending to these past meanings falls within the domain of explanation, as Ricoeur defines it. At its worst, it equates the interpretation of historical situations with the meaning of the text. In contrast, when interpretation is properly conceived as a process through which texts disclose "new modes of being" capable of giving the reader "a new capacity for knowing himself [sic]," reading may properly be understood as an activity of coproduction and cocreation between actors.[31]

Proof of Possibility: Two Conversations with Leviticus

While we saw in chapter 1 that the overwhelming tendency of critical scholarship on Leviticus has been to focus on the text as a historical object, a small contingent of interpreters has, in fact, shown how the priestly vision of life may disclose new modes of being for contemporary readers. Two examples stand out for their explicit focus on aspects of Leviticus that are rarely engaged in contemporary conversation, demonstrating an interpretive method much like that articulated by Ricoeur.

In their 2014 book *Maps and Meaning: Levitical Models for Contemporary Care*, Nancy H. Wiener and Jo Hirschman draw a connection between the spatial imagery of the wilderness camp depicted in Leviticus and the ways that certain roles in contemporary society occasion experiences of being "outside the camp." Their basic insight is that the levitical model of "how humans maintain their sense of orientation during times of both stability and transition" is a resource both for individuals in liminal or marginal periods of life, and for contemporary pastors and caregivers in their roles as companions and guides through these potentially disorienting experiences.[32] Wiener and Hirschman propose that "hospitals, nursing homes, and military bases are just a few of the contemporary corollaries of the Bible's *michutz lamachaneh*."[33] Turning to the account of the individual with צָרַעַת (*tzaraat*) in Leviticus 13–14 as

---

31. Felski, *Limits of Critique*, 12; 84; Ricoeur, *Interpretation Theory*, 94; see also "Biblical Hermeneutics," 64.
32. Wiener and Hirschmann, *Maps and Meaning*, 2.
33. Wiener and Hirschmann, *Maps and Meaning*, 2.

a case study, Wiener and Hirschman build on scholarly treatments of the passage by Jacob Milgrom, Mary Douglas, and various rabbinic sources to highlight the unique role of the priest in relation to the person with צָרַעַת ("the *metzora*"):

> The priest was present with the sick person from the initial inspection of a condition that might pose a threat to the broader community, beginning with weekly examinations of the lesions and continuing until the *metzora*'s death *michutz lamachaneh* or his full reintegration into the community. Through this steady presence, the priest offered to the *metzora* the possibility that he might find new anchors and a new sense of orientation as he adjusted to his new reality. Cut off from his family, from the community, and from formal ritual access to God, the *metzora* was nevertheless in regular contact with the priest. Despite his *tamei* status, the *metzora* was granted ongoing interactions with a person who embodied and represented *kedushah*. This is a powerful example of what accompaniment means—in the biblical context and for our own time too.[34]

Following this idea of a priestly model of accompaniment, Wiener and Hirschman explore concrete analogues in the role of contemporary pastors and caregivers, arguing that "Leviticus's accounts of the *metzora* [invite us] to imagine possibilities for healing and connectedness in contemporary *michutz lamachaneh* healthcare settings."[35] The *metzora*'s obligation to assume disheveled clothes and hair (בְּגָדָיו יִהְיוּ פְרֻמִים וְרֹאשׁוֹ יִהְיֶה פָרוּעַ), cover his upper lip, and announce himself as *tamei* (וְטָמֵא טָמֵא יִקְרָא; Lev 13:45) mirrors the biblical mourning practices, for example, which serves as a biblical precedent alerting caregivers to the fact that "illness is worth mourning over," and that mourning can be an important part of the patient's process of recognizing and accepting the reality of her situation.[36] They also note occasions in Exod 33:7–11 and Numbers 11–12 when the אֹהֶל מוֹעֵד (*Ohel Moed*) was pitched מִחוּץ לַמַּחֲנֶה (*michutz lamachaneh*) to suggest that the physical removal of the person with an illness from within the broader community need not mean the separation of that person from points of connection to the sacred. Instead, contemporary caregivers could draw on this precedent to explore ways that sacred space may be created within hospitals and care facilities where

---

34. Wiener and Hirschmann, *Maps and Meaning*, 71–72.
35. Wiener and Hirschmann, *Maps and Meaning*, 109.
36. Wiener and Hirschmann, *Maps and Meaning*, 112.

patients reside מִחוּץ לַמַּחֲנֶה (*michutz lamachaneh*), outside the nucleus of their broader communities, in order to "foster connections to God and people."[37] And in the *metzora's* eight-day purification process described in Lev 14:1–32, Wiener and Hirschman find an important recognition that the transition from illness back into the rhythms of the community is a gradual process, both spatial and temporal:

> Just as the *metzora* returned to the community slowly and by gradations, we too might find meaning in marking, naming, and honoring each step along the way. For example, a patient and her loved ones might choose to notice the different forms Shabbat takes when it is celebrated in a hospital setting, back home during one's recovery from a hospitalization, and then in synagogue when the person is well enough to begin returning to the contemporary *Ohel Moed*.[38]

In each of these examples of biblical precedents for mitigating the experience of illness as spiritual and physical isolation—by embracing mourning, facilitating connectedness, and marking transitions—Wiener and Hirschman discern that the levitical treatment of the *metzora* offers a rich resource for contemporary pastors and caregivers in accompanying patients on their journeys in the healthcare lifecycle. In Wiener and Hirschman's reading of Leviticus, the particularities of the scenarios related in the biblical text are not dismissed as irrelevant to a society shaped by a modern scientific understanding of illness and disease, nor are they rigidly transported from the culture of ancient Israel to contemporary Western culture without consideration of real differences—they do not suggest, for example, that individuals experiencing mysterious skin ailments be literally subjected to the procedures specified in Torah. Instead, they translate into analogous contemporary settings the meaning of the procedures surrounding the treatment of the *metzora* and the underlying values that shape them.

Another example of work that demonstrates the potential for transferability between biblical and readerly contexts is Ellen Davis's reading of the "wholesome materiality" of Leviticus.[39] Davis reads the biblical law codes in conversation with contemporary agrarian writers such as Wendell Berry and Wes Jackson to observe that "Leviticus articulates, perhaps

---

37. Wiener and Hirschmann, *Maps and Meaning*, 129.
38. Wiener and Hirschmann, *Maps and Meaning*, 133.
39. "A Wholesome Materiality" in Davis, *Scripture, Culture, and Agriculture*, 80–100.

more fully than anywhere else in Scripture, a theologically profound vision of the complexity and interdependence of the created order. Further, it grapples with the difficult question of how humans may responsibly participate in that order."[40] Davis's point of entry for bringing this observation into conversation with contemporary concerns is the associative, analogical way of thinking that Mary Douglas identified in the logic of Leviticus, as we saw in chapter 1.[41] Building on Douglas's insight, Davis finds a contemporary correspondence in the ecological sensibilities of agrarian writers, for whom analogy is "crucial for understanding why there is a vital connection between the health of soil and the health of human beings."[42] She focuses on how the writers of Leviticus 19 illustrate what holiness looks like "on the ground" through "a string of concrete examples" that "reckon deeply, imaginatively, and creatively with the stuff of ordinary life," including the cultivation and harvesting of crops.[43] Examining the levitical prohibition of polycropping (Lev 19:19), Davis "extends the analogy" to contemporary agricultural practices to consider the moral and ethical dimensions of modern genetic technology in seed production in light of the ecological vision reflected in the biblical text.[44]

Davis observes that transgenic engineering, used since its development in the 1970s and '80s to boost productivity and increase resistance of food crops to pests and disease, is conspicuous for its divergence from the practices that have shaped agriculture for millennia: "Whereas traditional hybridization mixes genes among varieties within a species or between closely related species," Davis writes, "transgenic engineering devises crosses between kingdoms: plant, animal, bacterial, and viral."[45] This raises a number of concerns for both ecology and human health, the full implications of which have not yet been realized. At the same time, too little attention and funding has been devoted to other forms of genetic technology "that can be used to speed and improve traditional breeding processes and increase genetic diversity for food crops."[46] Returning to the biblical prohibition of planting mixed seed, Davis suggests that the prohibition reflects a "regard for the integrity of the created order" that

40. Davis, *Scripture, Culture, and Agriculture*, 83.
41. Douglas, *Leviticus as Literature*, 13–29.
42. Davis, *Scripture, Culture, and Agriculture*, 84.
43. Davis, *Scripture, Culture, and Agriculture*, 85.
44. Davis, *Scripture, Culture, and Agriculture*, 87.
45. Davis, *Scripture, Culture, and Agriculture*, 88.
46. Davis, *Scripture, Culture, and Agriculture*, 89.

is absent in the technologies of transgenic engineering.⁴⁷ This seemingly arcane and obscure levitical prohibition thus becomes a clear point of contact between our own world and the world of the biblical writers, revealing an area where the logic of the biblical codes "should guide us in determining what might constitute holiness with respect to our culture's scientific, agricultural, and eating practices."⁴⁸

Davis's articulation of the way that the logic of levitical agricultural practices may inform contemporary food production skillfully balances attention to the context-bound details of the text—שָׂדְךָ לֹא־תִזְרַע כִּלְאָיִם ("your field you are not to sow mixed," Lev 19:19)—with attentiveness to the transferable values that they display. "It would be crude and overly literal," Davis notes, "to argue that the prohibition has found its ideal expression in industrial-scale monoculture, a practice that eliminates both small farmers and local food systems even as it exhausts the land."⁴⁹ Davis's problem with this sort of facile literalism is not that it is literal, per se. It is that neglecting to take account of the cultural and contextual differences between the biblical world and our own in this case works against honoring the interconnectedness of the created order that the biblical prohibition sought to reinforce. What Davis has done instead is to probe the symbolic significance of the prohibition, and then look for contemporary correlates where it may serve as a practical guide in discerning wise agricultural habits.⁵⁰ The result is a demonstration that the direction of thought that Leviticus opens up can be a valuable resource for the practical concerns of contemporary readers.

In these two examples, the horizon of the text has been engaged in practical, generative conversation with specific interpretive contexts in the present moment, one pastoral and one ecological. This is a marked contrast to the tendency of critical scholarship to focus on the text as an object to be explained rather than a potential new event of discourse that existentially involves the reader and her lived experience in the "world-propositions," as Ricoeur wrote, of the text. But the reasons for this weakness in scholarship, I suggest, are more complex than a lack of interest or desire on the part of readers. The kind of maximal interpretation that produces an event of discourse may be the exception rather than the

---

47. Davis, *Scripture, Culture, and Agriculture*, 90.
48. Davis, *Scripture, Culture, and Agriculture*, 90.
49. Davis, *Scripture, Culture, and Agriculture*, 87.
50. Davis, *Scripture, Culture, and Agriculture*, 91.

norm in readings of Leviticus in part because of the exceptional difficulty of this particular text.

Possibility—Not Inevitability

The strangeness of Leviticus in both subject matter and literary style seems in many ways to inhabit a space incompatible with that of the reader, challenging the possibility of meaningful exchange. Pentateuchal scholar Thomas Mann vividly articulates the problem in his observation that even the best readerly intentions can "founder on the shoals" of the chronological, cultural, or conceptual difficulties that Leviticus presents, stopping short of translating its strangeness into existential categories that are meaningful within contemporary discourse.[51] This is a different problem than the bias against priestly interests or fragmentation of the text that has contributed to the neglect and misunderstanding of the book. This is a question of whether the majority of the book's content and subject matter is simply too distant, and too strange, to be worth bringing into conversation.

In his study of the book of Numbers as Christian Scripture, Richard Briggs considers the question of whether some texts or parts of them may reflect values or assumptions about the world to which contemporary communities of faith cannot ascribe. Briggs observes that Numbers is a difficult book both because it is obscure to many readers (as is Leviticus) and because there are parts of it that are often considered morally and/or theologically problematic (as with Leviticus).[52] The account of Korah's rebellion in Numbers 16, for example,

> is an obvious stumbling block for many (if not most) readers of holy scripture today, and confirms the suspicions of most (if not all) unsympathetic readers that the Old Testament is best left where it is thought to belong, that is, in the past, a reminder of how not to live, or at least how not to think of God.[53]

This description could easily be assumed to be referring to Leviticus. Its extensive treatment of obsolete sacrificial procedures and obscure rules (i.e., avoiding mixed materials in Lev 19:19), along with passages that are morally problematic for twenty-first century readers—the death penalty

---

51. Mann, *The Book of the Torah*, 113.
52. Briggs, *Theological Hermeneutics*, 2.
53. Briggs, *Theological Hermeneutics*, 118.

in exchange for blasphemy, adultery, or failing to respect one's parents, for example (Lev 23:13–16; 20:9–10)—present difficulties that make the process of interpretation genuinely more complex than most texts, ancient or modern. Briggs ultimately argues that Numbers 16 need not be abandoned to the annals of history and instead "propels attentive readers to reach for altogether other ways of thinking that might yet turn out to offer a word of life to the world in which today's readers live."[54] To get to this kind of reading, Briggs takes seriously the ways in which the text tests the limits of transferability between the horizons of text and reader. This includes, for example, the possibility that when removed from the "framework of priesthood and holiness that permeates the horizon of the text" the moral vision of the narrative may be rendered incoherent and thus irrelevant to contemporary contexts. In other words, Briggs writes, "the fusion of horizons [may be] understood, offered, and then declined."[55] This is a real difficulty to be worked through, and Briggs's approach cautions against minimizing or avoiding such difficulties. If an interpretation is to speak compellingly to contemporary concerns, it must acknowledge that some texts push the interpretive capacities of their readers beyond the realm of the desirable. Only when difficulty has been identified and acknowledged can the possibility of bringing a text into productive conversation be a viable option.

In literary style, too, Leviticus presents a unique challenge to readers. We observed in chapter 1 that the unique blend of cultic instructions, brief narrative passages, and portrayal of ritual activities has frustrated attempts to describe the book's overarching literary character through the traditional framework of genre analysis. I have also suggested that these interwoven features are ultimately relativized in the text/reader relationship by the book's self-presentation as discourse, and that this should guide any inquiry into how the text communicates with its readers. One important aspect of this is that Leviticus does not merely portray an event of discourse, but an event of *divine* discourse, in contrast to the discourse of Deuteronomy ("These are the words which Moses spoke to all Israel..." Deut 1:1), for example, or other books with more conventional narrative prose. The result is a certain elevation of style and language that adds another layer of complexity to the task of discerning the direction of thought that the book may open up for its readers.

---

54. Briggs, *Theological Hermeneutics*, 118. See also 1–14, and especially 129–55 for his complete discussion of Numbers 16.

55. Briggs, *Theological Hermeneutics*, 140, 155.

INTERPRETING DISCOURSE 53

Examining the literary qualities of the priestly texts, Hannah Liss has observed an overlap between some of the characteristics that scholars have attributed to the priestly literature, and hallmark features of biblical Hebrew poetry.[56] Meir Paran's analysis of the Priestly Code, for example, suggested that parallelism and reduplication, standard techniques of biblical poetry, are stylistic devices also characteristic of the Priestly Code.[57] The overlap is not encompassing enough to classify Leviticus as poetry, per se—there are clear differences between the priestly literature and Hebrew verse as it appears in the Psalms, Song of Songs, or other short poetic units (i.e., Judges 5:2–3; Exod 15:1–18; and Num 21:17–18), namely that Leviticus utilizes definite articles, accusative markers, relative pronouns, and conjunctions in a way that Hebrew poetry does not—but this observation does call attention to the ways that the style of Leviticus differs from the ordinary discursive prose of Hebrew narrative.[58] A consideration of some of these features demonstrates how the language and style of Leviticus adds a level of complexity to the interpretive task.

The most obvious stylistic device is the highly structured patterning that Leviticus displays through its repetition of words, phrases, and themes. David Damrosch notes, for example, that chapters 1–7 display careful literary construction, particularly in chapters 1–3, which "show a consistent triadic form" in their description of three kinds of offerings (the עלה [*olah*], the מנחה [*minchah*], and the זבח שלמים [*zevach shelamim*]), each divided into three sub-sections.[59] The result is "a certain lyrical aspect," Damrosch observes, with each short section functioning like a stanza.[60] In chapter 1, the phrase רֵיחַ נִיחֹחַ לַיהוָה emerges as a refrain at the conclusion of each stanza:

---

56. Liss, "The Imaginary Sanctuary," 663–89.

57. Paran, *Forms of the Priestly Style*, 28–173 (Heb.). See also Milgrom's discussion of Paran's contribution in *Leviticus 1–16*, 38.

58. While attempts to identify the defining characteristics of Hebrew poetry are widely debated, there is rough consensus surrounding some of its primary features, concisely summarized by Adele Berlin in "Reading Biblical Poetry," 2097–2104. My comments here are also informed by the more extensive studies of Berlin, *The Dynamics of Biblical Parallelism*; Robert Alter, *The Art of Biblical Poetry*; David L. Peterson and Kent Harold Richards, *Interpreting Hebrew Poetry*; and James L. Kugel, *The Idea of Biblical Poetry*.

59. Damrosch, *Narrative Covenant*, 263–64.

60. Damrosch, *Narrative Covenant*, 264.

וְהִקְטִיר הַכֹּהֵן אֶת־הַכֹּל הַמִּזְבֵּחָה עֹלָה אִשֵּׁה רֵיחַ־נִיחוֹחַ לַיהוָה	And the priest is to turn all-of-it into smoke upon the slaughter-site, for an offering-up, a fire-offering of **soothing savor for YHWH** (Lev 1:9b).
וְהִקְרִיב הַכֹּהֵן אֶת־הַכֹּל וְהִקְטִיר הַמִּזְבֵּחָה עֹלָה הוּא אִשֵּׁה רֵיחַ נִיחֹחַ לַיהוָה	And the priest is to bring all-of-it near and turn it into smoke upon the slaughter-site: it is an offering-up, a fire-offering of **soothing savor for YHWH** (Lev 1:13b).
וְהִקְטִיר אֹתוֹ הַכֹּהֵן הַמִּזְבֵּחָה עַל־הָעֵצִים אֲשֶׁר עַל־הָאֵשׁ עֹלָה הוּא אִשֵּׁה רֵיחַ נִיחֹחַ לַיהוָה	And the priest is to turn it into smoke upon the slaughter-site, upon the wood that is upon the fire: it is an offering-up, a fire-offering of **soothing savor for YHWH** (Lev 1:17b).[61]

The refrain is then repeated another seven times throughout the book, periodically reemerging as a sort of *leitmotif* reminiscent of other refrains in biblical poetry such as those found in Psalm 136 (כִּי לְעוֹלָם חַסְדּוֹ, "For His steadfast love endures forever") or Psalms 42:6, 42:11, and 43:5 (מַה־תִּשְׁתּוֹחֲחִי נַפְשִׁי, "Why are you cast down, O my soul?" etc.).[62] Other notable examples of repetition in Leviticus include the exact repetition or repetition with minor variations of the description of the fat that is to be included in the offering (Lev 3:3b–5, 9b–19, 14b–15; 4:8b–9; 7:3b–4) and the well-known repetition of the refrain "I am YHWH" (אֲנִי יְהוָה) throughout chapters 18–22, with particular frequency in chapter 19.

A more complex technique than repetition is thematic parallelism, which Douglas found to be one of "Leviticus' favourite literary form[s]."[63] In this form, the second phrase (B) expands and defines the first phrase (A), as in Lev 22:10:

וְכָל־זָר לֹא־יֹאכַל קֹדֶשׁ	Any outsider is not to eat the holy-donation;
תּוֹשַׁב כֹּהֵן וְשָׂכִיר	A settler (belonging) to a priest, or a hired-hand,
לֹא־יֹאכַל קֹדֶשׁ	is not to eat the holy-donation.

---

61. Translation from Everett Fox, *The Five Books of Moses*.

62. Lev 2:2, 9; 3:5; 4:31; 6:21; 17:6; 23:18. A variation of the phrase also appears in 2:12, but is shortened (לְרֵיחַ נִיחֹחַ) to alert listeners to a crucial difference between this situation and other instances where the phrase appears: grain offerings made with leaven or honey should *not* be burned on the altar: לֹא־יַעֲלוּ לְרֵיחַ נִיחֹחַ.

63. Douglas, *Leviticus as Literature*, 48.

Here the "outsider" (זָר, *zar*) of the first phrase is explained and identified in the second phrase as anyone in close enough proximity to the priestly household to necessitate clarification regarding who was supposed to eat what.

Even more complex is the chiastic form, which we noted in chapter 1 as one of the features that Milgrom often cited as evidence of a careful editing process that produced the final form of the book. Milgrom notes that this technique appears throughout the book but is particularly frequent in sections designated by source criticism as belonging to the Holiness Code, which he pointed out is uniquely "characterized by an intricacy and artfulness of construction."[64] Rather than building a linear climax in emphasis of a particular theme or point, chiasm functions to draw attention to a central point, X, by flanking it with a series of mirrored parallels, as in A B C X C' B' A. Milgrom analyzes Lev 16:29–31 as a paradigmatic example of this structure, as follows:

- A. And this shall be for you a law for all time:
    - B. . . . you shall practice self-denial;
        - C. and you shall do no manner of work . . .
            - X. For on this day shall purgation be effected on your behalf to purify you of all your sins; you shall become pure before YHWH.
        - C'. It shall be a sabbath of complete rest for you,
    - B'. And you shall practice self-denial;
- A'. It is a law for all time.

Through this technique, the central point of a thematic unit can be located literally at the center of the literary unit, while also allowing the supporting points to be emphasized and developed through repetition in the mirrored parallels.

Mary Douglas's argument that the literary structure of Leviticus is an analogue to the architecture of the desert tabernacle was, in fact, a further development of this idea that the priestly writers used highly complex patterning devices as techniques for emphasizing content and highlighting key themes.[65] We noted in chapter 1 how Douglas suggested

---

64. Milgrom, *Leviticus 1–16*, 39.

65. Although Douglas's discussion of the literary structure is gradually developed throughout her book, a clear statement of the overall schema appears in *Leviticus as Literature*, 222–31.

that Leviticus 1–17 forms a literary ring in which chapters 11–16 expand and complete chapters 1–7 and should thus be read in light of one another. In this mapping, chapters 8–10 (the account of the dedication of the tabernacle and ordination of the priests) form the midpoint of the circle, and chapter 17 functions as the "latch," closing the ring by summarizing the key points of the sacrificial instructions begun in chapter 1. In spatial analogy, chapters 1–17 would thus represent the outer court, which is the primary location where the activities prescribed in these chapters are to take place, that is, "at the entrance of the tent of meeting" (פֶּתַח אֹהֶל מוֹעֵד; 1:3, etc.; 17:2–9). The next unit is shorter, consisting of seven chapters (chs. 18–24) to signify the smaller space of the inner sanctuary, and the smallest unit (chs. 25–27) completes the book as the literary analogue to the Holy of Holies, both sections thematically reinforcing their literary spatial analogies. The only two narrative passages in the book, chapters 10 and 24:10–23, stand at the midpoint of each ring to form structural and conceptual "screens" between the imaginary rooms, warning readers of major thematic transitions in correspondence with increasing proximity to the divine.[66] As the most intricate of the patterning devices that Leviticus exhibits, these interconnected chiastic units communicate multiple layers of significance. Tracing the book's direction of thought, on this account, is dramatically enhanced by the reader's ability to discern the patterns that are being played out literarily.

Along with these highly structured patterning devices, Leviticus also exhibits a certain density or terseness of language that is characteristic of poetry.[67] Words and phrases are repeated and woven into complex patterns of parallels and chiasm, conveying a seeming aesthetic delight in the minute details of the instructions being prescribed, but the significance of performing a precise sequence in this precise way may go unexplained. Similarly, a prohibition may simply be stated, seemingly with no rationale or justification; instead, Leviticus "adds another similar instruction and another and another" as in 19:19:[68]

---

66. Douglas, *Leviticus as Literature*, 195–217.

67. Berlin notes, for examples, that "biblical poetry is a type of elevated discourse, composed of terse lines, and employing a high degree of parallelism and imagery." In "Reading Biblical Poetry," 2098.

68. Douglas, *Leviticus as Literature*, 18.

INTERPRETING DISCOURSE 57

בְּהֶמְתְּךָ לֹא־תַרְבִּיעַ כִּלְאַיִם	Your animal, you are not to (allow to) mate (in) two-kinds;
שָׂדְךָ לֹא־תִזְרַע כִּלְאָיִם	your field, you are not to sow with two-kinds;
וּבֶגֶד כִּלְאַיִם שַׁעַטְנֵז לֹא יַעֲלֶה עָלֶיךָ	a garment of two-kinds, *shaʿatnez*, is not to go on you (Fox).

This creates a sort of "presentational" literary style, in the sense that it presents a series of instructions or descriptions of processes, but leaves the work of discerning their significance and relationship to one another up to the reader.[69] A certain density of meaning results, exceeding what is apparent on the surface in the same way that poetic forms of expression harbor more than meets the eye. It is a mode of communication in which "the surface is the depth," as Robert Alter has written of biblical poetry, "so that through careful scrutiny of the configurations of the surface"—the repetition of words and phrases, the careful patterning of literary units, the juxtaposition of one instruction with another and another—"we come to apprehend more fully the depth of the poem's meaning."[70]

Together, these techniques shape how the text communicates, suggesting that not all interpretive approaches will be equally suited to discerning the direction of thought that it opens up. Commenting on the symbolic nature of the subject matter that Leviticus is dealing with, Ellen Davis recommends, for example, that Leviticus be read "poetically, with close attention to the carefully crafted language in which the teachings are set forth, and with an eye to the core mystery to which they point."[71] Poetic forms of language, or styles of communication such as we encounter in Leviticus, invite reflection, foster questions, and present difficulty. Engaging in this kind of dialogue requires readers to slow down, and to probe beyond what is immediately apparent on the surface to the deeper connections that can only be formed through familiarity and a habit of association with the text's unique mode of communication.

Conclusion

Ricoeur's notion of the task of interpretation as engaging the written text in an event of discourse in the present moment offers an avenue of approach

---

69. Douglas, *Leviticus as Literature*, 18–19.
70. Alter, *The Art of Biblical Poetry*, 256.
71. Davis, *Opening Israel's Scriptures*, 63–64.

for pursuing the question of whether the reader's encounter with the discourse of Leviticus may be generative of new ways of thinking and new forms of life in a way that is analogous to Israel's encounter with the divine discourse at Sinai. Following Ricoeur, Leviticus can be seen as a potential new event of discourse, and what is to be interpreted in it is the direction of thought that it opens up for readers in new interpretive contexts.

We also observed two such examples of this kind of interpretation, in which specific aspects of the vision of life that Leviticus articulates were brought to bear on contemporary pastoral and ecological situations. These examples are the exception rather than the norm, however, which prompts the question of why, even in light of increasing interest and renewed respect for Leviticus over the past half-century, serious engagement with the book's vision of life often remains confined to the realm of historical scholarship while the text's ability to speak beyond its originating context has been muted. I have suggested that this may not wholly be attributable to a lack of interest or desire on the part of interpreters, since Leviticus poses uniquely difficult interpretive challenges in both content and style. Instead, it indicates that what is needed is a clearer articulation of what is involved in the process of bringing a difficult text into conversation with contemporary concerns. If the aim of interpretation is to discern the direction of thought that the text opens up in new interpretive contexts, how is this to be done? What is involved in the process of interpretation, so conceived?

3

On Difficulty

"But difficult things are what we were set to do, almost everything serious is difficult, and everything is serious."

—RAINER MARIA RILKE[1]

OBSERVING THAT LEVITICUS PORTRAYS an event of discourse that includes the reader in its address has led us to ask what this means for readers now encountering the book. In the previous two chapters we saw promising support for the idea that Leviticus has the capacity to speak meaningfully in contexts beyond its historical situation, and have reinforced this notion with a hermeneutic of discourse that defines a text as a potential conversation partner. In this construal of what a text is and what is to be interpreted in it, reading is understood to be an active, dynamic encounter between text and reader. It is a space of possibility and productivity, where new ideas are given the chance to take root in the ever-changing landscape of human experience. And so the task of interpretation becomes nothing less than an invitation to join this ongoing conversation; to apprehend the world proposed by the text, and to orient oneself in relation to it.

---

1. Rilke, *Letters to a Young Poet*, 17.

The problem, however, is that this is no easy task, and history has shown Leviticus to be an exceptionally difficult conversation partner. Having clarified our interpretive aim as "the art of discerning the discourse in the work," we now take a closer look at what is involved in that process, and how it might go awry.[2] Our guide through this discussion will be George Steiner, as he engaged the topic in his classic essay "On Difficulty." Following Steiner into an investigation of three main types of difficulty—contingent, modal, and tactical—we will use these as a framework for clarifying the unique difficulties encountered in Leviticus and the interpretive moves that they require. We will then explore how the notion of difficulty informs our hermeneutic of discourse to suggest that difficult texts may, in fact, be uniquely capable of enriching and expanding the horizons of their readers.

The chapter will conclude by introducing three exegetical probes that will put this theoretical work to the test, seeking in each case to identify the direction of thought that the text opens up in order to suggest possible avenues for new conversations.

Articulating the Task: Understanding (and) Difficulty

It seems to be stating the obvious to say that some texts are more difficult than others, but what, exactly, does that mean? Difficult how? Difficult for what–and for whom? "Difficult to understand," of course, but what does it mean to "understand"? This is the question at the heart of Steiner's inquiry into difficulty: what does it mean to say that a text is difficult to understand?

As articulated primarily in *After Babel* (1975) and *Real Presences* (1989), Steiner's notion of understanding resonates strongly with Ricoeur's conviction that we understand a text when we have learned to recognize "the sort of world that a work projects" and respond to it accordingly.[3]

---

2. Ricoeur, *Hermeneutics*, 101.

3. Ricoeur, "Biblical Hermeneutics," 82. While Steiner and Ricoeur shared a philosophy of language as creative and a view of the task and aim of interpretation as existentially or phenomenologically active, this similarity in their thought stems more from their adherence to philosophical hermeneutics in the tradition of Martin Heidegger and Hans-Georg Gadamer than from direct interaction with one another's work. Steiner reflects an awareness of Ricoeur's work in *After Babel* (see p. 313, n. 1), but mentions it only in passing. For an informative discussion of the philosophy of language that is reflected more broadly in the hermeneutics of Ricoeur and Steiner, in contrast to the view of language as it is understood in the rational empiricist tradition,

At minimum, this involves a basic knowledge of the object in question, but like Ricoeur, Steiner also argues that the ability to explain various aspects of a text's form, contents, or history is only the first step toward truly understanding what drives it—its force of life and *raison d'etre*. For Steiner, the fullest sense of understanding is that "aha!" moment when a reader finds common ground with something in the text. At times this happens naturally, but at other times such resonance occurs through a gradual process; as the reader's understanding of the text grows, so does the text's capacity to "speak." Steiner conceives of this process as an activity of translation, broadly conceived, in which the particularities of the text—including its language, culture, and worldview—become relatable to the reader. Steiner's key insight here is that interpretation is a concentric process, rippling out through multiple levels of apprehension.[4] Grounded in this "aha" moment of resonance and recognition, understanding is much more than the ability to explain what the text says: it is the ability to recognize and articulate the possibilities that the text creates within one's own lived experience.[5]

So what makes this kind of understanding difficult to attain? Steiner names three types of difficulty that find particular resonance for readers of Leviticus, and which we will examine in turn: *contingent*, *modal*, and *tactical*.[6] For each of these difficulties, we will also consider how they may arise within Leviticus, what interpretive skills they require, and how they may have previously been approached in scholarship.[7] Our aim is to find ways to navigate extraordinary challenges to the interpretive process without losing sight of the goal: namely, the direction of thought a text invites its readers to follow.

---

see Taylor, *The Language Animal*, 1–50.

4. Steiner, *On Difficulty*, 24. Steiner elaborates on this idea in his articulation of a multi-dimensional hermeneutic motion that begins with trust and culminates in reciprocity. To commit oneself to the time and effort required to understand a given text, Steiner observes, is to risk disappointment; to read at all is to trust that it will not be a waste of time. Having found something worthwhile, the reader reciprocates this "gift" by bringing the resources of the text to bear in her own world of ideas and action, thus infinitely expanding its range and influence. See Steiner, *After Babel*, 312–19.

5. Steiner, *Real Presences*, 7–8; *After Babel*, 312.

6. Steiner also identifies a fourth type of difficulty which he terms "ontological," but it is so narrow as to be descriptive only of certain types of deconstructionist modern poetry, and thus not useful for the present inquiry. See *On Difficulty*, 40–47.

7. To be clear, Leviticus makes no appearance in Steiner's own reflections on difficulty; the connections I draw here are entirely of my own making.

Contingent Difficulties: Doing Our Homework

The first difficulties encountered in any text are simply the things that need to be looked up. They are the most obvious and most numerous, the things that "stick like burrs to the fabric of the text" and disrupt an easy flow of comprehension.[8] Steiner calls these "contingent" difficulties because they hinge on the reader's own breadth of knowledge or lack thereof. Originating with the reader who knows less than the text "knows," this type of difficulty poses an interpretive challenge primarily in the sense that there is homework that must be done to unpack the basic meaning of the text's words and ideas.

Contingent difficulties are obstacles to understanding insofar as they need to be looked up, but their distinguishing characteristic is that they *can* be looked up: they are questions that have discoverable answers, given time and worlds enough. In some respects, then, they are not actually that difficult. But Steiner is quick to point out that looking things up can quickly become a complex and arduous process, occupying the vast majority of our attention and producing the illusion that interpretation consists primarily of research: of investigating everything that can be investigated. To gain a sense of the range of this class of difficulty we will consider several examples, ranging from the simplest to the most complex.

The simplest difficulties arise at the lexical level with words that are archaic, idioms and dialects that are unfamiliar, or arcane or technical vocabularies unknown in the readerly context.[9] The animal taxonomies of Leviticus 11 provide a prime example of this. What, for instance, is a *daman* (שָׁפָן), a *bustard* (רָחָם), or a *hoopoe* (דוּכִיפַת) (Lev 11:5, 18–19, NJPS)? A quick dictionary search clarifies: a *daman* is a sort of hyrax, or rock badger; *bustards* and *hoopoes* are birds. But we also find that תַּחְמָס (11:16) is variously rendered *nighthawk* (NJPS), *short-eared owl*, or *kestrel* (Milgrom), and שָׁלָךְ may be a *fisher owl*, *stork*, or *pelican*, translations that do little to provide clarity.[10] Looking things up has afforded the awareness that we are reading a list that encompasses a wide variety of birds, but the precise differences between them that were assumed by the priestly writers have now been lost to us. With the philological tools

---

8. Steiner, *On Difficulty*, 27.
9. Steiner, *On Difficulty*, 20.
10. So Milgrom, *Leviticus*, 663.

of modern scholarship at our disposal, even at the most basic level of the single word identifications often remain "educated guesses."[11]

The technical vocabulary of the priestly literature takes this kind of difficulty to another level, pressing readers beyond the general meaning of certain words to their specialized use in the context of the cult. Baruch Levine points to Lev 1:4 as an example of the "complexity of language characteristic of Leviticus and of priestly writing in general."[12] In the first set of instructions for offerings that are to be brought to the tent of meeting, the verse describes part of the ritual:

> וְסָמַךְ יָדוֹ עַל רֹאשׁ הָעֹלָה
> וְנִרְצָה לוֹ לְכַפֵּר עָלָיו
>
> He [the worshipper] shall lay his hand upon the head of the burnt offering, that it may be acceptable in his behalf, in expiation for him. (Lev 1:4)

Within this short verse Levine notes five technical words or phrases that convey a depth of meaning that is not immediately apparent on a surface reading:

- The *olah* (הָעֹלָה) is not only "something that goes up" (*qal FS Ptc.*) but is the name of a particular type of sacrificial offering (*FS noun*);
- *Samakh* (סָמַךְ) "has a technical meaning in the context of ritual and law," and was a widespread practice with symbolic function in the ancient Near East;
- The verb *ratsah* (רצה) characterizes "both the favorable disposition of God and the suitability of the offering itself,"[13] highlighting this moment as paradigmatic of the religious experience;
- The verb *kipper* (כפר) most often carries a basic sense of "to expiate, or cleanse" in the context of divine forgiveness; its usage here raises a number of questions since there is no mention of the offerer having committed any offense against God;
- When followed by the preposition *'al* (עַל), *kipper* indicates expiation "on behalf of, in relation to," where elsewhere it may denote the physical contact of blood manipulation, as in "to expiate over, upon," a distinction that is important in understanding the precise nature of the procedure described in Lev 1:4.

---

11. Milgrom, *Leviticus*, 662. See also Levine, *Leviticus*, 68.
12. Levine, *Leviticus*, xviii.
13. Levine, *Leviticus*, xviii.

Parsing the precise meaning of technical priestly vocabulary is further compounded by the composite nature of the book, which reflects at least two distinct sources.[14] This has long been a central area of focus for source critics interested in what the distinction between P and H (and possible sub-strata within P) might indicate about the book's provenance and formation, but the distinction is also important for understanding how certain words function in the book's final form. Milgrom notes, for example, that P maintains a distinctively precise, technical meaning for שֶׁקֶץ in Leviticus 11. Normally connoting "something reprehensible" (cf. Deut 29:16; I Kings 11:5; Nah 3:6; etc.), the priestly writer uses שֶׁקֶץ exclusively for creatures that live in the water (v. 10), birds (v. 13), flying insects (v. 23) and reptiles (vv. 41–44), but not for quadrupeds (vv. 2–8, 24–28, 39–40), or the exceptional class of creatures that concludes the list (vv. 29–38). The priestly writer instead designates these as טָמֵא. Milgrom thus suggests that this indicates "a legal and ritual distinction between these two terms: שֶׁקֶץ refers to animals whose ingestion is forbidden but which do not pollute, whereas טָמֵא refers to animals that, in addition, pollute by contact."[15] Within the same chapter, however, we find the following:

אַל־תְּשַׁקְּצוּ אֶת־נַפְשֹׁתֵיכֶם	v. 43a	You shall not **defile** your throats
בְּכָל־הַשֶּׁרֶץ הַשֹּׁרֵץ		with any creature that swarms.
וְלֹא תְטַמְּאוּ אֶת־נַפְשֹׁתֵיכֶם	v. 44b	You shall not **contaminate** your throats with any swarming creature that moves upon the earth (Milgrom).
בְּכָל־הַשֶּׁרֶץ הָרֹמֵשׂ עַל־הָאָרֶץ		

The two phrases are almost identical, appearing parallel to one another as equivalent terms in the structure of 11:43–44.[16] But here שֶׁקֶץ and טָמֵא are used as synonyms, complicating the legal distinction that seems apparent from the rest of the chapter. It is unlikely that this reflects a careless mistake on the part of the priestly writer. Instead, Milgrom suggests, "the use of *ṭimmēʾ* as a synonym of *šiqqēṣ* indicates a different source from the previous verses of this chapter, in which these two terms differed radically in meaning."[17] Within a single chapter we thus find two different sets of

14. For a brief introduction to the composition of Leviticus 1–16, for example, see Milgrom, *Leviticus 1–16*, 61–63.

15. Milgrom, *Leviticus 1–16*, 656.

16. Milgrom, *Leviticus 1–16*, 683.

17. Milgrom, *Leviticus 1–16*, 687. Milgrom's attribution of 11:43–45 to H is confirmed by Israel Knohl, who has contributed one of the most complete analyses of the

fingerprints on the same two words. While P scrupulously differentiated between them, "H blurs P's distinction between *šiqqēṣ* and *ṭimmē'*," each imprinting their distinct theological traditions.[18]

Included within the scope of things to be looked up are the range of connotations that a word can evoke intertextually or in reference to bodies of knowledge that are implicated by the text. Steiner writes that, especially in poetic and highly stylized texts, a word can be "an energized field of association and connotation," reaching out to a "multiplicity of meanings" that enrich and deepen the meaning of the text at hand.[19] Revisiting the creatures of Leviticus 11 for an example, we might ask why the priestly writer differentiates between certain animals as שֶׁקֶץ and others as טָמֵא. No answer is forthcoming in Leviticus itself, so Milgrom turns to the broader context of priestly thought. The animals designated שֶׁקֶץ, we recall, include those that live in the water, birds, flying insects, and reptiles. What do these animals have in common? The answer is found not in Leviticus, but in Genesis:

> Now, it can hardly be an accident that the very species that are *šeqeṣ* and . . . do not contaminate by contact have, according to the priestly creation story, their origin in water: "God said, 'Let the waters bring forth (*yišrĕṣû*) swarms (*šereṣ*) of living creatures, and birds that fly above the earth across the expanse of the sky'" (Gen 1:20). Thus both fish and birds were created from (and by) the waters.[20]

This provides a partial clue: In the priestly tradition, these creatures share a watery origin. But what does this have to do with their capacity to contaminate? Turning back to Lev 11:29–38 we find that water cut off from its source conveys impurity, while the source itself remains intrinsically pure. By analogy then, creatures that come from the waters,

---

differences between P and H and "demonstrated masterfully that on the basis of style, idiom, and ideology, H can be separated from P and that a comparison of the two resultant blocks proves conclusively that H is later than P and indeed has redacted P" (Milgrom, *Leviticus 1–16*, 13). Knohl's thesis as a whole has been met with wide acceptance, and while there is some disagreement over the attribution of particular passages to either P or H, 11:43–45 as a later addendum to P by H does not seem to be in question.

18. Milgrom, *Leviticus 1–16*, 15.
19. Steiner, *On Difficulty*, 21.
20. Milgrom, *Leviticus 1–16*, 658.

like the waters...do not contaminate by touch. Yet reptiles (*šereṣ*), which are creatures of both water (Gen 1:20) and land (*remeś*, Gen 1:25, 26) do not contaminate in the main (*šereṣ*, vv. 41–43), but some do (*ṭāmēʾ*, vv. 29–38)... Thus the Priestly distinction between animal carcasses that are *ṭāmēʾ* and those which are *šeqeṣ*... is rooted in the Priestly scheme of creation.[21]

In this example, a single word, שֶׁקֶץ, points to subtle nuances of meaning within Leviticus itself, while also drawing us out to the larger sphere of priestly thought. Beyond this, a word or phrase can extend to even broader systems of thought when it implies knowledges that have been lost to contemporary readers. Steiner cites "mythologies, the names of stars, [or] topography" as examples: looking these things up in the dictionary may provide an etymological frame, but then the "unnumbered furnishings of reality through which [a text] incarnates and makes concrete" must be gathered.[22]

Leviticus is replete with such cases. We have looked up *daman* (הַשָּׁפָן, Lev 11:5), for example, to discover that it is a rock badger—but what is a rock badger? Where do they live, and who would have the opportunity (or inclination) to eat them? What kind of world does the naming of a rock badger invoke? Some knowledge of the topography, climate, and ecosystem of the Middle East is necessary for answering these questions, so we scour for references to the rock badger in the folk lore or literature of these regions, turning from the dictionary to the encyclopedia to learn that the rock badger is a mammal of the order *Hyracoidea*, native only to Africa and southwest Asia, and is "characterized by small hooves on the first and third digits of the hind foot."[23] It is still not completely clear why the שָׁפָן, in particular, has been mentioned here, but the reader begins to understand that there is more to it than a passing mention of a small furry rodent. A whole world is implied in the naming of a rock badger, opening up a portal into the wilderness camp envisioned by the priestly writers.

Similarly, contingent difficulties might present themselves as puzzling absences or omissions in a text that are inexplicable without some knowledge of the concrete particularities of its provenance. Milgrom recounts just such a difficulty in his observation that, unlike the lists of land animals and birds given in Leviticus 11 and 20, not a single fish is

21. Milgrom, *Leviticus 1–16*, 658.
22. Steiner, *On Difficulty*, 21–22.
23. *Encyclopedia Britannica*, s.v. "hyrax, mammal," accessed April 2024, https://www.britannica.com/animal/hyrax.

specifically named apart from a general description of characteristics that make it an acceptable food source. Why might this be? Milgrom hypothesizes several reasons, including limited access to fresh-water streams and lakes due to geography and shifting political territories. A similar silence surrounding marine life throughout the Hebrew Bible suggests that the Israelites were not fishermen and had only a limited knowledge of aquatic species. And yet Israel's close proximity to the fertile Mediterranean poses a puzzling complication to these hypotheses: How is it possible that the Israelites had such a rudimentary knowledge of the "rich variety" of marine life contained within its waters?[24]

The question remained open until Milgrom heard a lecture given by Eugene C. Haderlie in 1973 on ecological changes in the marine life of the Suez Canal, and learned that it was not until the opening of the Canal in 1869 that the characteristics of the eastern Mediterranean as we now know it began to take shape.[25] Milgrom explains that,

> with the opening of the Suez Canal in 1869 the rich marine life of the Red Sea began to migrate successfully to the Mediterranean. [Professor Haderlie] explained that the eastern Mediterranean had a very low nutritive capacity due to the fact that the rich silt of the Nile flowed counterclockwise along the coasts of Israel and Lebanon but in currents that were too deep for most fauna to reach until it surfaced in the Aegean Sea. The import of his statement did not strike me until I left the lecture hall. This means, I realized, that before the canal, before the Red Sea fauna had penetrated the Mediterranean, the eastern Mediterranean littoral was an impoverished area for marine life . . . The implications of this scientific finding for the present pericope are unambiguous and decisive. The Israelites were unacquainted with fish not because they had no contact with the sea but, to the contrary, the sea with which they had no contact was virtually devoid of fish.[26]

And so a solution to "the enigma of the unnamed fish" is found, grounded not only in the geography of the Southern Levant, but also in the changes that have occurred in the region between the time of the biblical writers and the Mediterranean as we now know it.[27] Relying only

---

24. Milgrom, *Leviticus: A Continental Commentary*, 112.
25. Milgrom, *Leviticus: A Continental Commentary*, 112.
26. Milgrom, *Leviticus: A Continental Commentary*, 112.
27. Milgrom, *Leviticus: A Continental Commentary*, 112.

on current knowledge of the Mediterranean would lead to incorrect assumptions about what it would have been like during the time of the biblical writers, and a resulting misreading of what the priestly writers may have intended in their laconic naming of fish.

One final illustration of the depth and breadth of contingent difficulties involves what Steiner calls "complex" or "arduous words." He points to concepts such as "Nature," "Fortune," and "Native Honor," in Shakespearean literature as examples of thing that must be looked up, and which "lead from the dictionary and Shakespeare-concordance to the study of the very most dense, central topics in Elizabethan thought" and all the way out to the "far edges of Elizabethan and Shakespearean cosmology."[28] In the study of biblical texts, deciphering the full implications of complex words almost always includes drawing upon the historical knowledges of multiple fields of specialization to fill in the rough outlines indicated by the basic lexical meaning of the word, including archaeology, anthropology, sociology, philology, and theology.

One such complex word from the priestly vocabulary makes its first appearance in Lev 4:2–3, where we read of the instructions for the חַטָּאת (hattat). The chapter explains what should be done when someone sins (חָטָא, hata): A sin-offering (חַטָּאת) is to be brought to YHWH. Translating חַטָּאת as "sin-offering" seems appropriate in this context, since there is an apparent equivalence between the action (חָטָא) and the procedure for its reparation (חַטָּאת). Things become more complicated, however, when the same offering reappears in the context of the purification rite for the parturient described in chapter 12. When the allotted period of time has passed, the woman is to bring the same offering, the חַטָּאת, to the tent of meeting (Lev 12:2–8). If the essential meaning of the חַטָּאת as a "sin-offering" was assumed on the basis of its usage in chapter 4, its use in chapter 12 presents either a theological or etymological problem. Are we to infer that the priestly writers equate childbirth with sin? This seems unlikely, not only on logical grounds but also in light of the absence of any explicit reference to חָטָא, such as appeared in chapter 4.

Perhaps, then, it is a problem of translation. חַטָּאת has traditionally been rendered "sin-offering," which has the benefit of reflecting the noun's relation to its verbal root, which generally means "to sin" or "miss a mark" (*qal*). But חטא may also mean "to cleanse from sin" or "to bear the loss of a thing" (*piel*). So if the nominal form חַטָּאת indicates an offering that

---

28. Steiner's identification of "complex words" draws on William Empson's study, *The Structure of Complex Words*. See *On Difficulty*, 25–26.

likewise sometimes has to do with sin and sometimes does not, which meaning should the translation reflect? Is it a sin-offering, a purification-offering, or both? If the חַטָּאת names a single rite that is always performed in the same way, it would be misleading to translate it differently according to its presumed function in different contexts. However, choosing one translational option to the exclusion of the other is equally misleading in that it reflects only one dimension of the word's range.

The broader question underlying the difficulty of translation is what the חַטָּאת meant and what it represented in the thought-world of Leviticus, and so here the difficulty leads us out from lexical questions to the scholarly discussion surrounding the meaning and function of the חַטָּאת, both as it appears in Leviticus and as it is illuminated by its ancient Near Eastern context. In recent years, the traditional translation of the חַטָּאת as "sin-offering" has largely been abandoned in favor of Milgrom's persuasive argument that "purification offering" is a more accurate reflection of the function of the offering as indicated by the range of contexts in which it appears.[29] Milgrom explains:

> The very range of the *ḥaṭṭā't* in the cult gainsays the notion of sin. For example, this offering is enjoined upon recovery from childbirth (chap. 12), the completion of the Nazirite vow (Num 6), and the dedication of the newly constructed altar (Lev 8:15; see Exod 29:36–37). In other words, the *ḥaṭṭā't* is prescribed for persons and objects who cannot have sinned.[30]

Milgrom further observes that the blood of the חַטָּאת *"is never applied to a person."*[31] After the animal has been slaughtered, the priest

---

29. While Milgrom intended to ground his argument "contextually, morphologically, and etymologically" it is my view that the strength and weight of his thesis lies on the contextual side of that triangle. Joseph Lam has compellingly challenged the etymological and morphological planks of Milgrom's argument, namely that the חַטָּאת appears as a *piel* derivative and "its corresponding verbal form is not the *qal* . . . but the *pi'el* (e.g., 8:15), which carries no other meaning than 'to cleanse, expurgate, decontaminate.'" Lam has argued, in part, that Milgrom assumed an oversimplification of the morphology of the חַטָּאת and its corresponding verbal forms; see Joseph Lam, "On the Etymology of Biblical Hebrew," as well as Christophe Nihan's response to Milgrom's interpretation, which Lam cites: *From Priestly Torah to Pentateuch*, 183–84. In my view, it is of even greater relevance that the morphological element of Milgrom's argument is barely developed, constituting only three brief sentences before he immediately returns to an appeal to the "purifying *function*" (my emphasis) of the offering on contextual grounds (Milgrom, *Leviticus 1–16*; 253).

30. Milgrom, *Leviticus 1–16*, 253.

31. Milgrom, *Leviticus 1–16*, 255. Italics in the original.

brings some of the blood into the tent of meeting, where he sprinkles it in front of the curtain of the sanctuary, daubs it on the horns of the altar, and pours it out at the base of the altar (see Lev 4:4–7; 8:15; 16:14–19). "The *ḥaṭṭā't* blood, then," Milgrom concludes, "is the purging element, the ritual detergent" that purges not the person bringing the offering, but rather the sanctuary and its sancta.[32] The sanctuary cannot have "sinned," just as it seems implausible that the parturient should be guilty of "sin," and yet the חַטָּאת is still required. On these grounds, Milgrom concludes that there can be no intrinsic connection between sin and the meaning of the חַטָּאת. In support of this exegetical argument Milgrom also cites the Hittite ritual of smearing sacrificial blood on the appurtenances of the temple, as well as the central role that temple purification played in Mesopotamian and Egyptian cults.[33] As such, his case for translating the חַטָּאת as "purification offering" has been widely accepted on both historical and theological grounds.[34] This recognition that sin and impurity were not synonymous in the priestly theology also marked significant progress in reclaiming P from the long Wellhausian tradition discussed in chapter 1 of dismissing the priestly literature as a crusty relic of dead religion.[35]

Clarifying the lexical and contextual range of the חַטָּאת, however, is only the first step in deciphering the full implications of its cultic function and theological significance. According to Leviticus 16, the purification effected by the חַטָּאת was not an end in itself but served the larger goal of making atonement (כִּפֶּר) "for the sanctuary, from the uncleanness of the people of Israel, from their transgressions, for all of their sins" (Lev 16:16).[36] This raises further complications for understanding the meaning of the חַטָּאת. If we are going to understand the full significance of its

---

32. Milgrom, *Leviticus 1–16*, 254–25.

33. Milgrom, *Leviticus 1–16*, 254, 256.

34. Milgrom's argument that the חַטָּאת is a purification offering has been particularly well-received among American biblical scholars, while arguments for propitionary understandings of Israelite sacrifice continue to be defended among continental scholars, notably Hartmut Gese and Rolf Rendtorff.

35. By "the priestly theology" I refer only to the theological thinking that undergirded the sacrificial system, as broadly defined. This should not be confused with the assertion that "a" priestly theology can definitively be identified across the strata of priestly literature.

36. The first חַטָּאת of *Yom Kippur* had been brought for Aaron and his household (vv. 3–14); vv. 15–16 describe the second חַטָּאת of *Yom Kippur*, which is for the entire congregation, thereby concluding the purgation ritual and summarizing its function.

function, we need to understand what it was thought to accomplish, and this leads us into the realm of another complex word: כִּפֶּר (*kipper*).

Like חַטָּאת, the precise meaning of כִּפֶּר is difficult to pinpoint. Milgrom argued that the traditional translations of "atone" or "expiate" reflect the latest developments in the history of a word that originally indicated a physical rubbing or wiping movement. The biblical range of כִּפֶּר eventually came to include the notion of a "substitute" or "ransom," as expressed in the idea of a scapegoat carrying away the impurities ascribed to it (Lev 16:10, 21–22).[37] Only "the final stage in the evolution of the verb *kippēr*," Milgrom observed, "yields the abstract, figurative notion 'atone' or 'expiate' [meaning that] the offerer is cleansed of his impurities/sins and becomes reconciled, 'at one,' with God."[38] Milgrom thus concluded that that the most appropriate translation of כִּפֶּר in its ritual function in connection with the חַטָּאת is "to purge."[39] In support, he noted that the synonyms which accompany כִּפֶּר in biblical poetry and ritual texts also pertain to cleansing or purification, and that the word is derived from cognates meaning to "cover" or to "wipe."[40] While the semantic range can accurately include both "wiping on" and "wiping off," Milgrom favored "wiping off" in ritual texts because of his understanding of purification as a removal of impurities that have accumulated.[41]

Milgrom's preference for the earliest meanings of ritual terms makes his interpretation vulnerable to criticisms that his translations fail to reflect the appropriate depth and richness that the terms encompass.

---

37. Milgrom traces the logic of this development in noting that if the verb denoted physically wiping a substance away, the cloth that was used for cleaning had to be disposed of, carrying the impurities away with it. Milgrom, *Leviticus 1–16*, 1080.

38. Milgrom, *Leviticus 1–16*, 1083.

39. Milgrom holds to this view even though, as has been noted, a range of meanings can comfortably coexist in how כִּפֶּר is conceptualized. It would seem that he does this by locating subtle differences in usage in the different prepositions that are used in conjunction with כִּפֶּר, rather than attributing different meanings to the semantic range of the verbal root itself. He notes, for example, that "the purposive *waw* [as in 16:6] is equivalent to *lamed* (Ibn Janaḥ; Abravanel) and means 'in order to'" (1018), while "the preposition *'al* following the verb *kippēr* always means 'for, on behalf of'; thus "*kippēr* takes on the more abstract notion 'to expiate'" in 16:10. *Leviticus 1–16*, 1023.

40. Synonyms of כִּפֶּר include, for example, *hēsîr* "remove" (Isa 17:9), *ṭihar* "purify", and *ḥiṭṭē'* "decontaminate" (Lev 14:48, 52, 58). Milgrom, *Leviticus 1–16*, 1079.

41. "As has been demonstrated," Milgrom summarizes, "*kippēr* in all instances of the *ḥaṭṭā't* offering bears this meaning exclusively." While I agree that this meaning *can* be accepted in all instances of the חַטָּאת, I think that the etymological foundation that Milgrom lays for כִּפֶּר actually supports a more spacious, multivalent understanding of כִּפֶּר than he himself embraces. Milgrom, *Leviticus 1–16*, 1080.

Critics argue that Milgrom's idea of the blood of the חַטָּאת as "ritual detergent," envisioned as an almost mechanical means of dealing with the "aerial quality of biblical impurity," overshadows the ultimate goal of purification as it is seen to take shape in Leviticus more broadly.[42] Nehemia Polen, for example, argues that Milgrom's emphasis on the earliest meanings of חַטָּאת and כִּפֶּר led him to focus reductively on the purgative aspect of Yom Kippur. Polen reasons that the priestly conception of purification is more theologically and relationally complex, encompassing a wider range of meanings than did its Near Eastern counterparts. While comparative evidence can lend valuable insight to the interpretation of biblical ritual, as Milgrom had pointed out, Polen cautions that cultural parallels cannot do justice to "the narrative arc that situates Leviticus alongside Genesis and Exodus, books that have already introduced the core themes of covenant, relationship between leader and people, and—most importantly—the attraction and dangers of intimacy with the divine." Yom Kippur is not just laundry day, "an archaic riddance procedure," Polen concludes; "it is central because it enacts restoration of relationship and intimacy with the One whose Glory inhabits the Holy of Holies."[43] Indeed, while Milgrom illuminated the nuances within the range of meanings encompassed by חַטָּאת and כִּפֶּר and contributed much to our understanding of their functions at different stages in their evolution, he did not convincingly justify his preference for their earliest "pristine" meanings.[44] Nor is his argument that the translation of חַטָּאת must reflect its range of meanings ultimately reflected in his practice. In choosing "purification offering" over "sin-offering" he effectually chose the common denominator of the range of the חַטָּאת, rather than reflecting the breadth of its applications.[45]

This discussion of חַטָּאת and כִּפֶּר as examples of complex or arduous words highlights the ways that contingent difficulties ripple out from the (seemingly) simple necessity of looking up the meaning of a word or phrase, to concentric circles of interconnected knowledges including morphology, archaeology, anthropology, and theology, as each area of specialization casts further light on the meaning of a ritual now lost to our everyday awareness. Contingent difficulties thus span a wide range of interpretive challenges, from the simplest to the most complex.

42. Milgrom, *Leviticus 1–16*, 257.
43. Polen, "Vayikra," 63, 67.
44. Milgrom, *Leviticus 1–16*, 254.
45. Milgrom, *Leviticus 1–16*, 253.

Consequently, the homework of looking things up can be "mountainous," opening up new lines of inquiry in successive levels of complexity and nuance.[46] We have defined contingent difficulties as questions that are theoretically possible to answer, but in practice this order of difficulty may exceed the capacity of a single interpreter, or even a generation of interpreters. It is possible that only some parts of a text's whole may be clear at a given time, within a given sum of interpretive knowledge. Milgrom's experience of being unable to explain Leviticus's lack of detail concerning the marine life of the Mediterranean until he learned of the changes that occurred in the region with the opening of the Suez Canal is a case in point.

We have considered the range of contingent difficulty at great length because these are the kinds of questions that tend to occupy the vast majority of modern critical treatments of Leviticus, and for good reason. Contingent difficulties are the first obstacles to be addressed if a text is to be understood, and they cannot be circumvented. But while the explanatory powers of looking things up may go a long way toward translating a text's direction of thought into terms that are meaningful within the reader's lived experience, what if something in the text still "holds against us"?[47] Stopping at this point would leave the interpretive process incomplete. Beyond the realm of contingent difficulty lies another obstruction, in which the text inhabits a mode of existence that is in a deeper sense unfamiliar and inaccessible to the reader.

Modal Difficulties: Thinking with the Text

The first difficulties encountered in a text highlight what we do not know; another kind of difficulty is at play when we cannot relate to it. Even though its basic meaning may be clear at a cognitive level, something about the mode of being that the text reflects, the way that it communicates, or the vision of life that it projects can be felt to be incomprehensible: a disconnect inheres between text and reader such that we do not feel addressed or compelled by it. This experience can occur in any introduction to something new, but it is intensified when we encounter texts in which almost nothing seems to speak to our experience of life or our ways of understanding the world. Steiner calls this a "modal

46. Steiner, *On Difficulty*, 26, 30.
47. Steiner, *On Difficulty*, 28.

difficulty" that arises from the reader's particular position in relationship to the text, rather than in something intrinsically unintelligible in the text's own logic or mode of communication. The problem is not that the text is incoherent, but that it "articulates a stance toward human conditions which we find essentially inaccessible or alien."[48]

This disconnect is not just a matter of taste or aesthetic preference, Steiner argues, but rather a "failure of summoning and response [that lies] wholly outside the categories of 'liking' or 'disliking.'"[49] This is a particularly useful way of thinking about the attitudes of many readers toward Leviticus. The overwhelming sense of its unrelatability may have less to do with matters of taste and true dislike than with the fact that there is a basic disconnect at the level of summoning and response. Steiner observes that even after we have done our homework and have a good idea what a text is about, understanding may remain at a cerebral level that has not yet penetrated beyond the surface features of the text to feel "called upon" or "answerable to" it.[50]

Modal difficulties can result from any number of factors particular to a given text and its reader(s), but Steiner names two that we have already addressed as factors contributing to the unique difficulty of Leviticus: the text's content, and its form or style. In content, for example, we understand that the sacrificial and purity systems structure the daily life of the wilderness community in the embodiment of holiness. For most readers, however, these are not familiar forms of life. Leviticus remains firmly anchored in the world of post-exilic sixth century Yehud, as a foreign artifact viewed from afar. In form, or what Steiner calls its "performative means," we have seen that Leviticus "enacts language" in particularly challenging ways: it is a literary presentation of discourse that is non-linear and non-discursive, and it resembles a variety of genres including law, narrative, and poetry, without exactly conforming to any of them.[51] Its mode of communication as poetic discourse is unfamiliar to modern readers, disrupting the habits of reading to which we are largely accustomed.

Identifying this sense of disconnect and unrelatability—that is, recognizing that aspect of difficulty that arises from a fundamental difference between the mode(s) of being that the text reflects and our own ways of

48. Steiner, *On Difficulty*, 28.
49. Steiner, *On Difficulty*, 29.
50. Steiner, *On Difficulty*, 29.
51. Steiner, *On Difficulty*, 28.

thinking and being—does two things. First, it guards against a false familiarity that elides real difference and circumvents the aspect of interpretation that is all about translating the unfamiliar into meaningful terms. Second, and following from this, it enables the genuine "fusion of horizons" that is predicated on an essential difference between self and other.

Steiner distinguishes between contingent and modal difficulties primarily on the basis of a single criterion: can the difficulty be resolved by looking something up, or not? Steiner observes a tendency among modern interpreters to minimize or "efface this distinction" by denying or ignoring the substantial differences in modes of being between text and reader. He writes scathingly that,

> we may have to look up even the most elementary of scriptural, mythological, historical, literary or scientific terms and references; but we claim confident empathy with Benin bronzes, the shadow-dramas of Indonesia, the ragas of India and every genre and epoch in Western art ... We are ashamed to concede any modal inhibition, to confess ourselves closed to any expressive act however remote from our own time and place.[52]

Steiner's critique targets an intellectual arrogance that cannot admit a limited grasp of other ways of understanding, but premature appropriation of a text's resources may just as easily spring from an underdeveloped awareness of the extent of cultural and historical distance, or even an earnest philosophical commitment to cultural universalism. Among biblical interpreters, reluctance to admit a sense of incongruity may arise from religious commitments having to do with the text's status as Scripture and the belief in its universal applicability.

Whatever the cause, failing to recognize or acknowledge modal difficulties produces the same result: premature applications of the text to contemporary situations that are neither true to the substance of the source-text nor sustainable within their new configurations. The most obvious example of this is the way that Lev 18:22 and 20:13 have been read as a literal prohibition of all forms of homosexuality in any circumstance.[53] The debate over how to interpret these two verses has

---

52. Steiner, *On Difficulty*, 32.

53. See, for example, the statement that appears on the website of the Family Research Council: "The consensus of orthodox Evangelical scholarship remains consistent and overwhelming: The Bible teaches from Genesis through Revelation that homosexual conduct is a violation of the will of God." Schwarzwalder, "The Bible's Teaching on Homosexuality."

had a far-reaching influence for centuries, in both religious and secular spheres. As Idan Dershowitz wrote for *The New York Times*, "No text has had a greater influence on attitudes toward gay people than the biblical book of Leviticus."⁵⁴ Complicating the debate among people who intend to take the Bible's position seriously is the problem that "the Bible does not unambiguously endorse any position."⁵⁵ As we saw in chapter 1, Jacob Milgrom argued that the biblical prohibition is strictly limited to Jewish males living in the holy land, and otherwise has no bearing on contemporary debates over the morality of committed same-sex unions.⁵⁶ In contrast, literalists such as Robert Gagnon argue that "same-sex intercourse constitutes an inexcusable rebellion against the intentional design of the created order."⁵⁷ This unequivocal condemnation of homosexuality reflects a willingness to transfer certain biblical prohibitions to modern frameworks without fully reckoning with the contextual limitations and interpretive challenges that Milgrom and others have observed.⁵⁸ In its most extreme forms, such transference becomes a form of proof texting that dislocates elements of the text not only from their literary context, but also from their embeddedness in the cultural and cognitive structures that make them meaningful.⁵⁹ As is usually the case, there is more at stake

54. Dershowitz, "The Secret History of Leviticus," excerpted from, "Revealing Nakedness."

55. Davis, "Reasoning with Scripture," 514.

56. See Milgrom, *Leviticus 17*, 1786–1790; and *Leviticus: A Continental Commentary*, 197.

57. Gagnon, *The Bible and Homosexual Practice*, 37.

58. For a well-reasoned and carefully researched introduction to the key biblical texts, history of interpretation, and the broader cultural contexts that have influenced the debate, see Keen, *Scripture, Ethics, and the Possibility of Same-Sex Relationships.*

59. While Gagnon extensively considers the cultural and literary contexts informing Lev 18:22 and 20:13, he ultimately reads the prohibition of male homosexuality through the lens of his interpretation of human sexuality as portrayed in the priestly creation account of Gen 1:1—2:4a (an interpretation that is, in turn, guided by his reading of Paul; see Gagnon, *The Bible and Homosexual Practice*, 56–58; 289–96). Gagnon argues that the priestly "abhorrence" of male homosexual intercourse is "to be traced to its character as a flagrant transgression of the most fundamental element of human sexuality: sex or gender. Homosexual intercourse requires a radical 'gender bending' of human sexuality by the very creatures whom God placed in charge of the good, ordered creation" (140). This is a sort of canonical interpretation rather than facile proof texting, but its weakness as it applies to discerning the meaning of the prohibition becomes apparent in Gagnon's inability to demonstrate why the prohibition of male homosexuality should remain universally binding while others need not, such as refraining from intercourse when a woman is menstruating (Lev 18:19; 20:18) or wearing clothes of blended materials (19:19; see Gagnon, 120–21). I am grateful to Karen Keen for her helpful comments on Gagnon's interpretive method.

in this debate than a disagreement over methods of biblical interpretation: the history of one-dimensional literal interpretations of these texts has produced a cultural legacy of justification for the abuse and dehumanization of LGBTQ individuals. Ironically, this tragic legacy stands in stark contrast to the life-affirming values that inform the priestly view of life within its ancient Near Eastern context.

Leviticus 19:18 instructs members of the community to "enact-love toward your neighbor as [one] like yourself" (וְאָהַבְתָּ לְרֵעֲךָ כָּמוֹךָ), an injunction that extends similarly to the poor and non-Israelite landless by specifying that the edges of the fields and gleanings of the harvest are to be left as their livelihood (Lev 19:9–10).[60] This respect for life does not extend only to the human community, as Mary Douglas has shown: the priestly dietary regulations also provided clear boundaries to protect animal life from excessive exploitation at human hands, thus legislating holiness.[61] Even the land was included in the web of relationships through which Israel embodied the holiness that was necessary to their flourishing and survival in the face of the "high-voltage Presence in its midst," as Ellen Davis has demonstrated in her agrarian reading of Leviticus.[62] Interpretive shortcuts that fail to account for these broader dimensions of the priestly vision of life result in a caricature of "holiness" that is neither enriched nor expanded in new applications, but is instead rendered meaningless, destructive, or both.

Rather than effacing the distinction between text and reader, recognizing difficulty as the result of real differences between the text's mode of being and our own enables the genuine "fusion of horizons" that requires two different horizons in the first place. Properly acknowledged, modal difficulties confront us with the "inevitable parochialism," of our native ways of thinking and being in the world.[63] Encountering modal difficulty reveals the limitations of the reader's perspective and interpretive location, in turn providing a better understanding of the areas where the text challenges us to move toward new perspectives and new directions of thought. Modal difficulty thus highlights the aspect of interpretation that is a process of constructive acquaintance with something other than

---

60. Translation Davis, *Opening Israel's Scriptures*, 80.

61. Douglas, *Leviticus as Literature*, 1, 157.

62. Davis, "Reasoning with Scripture," 516; and especially, *Scripture, Culture, and Agriculture*, 80–100.

63. Steiner, *On Difficulty*, 40.

ourselves.[64] The difficulty cannot be resolved by looking something up, but instead asks us to lean toward the text to gain the perspective of its horizon. The movement is that of acquaintance, which is "to make or become familiar with something; to gain personal knowledge by experiencing; to get to know."[65] To see from the perspective of the text requires a familiarity that may need to be developed through long association and careful reflection, much like the approaches that Jacob Milgrom and Mary Douglas demonstrated toward Leviticus.

Douglas and Milgrom's ability to redirect the conversation surrounding Leviticus was the result of an interpretive stance that began with an interest in puzzling out the difficulties of contingency but ultimately recognized that a different order of difficulty was at play. Unsatisfied with the premature conclusions that had resulted from bias against the priestly literature and atomized treatment of the ritual laws, Douglas and Milgrom, in their own ways, immersed themselves in the cultural and conceptual perspectives of the text, regarding the strangeness of Leviticus as something like a cross-cultural encounter with the literary world constructed (or reflected) by the priestly writers. As we observed in chapter 1, their work of reading the purity and sacrificial systems as symbolic expressions of an overarching system of thought taught a generation of scholars and students to think with the priestly logic and see the symbol systems as culturally determined expressions of a deeper structure of societal values. Their work also demonstrates the close relationship between contingent and modal difficulties in the process of establishing a constructive acquaintance between text and reader. What began with looking things up led to sustained reflection and probing curiosity that spanned the course of their long and productive careers.

Curiosity, in fact, may be the fundamental interpretive skill that any encounter with modal difficulty requires. Ellen Davis writes of curiosity as a "virtue," insofar as it is "a genuine interest in the character and

---

64. Steiner's articulation of this describes a "reconstructive acquaintance" that is achieved when the reader has learned to relate to the text's mode of being. His point is to contrast an acquired empathy with an innate, instinctive ability to relate to the text, but he uses the word "reconstructive" to mean "regaining a cultural understanding that has been lost to the passage of time." This unnecessarily complicates his point in terms of the immediate text/reader relationship, since what he actually means to convey is an entirely *new* acquaintance. See *On Difficulty*, 32.

65. *Oxford English Dictionary*, s.v. "acquaint, v.", accessed April 2024, https://doi.org/10.1093/OED/3874729119.

perspective of the other."⁶⁶ It is an interest in the text precisely as other that energizes the experience of modal difficulty, transforming it from a sense of obstruction into an opportunity for growth and expansion. Moving toward the text to learn its logic and see from the perspective of its vision of life, we come to see things that we could not have seen before.

Learning to see from the text's perspective, however, is not the ultimate goal. To follow the text's direction of thought, we must turn our gaze back to the contemporary horizon to view our own situation in the present moment from the newly expanded perspective afforded by the text. Where modal difficulty confronts us with perspectives that lie outside the realm of familiarity and invites constructive acquaintance, a third type of difficulty challenges us to rethink what we thought we knew about reality and what is humanly possible.

Tactical Difficulties: Reconceiving Reality

Ellen Davis has suggested that "the genuine problem that Leviticus presents is its difficult theological grammar; its language is remote from that of 'ordinary' religious discourse, in our society *and probably in ancient Israel as well.*"⁶⁷ This perfectly captures the essence of yet another type of difficulty, in which unconventional uses of language and literary form are employed to arrest and redirect the reader's attention. These are not the kinds of difficulties that arise from a cultural or chronological distance between text and reader, but from a writer's attempt to communicate something that is outside the everyday realm of human experience, ancient or modern. Steiner thus aptly describes them as "tactical difficulties," produced by literary and grammatical tactics that authors resort to when normal, routine patterns of discourse are found to be inadequate. Steiner explains that,

> It is the poet's aim to charge with supreme intensity and genuineness of feeling a body of language, to "make new" his text in the most durable sense of illuminative, penetrative insight. But the language at his disposal is, by definition, general, common in use. Its similes are stock, its metaphors worn down to cliché.

---

66. Davis, *Preaching the Luminous Word*, 95.
67. Davis, *Scripture, Culture, and Agriculture*, 84. Emphasis mine.

How can this soiled organon serve the most individual and innovative of needs?[68]

This description of inadequate language as "common," and a "soiled organon" is particularly suggestive in light of the priestly concern with conveying a world where the categories of sacred and profane, of clean and unclean, are of the utmost importance. The priest's first responsibility was לְהַבְדִּיל בֵּין הַקֹּדֶשׁ וּבֵין הַחֹל וּבֵין הַטָּמֵא וּבֵין הַטָּהוֹר ("to make a distinction between the holy and the common, and between the unclean and the clean," Lev 10:10). But how does one delineate the realm of the holy in ordinary human language?

Rather than attempting to explain in discursive prose what is essentially inexplicable, the priestly writers worked to disclose the reality they envisioned by portraying an event of divine discourse in literary form. This technique allowed the priestly writers to approximate the divine encounter that Israel experienced at the Tent of Meeting, recreating Israel's experience for the readerly audience.

The notion of portrayal as a literary technique defines Leviticus's unique mode of communication in contrast to description. While "description" relies on a precise linguistic accounting of a situation, "portrayal" re-presents possibilities in fresh ways. Philosopher Charles Taylor further develops the notion of portrayal as one of three "dimensions of constitutive expression" through which certain works of art such as literature, music, or poetry articulate "new human meanings, [or] new existential possibilities." Taylor writes that portrayal is a "way of offering new models to understand human life" that is more flexible and fluid than description.[69] Through a variety of methods, portrayal "shows" rather than "tells."

In literature, portrayal allows an author to convey particular perceptions of reality or human possibilities without reliance on the generic requirements of narrative (i.e., character, setting, conflict, etc.), critical description ("the way things are"), or assertion ("the way things should be"). Though these elements may be included in a portrayal, they are often interwoven in flexible and unconventional ways to impress upon the reader a certain sense or insight that exceeds the descriptive capacities of ordinary language. This bears a striking resemblance to Steiner's description of unconventional literary methods as tools that authors use

---

68. Steiner, *On Difficulty*, 34.
69. Taylor, *The Language Animal*, 46, 235–37.

to disrupt "the inertias in the common routine of discourse" in order to "revitalize" and "reanimate lexical and grammatical resources."[70]

In Leviticus, portrayal functions as a literary technique that discloses an impossible vision of life as a human possibility, namely, that humans can safely coexist—and even flourish—in proximity to the divine presence. This portrayal runs simultaneously along two tracks: on one is a historical narrative portrayed as YHWH's address to Israel at Sinai, and on the other is an open-ended vision of life that exceeds the parameters of any single point in time. We will first consider how these two aspects are portrayed before concluding with a discussion of the unique interpretive difficulty that portrayal presents.

First, the narrative frame of the book identifies the discourse at Sinai as a historical event taking place at a fixed point in time: YHWH calls to Moses from the Tent of Meeting (וַיִּקְרָא אֶל־מֹשֶׁה וַיְדַבֵּר יְהוָה אֵלָיו מֵאֹהֶל מוֹעֵד; Lev 1:1), and addresses him with a series of instructions to be given to the people of Israel (דַּבֵּר אֶל־בְּנֵי יִשְׂרָאֵל וְאָמַרְתָּ אֲלֵהֶם; Lev 1:2). The *vayyiqtol* and *qatal* forms here and in 27:34 establish Leviticus as a unique event within the overarching pentateuchal narrative, continuing where Exod 40:34–35 left off.[71]

Within this narrative frame, however, a variety of unconventional literary techniques work together to expand the scope of this vision of life beyond the frame of the historical narrative. In chapter 2 we observed that the poetic characteristics of Leviticus elevate the language and style of the book beyond routine discursive prose to a mode of discourse appropriate to a portrayal of divine speech. This literary technique creates a certain grammatical flexibility as the spoken word is not confined to the parameters of genre or literary convention, and this comes to bear on the sense of time that is reflected in both the chronological progression and the grammar of the book.

The Sinai pericope is itself a unique focal point in the chronology of the Hebrew Bible. The fifty-eight chapters stretching from Exodus 19 through Numbers 10 occupy forty percent of the entire Torah, and yet, as Samuel Balentine notes, "the events that transpire at Sinai occupy just one year out of the 2,706 years that the Pentateuch covers between the creation of the world and the death of Moses."[72] This is a dramatic deceleration of time relative to the rest of Torah. Balentine further observes

---

70. Steiner, *On Difficulty*, 34–35, 40.
71. Levine, *Leviticus*, 4.
72. Balentine, *The Torah's Vision of Worship*, 120.

that the slowing down of the narrative tempo of these chapters suspends time in a way that links Sinai to the creation narrative of Genesis 1. He suggests that the Sinai pericope "recalls the heptadic patterning of the creation liturgy," as evidenced by Israel's arrival at Sinai six weeks after their departure from Egypt in a way that recalls "the six days of God's labor in the creation of the world."[73] Having arrived at Sinai, "the narrative tempo . . . changes. The seventh week now becomes the focus of extended reflection," Balentine writes, in which "the Torah envisions the sojourn at Sinai to be a *sabbath day experience,* a virtual suspension of time to enable the community to reflect on the importance of their covenantal commission to become partners with God."[74] The effect is to emphasize the events at Sinai as a "constitutive experience in the formation of the community."[75]

Furthermore, Sarah Musser observes that within this overall suspension of time at Sinai, the opening seven chapters of Leviticus slow down even further, spanning only a single day so that "chapters 1–7 and the sacrificial life they display are anchored to the time of the 'first day'" of creation.[76] Right before these chapters, the account of the building of the Tabernacle (Exod 35–40) was reported as having been completed "in the first month in the second year, on the first day of the month . . . just as YHWH had commanded [Moses]" (Exod 40:2, 16–33). Rather than following the completion of the Tabernacle with the account of its dedication, however, the narrative flow is interrupted by the insertion of Leviticus 1–7 and the detailed instructions for the maintenance of a sacrificial system that, in the chronology of the narrative, has not yet begun. Building on Balentine's observation of the connection between the Sinai pericope and the creation account of Genesis 1, Musser suggests that this "time-warp" separating the completion of the Tent of Meeting from the narrative of its inauguration in Leviticus 8–10 highlights the paradigmatic significance of the events portrayed in chapters 1–7. The book thus opens with a clear statement that what is of primary importance is not

---

73. Balentine, *The Torah's Vision of Worship,* 122–23; 126–27.

74. In the chronology of the Pentateuch this extended Sabbath lasts for eleven months, beginning with Israel's arrival at Sinai and concluding with the resumption of their journey to Canaan (Num 10:11). See Balentine, *The Torah's Vision of Worship,* 126–27. Italics in the original.

75. Balentine, *The Torah's Vision of Worship,* 120.

76. Musser, "Sacrifice, Sabbath, and the Restoration of Creation," 100.

the recounting of a historical narrative, but the projection of a vision of life that transcends any single point in time.⁷⁷

Reinforcing the disruption of chronology that occurs at the macro level, the book also conveys a sense of timelessness and indeterminacy at the grammatical level. The first set of instructions in Lev 1:2 (אָדָם כִּי־יַקְרִיב, "When anyone brings-near...") interrupts the narrative flow of *vayyiqtol* forms in 1:1 (וַיִּקְרָא ... וַיְדַבֵּר "And he called... and he spoke...") with an unusual fronting of the subject (i.e., subject-verb, vs. the verb-subject-object construction of standard Hebrew syntax), while the conjunction כִּי introduces a situation with no clearly defined chronology. As a temporal כִּי this would be the normal construction for introducing a legal text,⁷⁸ but in many instances within Leviticus כִּי is also conditional, indicating the "optional nature of the law that follows" or the procedures that should be followed should a particular situation arise (i.e., the instructions for the individual with צָרַעַת in 13:2).⁷⁹ The instructions are thus introduced as requirements for what should happen in a hypothetical scenario that may or may not transpire.

As the book continues, an unusual use of verbal forms emerges. Analyzing the language of Leviticus, John Sawyer observes that in comparison with other narrative books of the Bible, Leviticus is characterized by a "relative infrequency of plain statements of fact, describing what happened or how things actually are."⁸⁰ Sawyer continues:

> No book in the Bible has fewer *qatal* forms per 10,000 words than Leviticus; most have over twice as many. Similarly, no prose work (with the exception of Qohelet) has fewer *vayyiqtol* forms per 10,000 words than Leviticus. Conversely, *veqatal* forms are almost three times as frequent in Leviticus (721/603) as they are anywhere else. Deuteronomy, Ezekiel and some of the minor prophets come a long way behind in second place. The relative

---

77. Musser defines the significance of the events portrayed in Lev 1–7 as emphasizing the creative, redemptive purposes of the sacrificial system, writing that "the placement of the sacrificial legislation on the first day underscores the contention that the *telos* of sacrifice is creation's redemption" (100). This is a compelling explanation for the interpolation of chapters 1–7 between the accounts of the completion and dedication of the Tent of Meeting, but my interest is in the effect that this interpolation has on the reader's sense of time as it functions within the broader literary technique of portrayal.

78. Milgrom, *Leviticus 1–16*, 144; Levine, *Leviticus*, 4–5; Williams, *Hebrew Syntax*, §445.

79. Milgrom, *Leviticus 1–16*, 144; Williams, *Hebrew Syntax*, §446.

80. Sawyer, "The Language of Leviticus," 16.

frequency of *yiqtōl* forms, although not so high, is nonetheless above average for the Hebrew Bible as a whole.[81]

Some further insight into the aspect of Hebrew verbal forms clarifies the effect of this unusual literary technique. Bernard Comrie explains that the verbal forms convey unique perspectives of a situation or action that are inherently more fluid than the verbal tenses of English grammar:

> The [Hebrew] perfective looks at the situation from outside, without necessarily distinguishing any of the internal structure of the situation, whereas the imperfective looks at the situation from inside, and as such is crucially concerned with the internal structure of the situation, since it can both look backwards towards the start of the situation, and look forwards to the end of the situation, and indeed is equally appropriate if the situation is one that lasts through all time, without any beginning and without any end.[82]

The relative frequency of *veqatal* and *yiqtōl* forms in Leviticus thus seems to reinforce the sense conveyed by the irregular chronological progression: What is being portrayed here is not understood to be bound to a single historical location.

In another unconventional grammatical turn, the book describes itself as a collection of מִצְוֹת (*mitsvot*; Lev 7:37–38; 14:2; 16:29; 27:34) while curiously avoiding imperatives. In the entire book only forty-one imperatives are used, while "most books have three or four times as many";[83] and only in two places are they directed to the Israelites (9:3; 24:3), rather than to Moses or Aaron. Sawyer remarks that this language "seems almost to avoid the normal direct means of phrasing obligations," instead portraying a series of enactments that should, or could, or will be performed, depending on how the *yiqtōl* and *veqatal* forms are translated.[84]

Although not directly related to the sense of time that is conveyed, another layer of circumscribed indeterminacy arises from the fact that much of what is portrayed are enactments of ritual procedures. As such, vivid scenes emerge from the instructions that almost amount to

---

81. Sawyer, *Reading Leviticus*, 16–17.
82. Waltke and O'Connor, *Biblical Hebrew Syntax*, §29.6b citing Comrie, *Aspect*, 3–4.
83. Sawyer, *Reading Leviticus*, 16.
84. Sawyer, *Reading Leviticus*, 17.

dramatic presentations of the event.[85] Two interesting corollaries emerge from this to shape the unique communicative function of portrayal: First, the effect for readers is that of learning through observation in addition to instruction. While portrayal provides no commentary, it does supplement and expand the interpretive field by creating a "scene" that can spark insight in more flexible, intuitive ways. Second, because rituals are inherently symbolic and multivalent, readers will inevitably come to different conclusions about the significance of what is observed in the text, not only in a given moment but over the course of the text's lifespan. To some extent, the meaning that rituals express is not rigidly defined, but rather "fluid and mutable"; rituals hold open a space where a nuanced variety of meanings and significations may be equally valid.[86] The indeterminacy that ritual portrayal creates is also a defining characteristic of tactical difficulties as Steiner describes them, which create an intrinsic "rich undecidability" and provisionality so that meaning is intentionally "poised between alternatives of signification."[87] The effect is that the portrayal sparks the insight and perception of the reader, but not in static, precisely expressed ways. Within the given parameters of the specific ritual procedures that are prescribed there is a certain fluidity and flexibility of interpretation in which multiple meanings may be in play, over time and in any given moment.

The cumulative effect of these strategies in Leviticus is a blurring of a sense of time and perspective, which many interpreters have understood as presenting a vision of an idealized community. Bryan Bibb, for example, reads Leviticus as an "idealistic representation" of the world as the priestly writers thought it should be.[88] But more than that, Leviticus presents this ideal vision as a human possibility that the reader is invited to imagine herself as a witness to and participant in. Aware of the

---

85. David Damrosch makes much of the presentational character of the instructions, writing that "rather than simply prescribing the necessary details, the text stages the event, showing us a little ritual drama of interaction between the person offering the sacrifice, the priest and God." While I agree with his basic point, the contrast that he attempts to draw is unclear: how else would ritual procedures be prescribed? It seems that describing procedures that are physically enacted must inherently be highly visual, giving rise to vivid mental images in the reader's imagination. See Damrosch, *Narrative Covenant: Literature*, 264.

86. Davis, "Leviticus." Class lecture, Introduction to Old Testament Interpretation, Duke University Divinity School, Durham NC, 2012.

87. Steiner, *On Difficulty*, 40, 45.

88. Bibb, *Ritual Words*, 17–18; see also Damrosch, "Leviticus," 66.

narrative frame that portrays the event of discourse as occurring at a certain point in time with a defined situation and audience, the reader is also simultaneously drawn into the world of the text to share the perspective of the Israelite congregation hearing these words for the first time and looking into the possible futures that unfold before them. Bibb thus comments that the reader is "drawn into... interpretive engagement [that] follows the same contours of ritualization experienced by the characters in the story. We see and feel ourselves as participants within the community, standing alongside the priests as we watch every stroke of the knife, measuring our level of comprehension as the voice of God filters into our hearing."[89] In a real sense, new human possibilities are portrayed as an ongoing, open invitation to participate in bringing them into existence (Lev 26:3, 14–15).

These literary features together portray an impossible vision of life as a real possibility, namely that humans can coexist with a radically Other, dangerously divine presence "walking about in your midst" (וְהִתְהַלַּכְתִּי בְּתוֹכְכֶם; 26:12). Samuel Balentine describes this new possibility as the "Torah's vision of worship," which "summons the community of faith into a distinctive way of living that has the capacity to *shape* the given world, thus to bring it ultimately into conformity with God's own vision of the world's potential to be 'very good.'"[90] This is the overarching vision of the Pentateuch, of course, and not unique to Leviticus itself; but Leviticus discloses this vision in an unparalleled way, presenting the interpreter with a uniquely difficult challenge of translating the priestly vision of life into other contexts.

In fact, this difficulty of translation is another defining characteristic of tactical difficulties, including the tactic of portrayal. While portrayal sparks an "illuminative, penetrative insight," Steiner observes that "we cannot demonstrate or paraphrase [what is disclosed] grammatically."[91] This is because, as we have seen, tactical difficulties arise precisely when conventional uses of language are inadequate. With tactical difficulties, more than any other class of difficulty, form is content: so Taylor observes that "generally criticism struggles to articulate the portrayed through

---

89. Bibb, *Ritual Words*, 75.

90. Balentine, *Leviticus*, 11. Italics in the original. See also Balentine, *The Torah's Vision of Worship*, 59–77 and 148–76.

91. Steiner, *On Difficulty*, 34, 40.

description."⁹² The insights that arise through portrayal are "unsubstitutable," and cannot be "translated without remainder into other media."⁹³

The particular and tremendous challenge that tactical difficulties pose is that they convey what, in ordinary terms, is impossible, thus always remaining slightly out of our grasp and pressing us "to reach out toward more delicate orderings of perception," as Steiner writes, changing and expanding our capacity to envision what might be possible within the parameters of human experience.⁹⁴ The difficulty readers face in interpreting Leviticus is thus perhaps analogous to the difficulty the priestly writers faced in attempting to convey in literary form the divine encounter at the Tent of Meeting—the kind of encounter that exceeds the capacity of human language to describe.

The Generativity of Difficulty

The impossibility of exactly reproducing the insights disclosed through portrayal does not mean, however, that the text's direction of thought must remain out of reach of practical translation into meaningful contemporary categories. Translation may be approximate and not without remainder, but it is the claim of this book that difficulty—modal, contingent, and tactical—can prove to be fertile soil for generating new existential possibilities in the reader's own context. As we saw at the beginning of this chapter, the aim of translation is not replication of the text's forms of life in new applications, but the regeneration of its vision into new forms of life that are contextually appropriate. The conversation between text and reader is continually a new event of discourse, producing new insights in the reader's ever-changing horizon.

In different ways, each of the difficulties we have examined reflect a fundamental distance between text and reader: they are the gaps in our knowledge that must be filled, the alternative modes of existence that we must learn to recognize and relate to, or the existential possibilities that the text opens up in front of us. But while this distance is what makes interpretation inherently difficult, it is also what enables the encounter between text and reader to be generative. In chapter 2 we observed Paul Ricoeur's understanding of interpretation as nothing less than "an

---

92. Taylor, *The Language Animal*, 237.
93. Taylor, *The Language Animal*, 291.
94. Steiner, *On Difficulty*, 40.

attempt to make estrangement and distanciation productive" in the text/reader relationship, and this productivity would not be possible if the text did not introduce us to something fundamentally other or different.[95] Without this difficulty, there would be no opportunity for the text to enlarge, challenge, or enrich our understanding of what it is to be human, and human in relation to a transcendent Other. In a certain sense, the extent of a text's difficulty is also the extent of its generative capacity.

The priestly vision portrayed in Leviticus introduces a new (to us) and different way of life, but more than that, it is portrayed as a human possibility open to all; an invitation to imagine ourselves addressed by the discourse at Sinai, and to imagine a way of life shaped by these particular patterns and norms and ideals. Taken together and culminating with this tactic of existential portrayal, all the things that make the text difficult subtly, creatively, and non-coercively present the reader with new possibilities to imagine in the context of some other world, as well as an invitation to imagine how those possibilities might come to life for us.

Possibility is not inevitability, however. A text can only be as generative as the reader allows it to be, and this is risky as well as difficult. Coming to recognize the life-possibilities on offer in the vision of life that a text portrays is to risk being unsettled and destabilized and pressed into the hard work of what Taylor has called "regestalting," reevaluating and reshaping aspects of how we view and participate in the world we inhabit.[96] With tactical difficulty, a mode of disclosure that cannot objectively be explained or paraphrased, this existential dimension of interpretation comes unavoidably to the fore. More than contingent or modal difficulties, tactical difficulties preclude the possibility that the text can be understood at a safe, detached distance. At stake are the models of understanding through which we have structured our lives and beliefs, and the very point of tactical difficulty is to test the reliability of these models. "The gifted poet uses words to yield a changed perception of what we cavalierly call 'reality,' as though that were a fixed quantity," Ellen Davis warns; "but more than that, the poet's words change us. The best poems persuade us to think and act differently."[97]

The task of interpretation is now to respond to the possibilities on offer in front of the text by considering how the vision of life that it portrays may interact with the status quo of the reader's world. This is the

---

95. Ricoeur, *Interpretation Theory*, 44.
96. Taylor, *The Language Animal*, 46.
97. Davis, *Wondrous Depth*, 24.

final hermeneutical move we have had in our sights, the "new event of discourse" that was explored in chapter 2 with the help of Paul Ricoeur's theory of interpretation, and earlier in this chapter with George Steiner's notion of interpretation as being complete only when it "has so illuminated the source that new 'formats' of significance" become visible within the reader's own horizon.[98]

From Task to Text

The chapters that follow will seek to demonstrate this aspect of interpretation through three exegetical probes, in each case first identifying the text's direction of thought, and then asking how it may speak in contemporary contexts: What new perceptions, knowledges, or possibilities arise when the text's vision of life is brought into conversation with the readerly context?

In light of the central role that discourse plays in the priestly conception of how new forms of life are brought into existence—the creation account of Gen 1:1—2:4 being the paradigmatic statement of the constitutive power of language—the exegetical probes that follow will explore the following questions: What is the role of language in the priestly conception of life as it is portrayed in Leviticus? What does it do? How does it function within the community, and in the community's relationship to YHWH? And how important is it to structuring and sustaining the Israelite community in relation to YHWH?

Three focal points emerge as opportunities to engage these questions. First, chapter 4 will explore how sacrifice functions as a form of communication. YHWH speaks, but how does Israel respond? Just as the divine speech is mediated to Israel through Moses, the people (so it seems) cannot directly respond to YHWH; instead, an alternative mode of discourse in the form of the sacrificial system mediates Israel's range of responses. Through discourse, Israel learns the symbolic language of sacrifice that enables them to maintain an open line of communication with the divine.

Second, chapter 5 will examine the most explicit treatment of human speech in the book of Leviticus, the so-called narrative of the blasphemer that appears in 24:10–23. The narrative distills some of the most important themes of Leviticus, providing a window into the priestly

---

98. Ricoeur, *Interpretation Theory*, 92; Steiner, *After Babel*, 317.

vision of life that the book, as a whole, projects. The central role of speech in a narrative that deals with the most important themes of the book thus suggests that this narrative is particularly fertile soil for generating new forms of life in the discourse between text and reader.

Third, chapter 6 will explore how Leviticus 10 opens up a substantive reflection on the challenges and requirements of interpretation. This chapter directly engages the difficulties of interpretation through its literary portrayal of Aaron in the aftermath of the deaths of his sons, Nadav and Avihu, revealing a priestly understanding of interpretation as situational, unavoidable, and not completely safe. In the priestly vision of life, interpretation is essential to maintaining a life of human flourishing. An inevitable ambiguity and provisionality inheres even in divine discourse, necessitating an ongoing process of interpretation to discern the forms of life that lead to safety and to maintain the respect and freedom that are fundamental to healthy relationships.

In each of these exegetical probes, we will be looking for specific points of contact between the priestly conception of the constitutive function of discourse, and the ways that language is enacted in twenty-first century contexts. How does this vision inform our everyday uses of language within the various relationships that structure our families and communities? What is at stake in the event of discourse?

PART II

4

The Discourse of Sacrifice
Cultivating Communication

"A master translator can be defined as the perfect host."
—George Steiner[1]

The first series of תּוֹרֹת (*torot*) that comprise the opening chapters of Leviticus would seem to have little to do with discourse. The narrative frame portraying Israel's encounter with YHWH begins with divine speech as YHWH addresses Moses with the ritual instructions that are to be relayed to the Israelites: וַיִּקְרָא אֶל־מֹשֶׁה וַיְדַבֵּר יְהוָה אֵלָיו מֵאֹהֶל מוֹעֵד לֵאמֹר׃ דַּבֵּר אֶל־בְּנֵי יִשְׂרָאֵל וְאָמַרְתָּ אֲלֵהֶם ("And YHWH called to Moses and spoke to him from the tent of meeting saying, Speak to the Israelites..." Lev 1:1–2a). But as these instructions unfold at the literary level, the reader hears a single voice—is it Moses or YHWH?—evoking scenes of sacrifice: of animals selected and brought forward, blood sprinkled, flesh flayed and arranged on the wood that is upon the fire that is upon the altar, all of it ascending in smoke. Strictly speaking, there is no dialogue, only a series of actions portrayed with economy and efficiency. The voice of the narrator recedes from our awareness into the background as we watch these events unfold with a steady, certain rhythm.

---

1. Steiner, *Real Presences*, 146.

This absence of speech is not an indication that the opening discourse has come to an end, but that a significant shift is taking place in the patterns of communication that will structure the wilderness community from this point on. Israel's survival and identity as a nation depend on YHWH's continued presence (Exod 33:12–16), but the people's ability to host this presence has yet to be seen. Situated within the narrative arc of Torah at a crucial juncture in Israel's development as a nation—immediately following the completion of the Tent of Meeting where the divine presence is to take up residence—Leviticus begins by addressing an urgent question: Can humans learn to communicate in ways that sustain the continued presence of the divine and the consequent flourishing of the community? This chapter argues that the sacrificial system is the answer to this question, forming the template for the kind of respectful, reciprocal exchanges on which good relationships are built. Careful attention to the ways that the sacrificial system structures communication both between Israel and YHWH and among the Israelites themselves reveals that, for the priestly writers, discourse is a constitutive force in structuring and sustaining the Israelite community.

Sacrifice as Communication, from Three Perspectives

The claim that the sacrificial system holds a central function in structuring the community's patterns of communication finds support on three fronts: the socio-cultural function of ritual, the narrative context of the book of Leviticus, and the grammar of the sacrificial instructions.

First and most generally, there is broad agreement among sociologists, cultural anthropologists, and historians of religion that, as Mary Douglas summarized, all ritual is "preeminently a form of communication."[2] Drawing on the socio-linguistic work of Basil Bernstein, Douglas argued that the structures of ritual function much like linguistic forms insofar as they are "restricted codes" that enable the transmission of culture.[3] Both ritual and language are fixed forms that convey information through meaningful, recognizable patterns, creating

---

2. Douglas, *Natural Symbols*, 22. For a detailed account of how the view of ritual as communication is located within ritual studies, see also Catherine Bell, *Ritual Theory*, especially 23–43.

3. Douglas, *Natural Symbols*, 58; for more contextualization of this aspect of Douglas's work, see Fardon, *Mary Douglas*, 114.

"a two-way avenue for the communication of values and expectations."[4] Communication can take many forms, in other words, many of which do not depend on the spoken word. For example, Edmund Leach clarifies the expanse of human communication as a range of "expressive actions which operate as *signals, signs,* and *symbols,*" from the most basic elements of body language, facial expressions, and vocal inflection to the highly structured and culturally specific forms of ritual action.[5] The communicative function of sacrifice should thus not be overlooked simply because of the apparent silence of the ritual procedures; what is being portrayed here is a non-verbal mode of communication that is rich with meaning and expression.

Second, the narrative context of the book of Leviticus has primed readers to be alert to the idea that learning how to communicate with YHWH will be vital to Israel's development as a nation. The opening pages of Leviticus are not, of course, the opening pages of the story of Israel or of Israel's God; YHWH has spoken in many times and places, and since the days of Cain and Abel individuals have responded by bringing their offerings to YHWH (Gen 4:1–16). Language, too, regularly served to mediate the fundamental distance between human and divine. But as Rabbi Jonathan Sacks observes, this was a solution that worked for the patriarchs, while the discourse at Sinai presents a new situation that is a turning point in the relationship between YHWH and Israel. Israel's formation as a nation is an entirely new development, with new requirements.[6] And in the wilderness wanderings, the sufficiency of language to mediate the distance between human and divine has been tested and found wanting.

The scenario is this: newly liberated from the oppression of Egypt, the Israelites depend on Moses and Aaron to mediate the divine word. While they have seen YHWH's power and deliverance (Exod 4:30–31; 14:10–14, 30–31), they have heard only the voices of Moses and Aaron speaking on YHWH's behalf (Exod 4:12–17). Despite Moses's insistence that it is YHWH who brought them out of the land of Egypt and who is responsible for their sustenance (Exod 16:7–8), the people grumble (לון) against Moses and Aaron again and again for their failure to provide for their basic needs (Exod 15:24; 16:2; 17:3). In the wake of their deliverance from Egypt, the Israelites are consumed with a fundamental

---

4. Bibb, *Ritual Words*, 63. See also Douglas, *Natural Symbols*, 2, 54.
5. Leach, *Culture and Communication*, 9. Italics in the original.
6. Sacks, *Leviticus*, 11.

question about their nascent nationhood: Whom do we trust? Who will provide for us? "Is YHWH among us, or not?" (Exod 17:7).

So YHWH decides to settle the matter, saying to Moses, "I am coming to you in a thick cloud, so that the people may hear (שמע) when I speak with you, and so they may trust you forever" (Exod 19:9). But this proximity is more than the Israelites can bear, so they plead with Moses to continue in his role as mediator: "You speak with us, and we will hearken, but let not God speak with us, lest we die!" (Exod 20:18–21, Fox). With this, Israel's doubt about YHWH's presence and Moses's trustworthiness as mediator would seem to have been resolved, but the resolution immediately unravels. While Moses is on the mountain receiving the instructions for the sanctuary that is to be the locus of YHWH's earthly presence (Exod 25:8—31:18), the people panic. Recently unmoored from the bondage of tyranny, Moses's long absence engenders fears of abandonment and the prospect of leaderlessness is intolerable for them. In this new situation, without precedent, neither Aaron nor the people know what to do (Exod 32:2), and they grasp for substitutes. Again mistaking YHWH's deliverance for Moses's leadership (Exod 32:1), their confusion escalates to the point of seeking safety and security in the form of a molten calf. But these frantic attempts produce the exact opposite of the well-being they sought, resulting not only in the deaths of more than three thousand people (Exod 32:28), but also jeopardizing YHWH's promised presence. For their own safety, YHWH warns, "I will not go up in your midst—for you are a hard-necked people!—lest I destroy you on the way" (Exod 33:3). If the sights and sounds of YHWH's presence were too much for the people to bear, the real threat of abandonment is even more unbearable: "When the people heard this terrible word (הַדָּבָר הָרָע הַזֶּה), they mourned" (Exod 33:4), and the burden of leadership becomes too great for Moses to bear alone (Exod 33:7–13). Without YHWH's presence, there is no point in going up to the promised land, Moses argues; the identity and survival of the nation depend on this very thing (Exod 33:16). So YHWH relents (Exod 33:14, 17), reinstating the terms of the covenant (Exod 34:10–28) and taking up residence in the newly constructed Tent of Meeting (Exod 39:42; 40:34–48).

Again Israel finds themselves in a new situation: Not since the beginning of the world has YHWH walked about in the company of humankind (Gen 3:8; Lev 26:12), and now the two from the garden have become a multitude. But a history of botched communication stretches back even farther than the grumbling and idolatry of the wilderness, all the way to the twisted words that caused the first rift in the fabric of creation (Gen 3) and the first, most fundamental distance between human and divine. The narrative setting of the situation at Sinai thus frames a crucial element in this new situation of co-habitation: good communication. Establishing appropriate patterns of communication will be fundamental to allaying Israel's fears and enabling them to maintain a hospitable environment for the divine presence, thus creating and sustaining Israel's identity as a nation.

The third support for the claim that the sacrificial system functions centrally in structuring the community's patterns of communication is the grammar of the opening chapters of the book. The first seven chapters of Leviticus, commonly referred to as the sacrificial system,[7] do not, strictly speaking, deal with a "sacrificial" system; they deal with a system for "bringing-near." For contemporary readers, the notion of sacrifice has largely come to denote one of two things: either the animal sacrifice that took place in the ancient world, or any self-negating activity that represents personal cost and commitment, two senses that Moshe Halbertal designates with the shorthand "sacrificing to" or "sacrificing for."[8] In contrast, the generic term that Leviticus uses to designate a variety of offerings is קָרְבָּן (qorban), the nominal derivative of קרב that denotes "that which is brought near, presented, offered." While it is true that the activities portrayed in the first chapters of Leviticus involve bringing something to the altar, and that in most instances what is brought is an animal whose life will be returned to YHWH (i.e. Lev 1:3–9), it is significant that the primary term used to describe these processes does not intrinsically connote either death ("sacrificing to") or negation ("sacrificing for"). The קָרְבָּן, as Milgrom has further observed, is "not limited to offerings for the altar, but applies to any sanctuary gift, such as draft animals and carts (Num 7:3) or spoils of war (Num 31:50)"—offerings, in other words, that do not necessarily involve the death of an animal.[9] In fact, the Hebrew word that specifically denotes the sacrificial slaughter of an animal, זֶבַח (zevakh), does not make an appearance for two whole

---

7. See, for example, the way the book is outlined in Milgrom, *Leviticus 1–16*; Balentine, *Leviticus*; Levine, *Leviticus*; and Wenham, *The Book of Leviticus*.

8. Halbertal, *On Sacrifice*, 1. For further discussion of the imprecision that "sacrifice" introduces into the conversation, see Hénaff, *The Price of Truth*, 156–63; and Musser, "Sacrifice, Sabbath, and the Restoration of Creation," 1–11.

9. Milgrom, *Leviticus 1–16*, 145.

chapters, and is limited to the context of a specific type of offering, the זֶבַח שְׁלָמִים (*zevakh shelamim*, Lev 3:1).

The odd syntax of the phrase that begins the instructions further underscores the point that the opening chapters are about setting the parameters for Israel's approach to the divine presence. The phrase reads: אָדָם כִּי־יַקְרִיב מִכֶּם קָרְבָּן לַיהוָה (lit., "When anyone brings-near from among you a bringing-near to YHWH," Lev 1:2). We would expect the particle מִכֶּם to precede the verb, but instead it follows it. Although Milgrom can find no apparent reason for this unusual word order,[10] there is one obvious possibility: fronting the verb places the weight of emphasis squarely on the action that it sets in motion, so that everything that follows is subordinated to the movement of drawing-near. The prepositions used throughout the instructions for the offerings also reinforce the notion of movement. Both לְ and אֶל are prepositions of motion,[11] and Milgrom observes that in every instance of the construction יַקְרִיבֶנּוּ אֶל ("brings-near to," i.e., זָכָר תָּמִים יַקְרִיבֶנּוּ אֶל־פֶּתַח אֹהֶל מוֹעֵד יַקְרִיב אֹתוֹ, Lev 1:3) the object of the preposition is "either God (Num 16:5, 9), the altar (Lev 1:15; 2:8; [= Num 5:25] 6:7), the sanctuary entrance (Exod 29:4; 40:12; Lev 1:3), or the priest (Exod 28:1; Lev 2:8; 9:9)."[12]

So the first instructions that YHWH gives to the people are instructions to facilitate encounter. YHWH speaks "from the Tent of Meeting" (מֵאֹהֶל מוֹעֵד, Lev 1:1), the very purpose of which was to provide a point of contact, a meeting-place, between YHWH and Israel.[13] And the grammar of this encounter is not static, but dynamic; קרב is a movement word, the basic meaning of which is "to come near, approach."[14] In the context of the cult, the verbal form of קרב carries the specific sense of "to offer, present,"[15] but the movement that enables such offering holds priority over what is brought and what is done with what is brought, as various translators have recognized. Martin Buber found both "sacrifice" and "offering" insufficient,

---

10. Milgrom, *Leviticus 1–16*, 145.

11. Williams, *Hebrew Syntax*, §265, 297; Waltke and O'Connor, *Biblical Hebrew Syntax*, §10.4a; Gesenius and Kautzsch, §119r; Joüon and Muraoka, *A Grammar of Biblical Hebrew*, §133b.

12. Milgrom, *Leviticus 1–16*, 147.

13. Balentine, *Leviticus*, 27; Milgrom, *Leviticus 1–16*, 140. Milgrom also notes the significance of the divine discourse being addressed not only to Moses, but to all the people, אֶל־בְּנֵי יִשְׂרָאֵל, in contrast to other ANE cultic traditions that involved the priesthood while excluding the laity.

14. Kohler and Baumgartner, *HALOT*, s.v. "קרב."

15. Milgrom, *Leviticus 1–16*, 145.

instead translating קָרְבָּן as *Darnahung* ("nearbringing, forebringing, therebringing"); Everett Fox prefers "near-offering"; and Jonathan Sacks calls the קָרְבָּן the "coming close by bringing close."[16] The Israelites are not to come empty-handed (Exod 23:14), and how and what they bring is crucial to maintaining an open path of approach, but the point here is that it is the approach itself that is of fundamental importance. The grammar of sacrifice, as portrayed in the priestly texts, is a grammar of encounter. It is about facilitating interaction between two parties, enabling a proximity and correspondence that would not otherwise be possible. Sacrifice mediates communication and communion.[17]

Structuring Discourse, in Two Primary Ways

Approaching sacrifice as a mode of communication raises two questions: *what* does it communicate, and *how* does it communicate? As for the first question, since sacrifice "serves a multiplicity of functions" within the priestly system, it communicates many different things that have been well documented in the study of biblical sacrifice and the history of religion.[18] There are both voluntary and obligatory offerings; offerings performed on a regular, daily basis as maintenance of the cult, for specific life-events or situations that may arise, and at set times within the religious calendar. There are offerings to express thanks and celebration, and offerings to expiate and atone for impurity and either willful or inadvertent wrongdoing. Like language, the system is flexible and fluid, offering a range of expressions that "cover the gamut of the psychological, emotional, and religious needs of the people,"[19] and leading scholars to conclude that the sacrificial system cannot and should not be reduced to a single overarching motive or function. What sacrifice communicates depends on each particular situation, to the extent that it may be discerned.[20] So the answer to the question of "what sacrifice communicates"

---

16. Buber and Rosenzweig, *Scripture and Translation*, 77; Fox, *The Five Books of Moses*, 497; Sacks, *Leviticus*, 12.

17. Emphasizing the redemptive function of sacrifice, Musser puts it this way: "Sacrifice is not primarily concerned with death; it is oriented toward communion." "Sacrifice, Sabbath, and the Restoration of Creation," 109.

18. Levine, *Leviticus*, 3; see also Miller, *The Religion of Ancient Israel*, 106–30.

19. Milgrom, *Leviticus: A Continental Commentary*, 20.

20. Milgrom, *Leviticus: A Continental Commentary*, 20; Hubert and Mauss, *Sacrifice*, 50–60.

is necessarily descriptive, as it must attend to and be constrained by the social, historical, cultural, and literary contexts in which sacrifice occurs.

The second question is more interesting for its potential both to be descriptive of the priestly portrayal of sacrifice and to open up new directions of thought for readerly contexts: *How* does sacrifice communicate? What are the particular forms that enable exchange between YHWH and Israel, that is, between two radically different parties when a great deal is at stake? And what might we learn from this about the forms of communication that shape our own relationships and societies? These are huge questions, of course, and I will not pretend to do justice to them here. Instead, I would like to open up the conversation by examining two ways that the sacrificial system structures Israel's discourse. First, and centrally, it enables Israel's response to YHWH as a non-verbal, enacted form of communication. Second, it sets clear parameters around how the Israelites are to communicate with one another, a concern that is not entirely distinct from the primary objective of establishing a community capable of hosting the divine. From these focal points a view of discourse emerges as a constitutive force capable of altering reality, either sustaining or damaging the conditions necessary for human flourishing. For contemporary readers, these observations have the potential to generate new ways of thinking about what is possible and what is at stake in communicating with the "other" in freighted situations of encounter.

The Silence of Sacrifice: Communicating with the Divine

I have suggested that the relative absence of the spoken word in Leviticus's literary portrayal of sacrifice does not disqualify the endeavor of exploring how sacrifice functions as a form of communication. But it would be a mistake to leave it at this and gloss over the "literary" silence of sacrifice, taking it for granted as an insignificant variant within a range of communicative activities and behaviors. As we have noted, language functions centrally throughout the Hebrew Bible in mediating the divine-human relationship and, in the priestly view of divine speech, in creating and generating new forms of life. The dearth of reported human speech in this crucial moment of re-making patterns of communication is thus an intriguing detail worth further investigation: What comes to the fore when speech is replaced by alternative modes of communication? What does this reveal, if anything, about the priestly view of human speech and its function?

Highlighting its non-verbal character brings three features of this alternative mode of communication to the fore: the mediatory function of gifts, the unavoidability of proximity, and the significance of embodiment.

Gifts as Mediators

In the absence of words, something else must bridge the distance between self and other if any meaningful interaction is to take place. While each offering serves a unique purpose, if there is a common denominator uniting all the offerings presented in the sanctuary it is their basic function as gifts that create connection by mediating the distance between human and divine.[21]

Drawing on the work of Henri Hubert and Marcel Mauss on the social function of ceremonial gift exchange, Marcel Hénaff has demonstrated that ceremonial gift exchange is not primarily a moral gesture, such as an offer of charity or material assistance, or proof of the giver's magnanimity and selflessness.[22] This is also true of biblical sacrifice; Israel's offerings are a response to the divine initiative of creation, preservation, and communion, and the notion of sacrifice as an expression of self-denial and renunciation would have been unknown to the biblical writers.[23]

Nor is the offering of a gift primarily about the thing that is offered, though the gift must reflect the appropriate respect and esteem that it is meant to express. In specifying a range of economic brackets for the voluntary offerings, Leviticus prioritizes the participation of everyone in the community. An individual could bring a bull, a lamb or goat, or a bird.[24] Even grain could be an appropriate gift in the offering commonly understood to be the "poor man's burnt offering" (מִנְחָה, minha).[25]

---

21. Balentine, *Leviticus*, 28; Milgrom, *Leviticus 1–16*, 162.

22. Hénaff, *The Price of Truth*, 134. See also Hubert and Mauss, *Sacrifice*; and Mauss, *The Gift*.

23. Halbertal, *On Sacrifice*, 1.

24. With the exception of the זֶבַח שְׁלָמִים (Lev 3), which Milgrom suggests is because a bird would not have provided enough meat to be worth eating, which defeats the primary purpose of the זֶבַח שְׁלָמִים as providing meat for the table. Milgrom, *Leviticus 1–16*, 221–22.

25. Milgrom, *Leviticus 1–16*, 195.

Similarly, the instructions for the non-voluntary offering of the חַטָּאת (hattat) include explicit arrangements for situations in which the offerer cannot afford the required offering (אִם־לֹא תַגִּיע יָדוֹ דֵי שֶׂה, Lev 5:7, 11). These allowances reflect a system in which the most important thing is the exchange itself, from which no one was to be excluded on the basis of wealth. The purpose of gift-giving, Hénaff summarizes, "is neither the thing given (which captures the attention of economists), nor even the gesture of giving (which fascinates moralists)," but the formation or maintenance of a relationship that is expressed in the act of giving and receiving.[26]

It is worth noting that the use of a physical object to facilitate the interaction between two parties presupposes an awareness of the fundamental distinction between self and other, while simultaneously expressing a willingness to cross those boundaries. Hénaff writes that the extension of a "mediating object" from one person to another—a handshake, for example, or a hostess gift—is an extension of the self into "alien space" for the purpose of establishing a connection and demonstrating good will.[27] Similarly, "sacrifice recognizes, consecrates" and then crosses a boundary between the visible and invisible, the common and sacred, the human and the divine.[28] The altar and its proper maintenance is thus crucial to Israel's ability to communicate with YHWH, since it provides the means through which this boundary-crossing transfer occurs: the offering is turned into smoke (הִקְטִיר), ascending as a "pleasing odor to YHWH" (רֵיחַ־נִיחוֹחַ לַיהוָה, Lev 1:9).

Boundaries also presuppose the possibility of rejection, of course. Tracing the unpredictability of acceptance back to the first offerings of Cain and Abel and YHWH's unexplained rejection of Cain's offering (Gen 4:1–16), Moshe Halbertal argues that the word "offering" more accurately depicts biblical sacrifice than "gift," since a gift presumes acceptance, while an offering is open-ended; it is extended into a liminal space where it may yet be spurned. Halbertal observes that the difference between קָרְבָּן or מִנְחָה and the more generic biblical word for gift, מַתָּנָה (mattanah), reveals this "crucial gap . . . between giving and receiving."[29] קָרְבָּן and מִנְחָה are used exclusively in instances where a gift is offered from an inferior to a superior, "to stress the fact that the superior has

---

26. Hénaff, *The Price of Truth*, 141.
27. Hénaff, *The Price of Truth*, 132–35.
28. Hénaff, *The Price of Truth*, 182.
29. Halbertal, *On Sacrifice*, 10.

the privilege of rejecting the gift."³⁰ In this light, the precise instructions for the kinds of offerings that should be brought and how they are to be offered appear not as the demands of an exacting deity but as a gracious accommodation that works to mitigate the anxiety and risk of rejection by clarifying exactly what will be accepted and what will not: אֶל־פֶּתַח אֹהֶל מוֹעֵד יַקְרִיב אֹתוֹ לִרְצֹנוֹ לִפְנֵי יְהוָה ("to the entrance of the Tent of Meeting he should/will bring it near, *for his acceptance before YHWH*," Lev 1:3b).

So the offering given and received is ultimately about initiating or sustaining a relationship; the point is "to establish bonds of recognition."³¹ In this new situation, the sacrificial system is Israel's first opportunity to extend a concrete pledge of good faith that acknowledges their acceptance of YHWH's presence and desire for it to remain with them. The exchange of a physical object, visibly accepted or rejected, continues the cycle of reciprocity initiated by YHWH and mediates the distance between human and divine. Israel's voluntary participation in this exchange is thus their public commitment to maintaining an ongoing association with YHWH, a continual "procedure of reciprocal recognition" that keeps the lines of communication open, בַּבֹּקֶר בַּבֹּקֶר ("morning by morning," Lev 6:13).³²

Rethinking Proximity

Earlier we observed that the grammar of sacrifice is a grammar of encounter, of "coming-close by bringing-close." This takes on even deeper significance if the offering is understood to be the primary vehicle through which Israel expresses their receptivity to the divine presence. Bringing an offering is not simply what one must do in order to approach the divine, as if it were a kind of entrance pass guaranteeing safe passage; it is the entire reason for the approach. The distinction here is subtle, but important. One does not bring a gift in order to (safely) approach; one approaches because there is something one wishes to express, and which must be expressed through a gift. And so it is a coming-close *because* bringing close. A system that prioritizes physical offerings as a primary mode of communication is a system predicated on proximity.

30. Halbertal, *On Sacrifice*, 10. Halbertal addresses only the מִנְחָה, but the distinction holds true for the קָרְבָּן as well, which designates only those items that are offered to YHWH and never to a fellow human.

31. Hénaff, *The Price of Truth*, 18.

32. Hénaff, *The Price of Truth*, 114.

Indeed, this necessity of physical proximity permeates the sacrificial instructions: offerings must be brought אֶל־פֶּתַח אֹהֶל מוֹעֵד ("to the opening of the tent of meeting"; Lev 1:3 and throughout); at times the offerer must personally lay his or her hand on the head of animal offered (Lev 1:4; 3:2; 4:24), or prepare the מִנְחָה (*minha*) with the required oil and frankincense (Lev 2:1, 15); the שְׁלָמִים (*shelamim*) is to be brought with the offeror's own two hands (יָדָיו תְּבִיאֶינָה אֵת אִשֵּׁי יְהוָה, Lev 7:29–30; 8:27–28);[33] and the phrase לִפְנֵי יְהוָה ("before YHWH") is repeated fifty-nine times in Leviticus alone, more than one-fourth of the occurrences in the entire Hebrew Bible. Sacrifice is not a mode of communication that can be conducted from afar; the offering of a gift is simultaneously a recognition of the fundamental distinction between self and other, and a respectful crossing of the boundaries of distinction.

This tension holds together two moments in Israel's recent history as a redemptive alternative to either the presumption of constructing the golden calf in defiance of appropriate boundaries, or the fearful dependence on Moses as mediator in complete avoidance of approaching the divine (Exod 20:18–21). Sacrifice mediates between these two extremes, requiring the people's participation while teaching them appropriate forms of approach. Israel learns that boundaries exist not ultimately to keep things separate, but to enable a relationship between two parties in which both may maintain their dignity and distinction. The characterization of Leviticus as a "book of separations" is thus only half of the story.[34]

The Significance of Embodiment

It is widely understood that sacrifice is symbolic, but exactly what this means requires some clarification. In one sense, a symbol can mean that something (the sign) stands for, or represents, something else (the signified). A handshake can "symbolize" a greeting between strangers, a business agreement, or good sportsmanship, for example. So we might say that the symbol says something like "Nice to meet you," "I agree to these terms," or "Good game." At the same time and in another sense, however, these symbolic actions also do what they say: extending a hand to a stranger constitutes the introduction, closes the deal, or formally cedes victory to an opponent. Given a clear enough context, the verbalization

---

33. Milgrom, *Leviticus 1–16*, 430; Levine, 45–46.
34. Fox's phrase, as articulated in *The Five Books of Moses*, 499.

of the symbol's meaning is superfluous; the performative symbol doesn't need to be explained to accomplish and concretize a social exchange.

Biblical sacrifice is symbolic in this way, in that it is embodied and enacted communication that accomplishes what it displays in the context of the cult. Sign and signified are one and the same, not disconnected as if the ritual were a dramatic performance of an intangible, ethereal "reality" existing in another sphere. It is, rather, a concrete procedure of "world construction."[35] Mary Douglas's detailed analysis of how symbols function in relation to the social order demonstrated that in societies where symbols are highly valued and ritualism is strong, "symbolic action is held to be most certainly efficacious."[36] Her work on this topic followed a circle of French sociologists among whom Marcel Mauss and Henri Hubert had been influential, and reflects their view of sacrifice as functioning to generate and concretize social structures.[37] The insight that this school of thought lends is that if we view sacrifice as a form of communication, and find that it is also an "operative mechanism" that "produces what it shows," then we can see in the sacrificial system a view of communication as something that does more than convey information or exteriorize thoughts and beliefs.[38] Put simply, sacrifice says by doing.

So we can observe that the basically non-verbal character of sacrifice yields a mode of communication that is intrinsically efficacious, thereby minimizing the possibility of manipulation, equivocation, or dissembling. This idea will become clearer in the following sections as we examine the situations in which human speech comes directly into focus, but already we can draw some initial observations.

It is tempting to infer that the non-verbal, symbolic patterns of communication constituting Israel's primary mode of response to the divine discourse indicate an elevation of action over the spoken word. Conventional wisdom suggests that "actions speak louder than words" and "we need more than thoughts and prayers," as if language alone is either insufficient or ineffectual in moments of crisis. But this devaluation of the spoken word does not quite ring true within the priestly purview:

---

35. Gorman, *Ideology of Ritual*, 59.

36. Douglas, *Natural Symbols*, 8. Chapter 1 of this volume is an indispensable contribution to the broader discussion of symbolic action as a form of communication.

37. Douglas specifically notes the influence of the French sociologists associated with *L'Année Sociologique*, an academic journal of sociology founded by Émile Durkheim in 1898. See Douglas, *Natural Symbols*, xxxiii.

38. Hénaff, *The Price of Truth*, 185.

according to the priestly writers, the divine word spoke the world into being (Gen 1:1–2) and laid out the parameters for the tabernacle and cult (Exod 25–31).[39] Language is the first and most fundamental creative and generative force. Perhaps, then, what we see in the language of sacrifice is a distinction between the capacities of divine and human speech: Is it only the divine word that carries operative force, while humans must resort to more concrete, demonstrative modes of communication? This is not quite right, either. Throughout the book of Leviticus Moses is charged to communicate the divine word to the people and is assumed to be a wholly reliable verbal communicator. Similarly, Aaron is tasked with the ongoing responsibility of teaching and perpetuating these instructions among the Israelites (Lev 10:10–11).

In the broader context of the Sinai pericope, an important clue emerges about the effects of human speech: Israel has a dubious history with words, so that in this crucial moment of establishing good patterns of communication, too much is at stake to rely on human speech. The symbolic language of sacrifice takes center stage not because words are inconsequential, but because they can be untrustworthy.

In the moments leading up to the discourse at the Tent of Meeting the question of how Israel will communicate with YHWH has become critical. A key element of this scenario that we have not yet addressed is that on two occasions Israel had verbally expressed their assent to the terms of the covenant—כֹּל אֲשֶׁר־דִּבֶּר יְהוָה נַעֲשֶׂה (Exod 19:8; cf. 24:3–7)—but this commitment did not prove sufficient to hedge against the debacle of the golden calf (Exod 32). What happens after the reinstatement of the covenant in Exodus 34 is surely significant: first the construction of the Tent of Meeting (Exod 35:1—40:38), followed by the sacrificial instructions that begin in Leviticus 1. Human speech temporarily recedes from the narrative while these new spaces of encounter and new patterns of approach are put into place. These details, along with what we are about to observe in the reappearance of human speech in Leviticus 5, suggest a certain wariness about the effects of human speech in the foundational moments of establishing good patterns of communication.

---

39. Gorman, *Ideology of Ritual*, 49–52.

Disordered Speech: False Oaths and Deception

Creating Chaos: False Oaths in Leviticus 5:1, 4

Chapters 1–3 of Leviticus contain the instructions for the voluntary offerings, the עֹלָה (*olah*) the מִנְחָה (*minha*), and the זֶבַח שְׁלָמִים (*zevah shelamim*). The first mention of wrongdoing (חטא) appears in 4:2 with the instructions for the חַטָּאת (*hattat*), but at this point חטא is only a generalization; the sacrificial procedures for dealing with it are explained before the particular situations that require the חַטָּאת come into focus. The first sins that are specifically named in the book appear in 5:1–4, and form a chiastic unit that juxtaposes inappropriate speech with contracting impurity by coming into contact with either animal or human uncleanness:

5:1 Failure to testify
    5:2 Contact with animal uncleanness (טָמֵא)
    5:3 Contact with human uncleanness
5:4 Uttering an impulsive oath

This brief passage poses several intriguing questions. Why do the speech-acts of 5:1, 4 bracket the seemingly unrelated issue of coming into contact with impurity in 5:2, 3—do these things have anything to do with one another, and if so, what? Is there any significance to the fact that the first mention of human speech and the first mention of wrongdoing (חטא) appear in conjunction with one another? What, exactly, is the "wrongdoing" that these behaviors supposedly constitute—particularly since the person is said to have been unaware (נֶעְלַם)? And how can he or she have been unaware of having done these things in the first place, particularly in the scenarios of vv. 1, 4? I will take verses 1 and 4 in turn, examining them closely before turning to some observations about what they suggest about the role of speech.

The scenario in 5:1 is that someone (נֶפֶשׁ), any person within the community, hears a public call for information concerning something that has happened. The person was actually a witness to the matter and could provide testimony about something that he saw or heard, and yet he ignores the call and says nothing. According to the priestly writers, this is a wrongdoing (חטא) that incurs a penalty: in the ancient Near East, the קוֹל אָלָה (*qol olah*) denotes a custom of issuing a public proclamation to elicit more information concerning a crime that has been committed, and Milgrom explains that these calls were "enforced by a contingent curse."[40] Failure to speak up subjects the witness to the consequences of his silence: וְנָשָׂא עֲוֺנוֹ ("he must bear his punishment"). The specific consequences are not enumerated, but presumably it depended on what was at stake in the situation for which a witness was needed.

At first glance, the scenario in 5:4 appears to be the opposite of what was enumerated in 5:1. Instead of not saying what should have been said, a person thoughtlessly "blurts out an oath" (תִשָּׁבַע לְבַטֵּא בִשְׂפָתַיִם). The verb בטא denotes saying something impulsively or impetuously, and the redundancy of בִשְׂפָתַיִם (lit., "with lips") indicates that there is a particular issue with having sworn something out loud, regardless of whether the oath was for a good or a bad purpose.[41] The next part of the verse is difficult, reading וְנֶעְלַם מִמֶּנּוּ וְהוּא־יָדַע וְאָשֵׁם לְאַחַת מֵאֵלֶּה. Fox renders it as "and though (the fact) is hidden from him, he comes-to-know that he incurred guilt in (any) of these." Following the rabbis, Milgrom reads נֶעְלַם as indicating forgetfulness, which yields a slightly smoother translation: "though he has known it, the fact escapes him but (thereafter) he feels guilt in any of these matters."[42] In other words, the person did not implausibly utter an oath without being aware of it; he obviously knew of his action, but the matter had slipped his mind. The clause of 5:4b followed by 5:5 concludes the pericope to summarize the preceding verses with instructions for what should be done when the person becomes aware of having done wrong in any of these matters. Baruch Levine draws an important distinction between becoming objectively aware of having transgressed, and the subjective feeling of guilt in his observation that "according to cultic law guilt is not a function of awareness; it is a function of committing an act or failing to commit one."[43] So the phrase, הוּא־יָדַע וְאָשֵׁם literally reads, "he, being guilty, knew"; he becomes aware that he is—and has been—culpable.

Both of these situations have to do with speech—either saying something or not saying something—and both of them are considered instances of wrongdoing, as indicated by the opening clause (כִּי־תֶחֱטָא) and the concluding phrase confirming culpability. But why do these things constitute errors in the first place? To understand why these situations

---

40. Milgrom, *Leviticus 1–16*, 294.

41. Koehler and Baumgartner, *HALOT*, s.v., "בטא." See also Milgrom, *Leviticus 1–16*, 299.

42. Milgrom, *Leviticus 1–16*, 293.

43. Levine, *Leviticus*, 27.

appear in the context of the sacrificial instructions and how they inform an understanding of the function of language, we first need to understand the logic of why these are considered inappropriate uses of speech. While the two situations appear to be quite different from one another—one is a deliberate refusal to speak, and one is a careless blurting out of speech—they illustrate two different ways to commit the same error.

Both the failure to testify and impulsively uttering an oath are characterized by the verb חטא, but this introduces a complication: Milgrom points out that P uses the verb חטא exclusively to refer to inadvertent errors.[44] How can either of these things have been done inadvertently? Refusing to testify is obviously a deliberate, "if not brazen," action. But Milgrom observes that there is no evidence that the person *agreed to* the public imprecation that he heard (cf. Num 5:22; Deut 27:11–26), so no deception has actually occurred, which would be a more serious offense.[45] It is an error of omission, not commission. In these situations, Milgrom deduces, the error falls into a legal category that allows a deliberate sin to be demoted to the category of inadvertent sin, once the person realizes his transgression and takes the appropriate steps—we will return to this below.

Impulsively blurting out an oath is also obviously done deliberately, although it is easier to imagine inadvertence in a situation of saying something you didn't fully intend to say. But again, the situation hinges on a legal provision hinted at in the difficult phrase noted above, נֶעְלַם מִמֶּנּוּ: "the fact escapes him" (5:4). Commentators agree that the issue is not so much having uttered an oath thoughtlessly, but that once spoken an oath is legally binding and in this case the person has failed to fulfill his oath; it was of so little consequence to him that it immediately slipped his mind. Nonetheless, Milgrom argues that this, too, can be understood as an inadvertent error: there is no evidence that the person did not intend to fulfill the oath, only that he neglected to do so. The oath was sworn deliberately—if thoughtlessly—but, like the failure to testify, it was not a deliberate deception.[46] So both of these situations qualify as inadvertent errors that are expiable in conjunction with confession, as we will soon see. Herein lies the answer to their inclusion within a pericope dealing with inadvertent error, as well as the common thread uniting them: both

---

44. Milgrom, *Leviticus 1–16*, 229.
45. Milgrom, *Leviticus 1–16*, 314.
46. Milgrom, *Leviticus 1–16*, 313.

instances of inappropriate uses of language involve unfulfilled oaths that make a person vulnerable to consequences.

Now we are prepared to ask the more important question of what is at stake in these scenarios: Why are these things errors in the first place? What is so significant—and offensive—about unfulfilled oaths?

Milgrom offers two explanations, one historical and one cultic. First, he notes that unfulfilled oaths were universally condemned in the ancient world. Oaths, which invoked the name of a god or gods as leverage on behalf of a human endeavor, were understood to be a "risky undertaking," attracting unwanted attention from the gods, whose preferences and sensibilities were unpredictable; there was "no telling when or what supernal forces would be offended."[47] Better not to take the risk at all, and it was certainly unwise to undertake an oath on a whim or if there was a chance that you could be unable to fulfill it.

On cultic grounds, Milgrom argues that the juxtaposition of laws concerning unfulfilled oaths with situations in which a person may unwittingly contract ritual impurity (Lev 5:2–3) indicates that in all these situations the effect is the same: unfulfilled oaths and uncleansed impurity pollute the sanctuary, requiring the same procedures for expiation. So we can observe that speaking and hearing have the same practical effects as physical contact; they both are capable of causing impurity, and both require expiation.[48] For the priestly writers, there is no such thing as empty words.

While both of these explanations shed light on what is at stake here, neither is fully satisfactory. Milgrom has explained that these behaviors are dangerous because they pollute the sanctuary, but why do they pollute the sanctuary? What, exactly, is the problem? To find a better solution, we need to return to what we know to be the most fundamental thing about the priestly notion of speech:

בְּרֵאשִׁית בָּרָא אֱלֹהִים אֵת הַשָּׁמַיִם וְאֵת הָאָרֶץ
וְהָאָרֶץ הָיְתָה תֹהוּ וָבֹהוּ וְחֹשֶׁךְ עַל־פְּנֵי תְהוֹם
וְרוּחַ אֱלֹהִים מְרַחֶפֶת עַל־פְּנֵי הַמָּיִם
וַיֹּאמֶר אֱלֹהִים יְהִי אוֹר וַיְהִי־אוֹר
וַיַּרְא אֱלֹהִים אֶת־הָאוֹר כִּי־טוֹב
וַיַּבְדֵּל אֱלֹהִים בֵּין הָאוֹר וּבֵין הַחֹשֶׁךְ

At the beginning of God's creating of the heavens and the earth,

47. Milgrom, *Leviticus 1–16*, 313.
48. Milgrom, *Leviticus 1–16*, 315.

When the earth was wild and waste, darkness over the face of Ocean,
Rushing-spirit of God hovering over the face of the waters—
God said: Let there be light! And there was light.
God saw the light: that it was good.
God separated the light from the darkness.
(Gen 1:1–4, Fox)

Speech is a divine act that generates and brings order to the created world; God spoke, and it was so. The problem with unfulfilled oaths is not chiefly that they pollute the sanctuary, although they certainly do; the problem is that they are the opposite of generative speech that brings things into existence and brings order to human experience. They are false starts that leave things undone, creating only a liminal state that is neither one thing nor another. In 5:1, a person is confronted with a situation that calls for resolution that he is capable of providing, but he refuses to act as a witness so that the imprecation remains open-ended and unfulfilled. In 5:4, the situation is even simpler: swearing an oath sets something in motion, initiating a cause-and-effect that goes nowhere and does nothing. These uses of language open up a liminal space of incompletion in which things are not whole and sound, creating an environment that is transitional and indeterminate. Unfulfilled oaths, regardless of intent, generate chaos and instability.

Blurring Boundaries: Deceit in Leviticus 5:20–26

The second major occurrence of human speech also appears in chapter 5, with the first named sins that are intentional. The scenario opens in a similar fashion to 5:1: נֶפֶשׁ כִּי תֶחֱטָא ("when a person does wrong"; 5:21), but here includes an additional clause, וּמָעֲלָה מַעַל בַּיהוָה ("by committing sacrilege against the Lord"; Milgrom). This phrase brings to the fore another subtle detail concerning the verb חטא: in P, it is used exclusively to refer to sins against God.[49] The phrase מָעֲלָה מַעַל is somewhat opaque, since it is never defined in the Bible; analyzing the contexts in which it appears, Milgrom concludes that it is synonymous with the verb חלל, "to profane" (cf. Lev 19:12), and means "to commit sacrilege." All cases of מעל involve either 1) sacrilege against the Tent of Meeting and its appurtenances, or 2) sacrilege involving oaths, the topic of 5:20–26.

---

49. Milgrom, *Leviticus 1–16*, 229.

The issue involves doing any number of things to defraud one's neighbor, including purposefully deceiving (כחש) someone in a matter of an investment or partnership, committing robbery, exploiting a laborer or weaker party in a transaction, or finding and keeping something that is not yours. In brief: וְנִשְׁבַּע עַל־שֶׁקֶר עַל־אַחַת מִכֹּל אֲשֶׁר־יַעֲשֶׂה הָאָדָם לַחֲטֹא בָהֵנָּה, "by swearing falsely about any one of the things that a person may do and sin thereby" (Lev 5:22). Again we are confronted with an issue concerning oaths, but here they involve two additional elements: intentional deceit, and doubling-down when confronted or caught, denying any wrongdoing and refusing to come clean.[50] We have already noted some reasons for the priestly writers' dim view of oaths, but further details come to light in this context. All of the sins that are enumerated concern deceiving or defrauding another person within the community; why, then, are these considered sacrilege against YHWH (מָעֲלָה מַעַל בַּיהוָה)? Addressing this question along with the unfulfilled oaths of 5:1 and 5:4, Levine notes that "on the face of it, these are not cultic laws but, rather, laws of testimony."[51] But what, exactly, is the difference? For the biblical writers on this point, there is not a clear distinction; oaths have a tangible effect on both the social and cultic sphere. The question is, why?

We recall that oaths in the ancient world involved invoking the power of a deity, as reflected in Lev 19:11–12:

לֹא תִּגְנֹבוּ וְלֹא־תְכַחֲשׁוּ וְלֹא־תְשַׁקְּרוּ אִישׁ בַּעֲמִיתוֹ
וְלֹא־תִשָּׁבְעוּ בִשְׁמִי לַשָּׁקֶר וְחִלַּלְתָּ אֶת־שֵׁם אֱלֹהֶיךָ אֲנִי יְהוָה

> You shall not steal; you shall not dissemble; you shall not lie to one another.
> And you shall not swear falsely by my name, thereby desecrating the name of your God: I am YHWH.

The problem is not with swearing an oath in and of itself, per se; it is that swearing implicates YHWH so that the matter has consequences beyond a mere person to person altercation. Furthermore, when an oath is sworn falsely in order to deceive or defraud someone, "the Lord has been made an accomplice to the defrauding of man."[52] This is why false oaths constitute sacrilege (מעל) against YHWH: the sanctity of YHWH's holy name (e.g., Lev 20:3; Isa 57:15; Ezek 36:20–22; Amos 2:7; Ps 111:9) has

---

50. Milgrom, *Leviticus 1–16*, 336.
51. Levine, *Leviticus*, 26.
52. Milgrom, *Leviticus 1–16*, 337.

been damaged. Drawing a connection between the two groups of cases involving מעל—damage done to the divine name through oaths, and damage done to the sancta—Milgrom notes that מעל can be understood as something that causes a real alteration in the status of its object: "the sancta has been desecrated; it is now profane."[53]

An interesting juxtaposition that further illuminates the power of speech to alter reality occurs in Lev 19:11–16. In a restatement of the prohibitions against stealing, lying, or otherwise defrauding another person while swearing falsely, the following injunction appears:

לֹא־תְקַלֵּל חֵרֵשׁ וְלִפְנֵי עִוֵּר לֹא תִתֵּן מִכְשֹׁל וְיָרֵאתָ מֵּאֱלֹהֶיךָ אֲנִי יְהוָה

> You shall not insult the deaf, and before the blind you shall not place a stumbling block, but you shall fear your God: I am YHWH. (Lev 19:14).

Why is this here? There is an obvious thematic continuity in outlining the behaviors that constitute love of God and neighbor, structuring a society characterized by basic respect and equity. But there is also a deeper connection: insulting or slandering (קלל) another person is the opposite of blessing,[54] the antithesis of the life-giving divine word (cf. Gen 1:28; 2:3). The fact that the person cannot hear the insult is of no consequence; once spoken, an insult is as destructive as putting a stumbling block in front of the blind. Words have tangible effects in the physical world.

In this, too, YHWH is implicated. Milgrom observes that even if the insult is not heard by a person, YHWH hears. The concluding phrase, וְיָרֵאתָ מֵּאֱלֹהֶיךָ אֲנִי יְהוָה ("you shall fear your God; I am YHWH"; Lev 19:14) "implies that the weak and helpless, namely, the deaf and the blind, are under divine protection."[55] Similarly, going about as a slanderer (לֹא־תֵלֵךְ רָכִיל בְּעַמֶּיךָ; Lev 19:16) is incompatible with the divine presence that would walk among the people (וְהִתְהַלַּכְתִּי בְּתוֹכְכֶם; Lev 26:12), as the rabbis observe: "Of him who slanders, the Holy One, blessed be He, says: He and I cannot live together (לון) in the world."[56] Speech that does damage to others not only fails to reflect the divine image (Lev 19:2), but actively

---

53. Milgrom, *Leviticus 1–16*, 351, citing *Sipra*, Ḥobah par. 11:1. As it relates to the possibility of altering the status of the divine Name, we will return to this discussion in the following chapter.

54. Milgrom, *Leviticus 17–22*, 1638. The semantic range of קלל will also be examined more fully in the following chapter.

55. Milgrom, *Leviticus 17–22*, 1639.

56. Cited in Milgrom, *Leviticus 17–22*, 1644; from b. ʿArakhin 15b.

undermines the divine word, creating a world that is inhospitable to the divine presence.

Like unfulfilled oaths, then, deception also generates chaos and instability but of a different order. Rather than opening up a liminal space of incompletion and indeterminacy, deception does damage within the community by actively sowing distrust and disrespect, tarnishing the reputations of everyone involved, including YHWH. This is why sacrilege to the divine name is so dangerous: deception threatens the destruction of the entire community because it unravels the social fabric, blurring the boundaries between reality and delusion. Did a thing happen, or did it not? Whom can we trust? How do we know what is true?

Repairing Order: The Role of Confession

Speech does not play an exclusively destructive role in the processes of the sacrificial system, however. To the extent that it has the capacity to create chaos (as we will see more clearly in chapter 5), it also serves as an important element in undoing the damage of sin and reaffirming the divine order. Through confession, the destabilizing effects of neglect and deceit are stayed, setting a process of reparation in motion.

Confession appears in three cases in the book of Leviticus: first in conjunction with the sacrificial system in chapter 5, and later in the ritual of the scapegoat in chapter 16 and the hypothetical provisions for repentance for infidelity in 26:40–45. Only in chapter 5 does confession operate explicitly in conjunction with sacrifice, but in all instances, confession fulfills the same function: to begin the process of restitution and reparation. The process is simple and brief:

וְהָיָה כִי־יֶאְשַׁם לְאַחַת מֵאֵלֶּה וְהִתְוַדָּה אֲשֶׁר חָטָא עָלֶיהָ

> When he feels guilt/realizes that he has incurred guilt in any of these matters, he shall confess that wherein he did wrong (Lev 5:5).

Two observations arise: first, it is interesting that there are no further specifications concerning what constitutes confession, how it is to be performed, or what the individual is to say. In fact, none of the four instances in P that call for confession are forthcoming in these details (cf. Lev 16:21; 26:40; Num 5:6), a feature that is striking given the high level of specificity and precision that characterizes other ritual procedures.

This suggests either that the form of confession was familiar enough that it did not need explanation, or, more likely, that confession is fundamentally an act that requires the agency and self-reflection of the person who has committed the offense; there is no script for expressing the wrong you have done, since the purpose of confession is to bring to light what you have concealed or misconstrued or denied. You are responsible for finding the right words to undo these errors.

Second, Milgrom has observed that "confession is never required for inadvertences, but only for deliberate sins."[57] He explains that the rationale for this distinction is found in the fact that only inadvertences are expiable by sacrifice, which eliminates the possibility of forgiveness for sins committed intentionally. Confession fills this gap, functioning as a "legal device fashioned by the Priestly legislators to convert deliberate sins into inadvertences" and extend the reach of the cult to include those sinners otherwise excluded from the possibility of forgiveness and restoration.[58] "The repentance of sinners," Milgrom suggests, "through their remorse and confession, reduces their intentional sin to an inadvertence, thereby rendering it eligible for sacrificial expiation."[59] Intriguingly, Milgrom goes on to suggest that the significance of confession is more than a legal hoop to jump through; it reflects an awareness of the psychological effects of confession and repentance. A person's willingness to articulate the wrong he or she has done demonstrates recognition of the gravity of the offense and the damage it has done. It also expresses a seriousness about changing, and a desire to be restored not only to the community but to oneself. So Milgrom observes that "confession in P must be verbalized because it is the act that counts, not just its intention."[60] The verbalization is the act, a counterintuitive claim in a modern society in which words are not held to be consequential for effecting real change. Confession is the evidence and affirmation of remorse that sets restitution in motion.

Mary Douglas has suggested a slightly different logic for the role of confession in the ancient world, not altogether rejecting Milgrom's thesis but cautioning against overemphasizing a psychological rationale. Douglas observed that in the ancient world oracles functioned as a mechanism

---

57. Milgrom, *Leviticus 1–16*, 369.
58. Milgrom, *Leviticus 1–16*, 301.
59. Milgrom, *Leviticus: A Continental Commentary*, 58.
60. Milgrom, *Leviticus 1–16*, 301.

to "discover hidden sins."[61] Through divination, a person who had done something to damage the social contract while denying any culpability could justifiably be convicted and punished, thereby restoring justice within the community. The abolition of witchcraft in the priestly world (e.g., Lev 19:26, 31; 20:6, 27) created a vacuum that the laws regarding oaths and confession sought to fill. Douglas argued that these were legal provisions in which "the oath automatically turns a minor case between persons into a major case for priestly enquiry and priestly justice . . . the Levitical text uses the oath to raise a civil crime to the level of sacrilege. It is a standard technique for appealing to a higher court."[62] At the same time, however, the Levitical system shifts the weight of responsibility for deception—and, ultimately, truth-telling—from the impersonal workings of a priestly oracle to the individual who has perpetrated the crime. This reflects a stunning recognition by the priestly writers that genuine social harmony cannot be achieved through merely external means, enforced by society and imposed upon a suspected perpetrator. When a person has knowingly and purposefully done harm to the community, full restoration cannot occur without her own acknowledgement of the damage done.

Douglas's explanation of the function of oaths and confession as a substitute for divination further highlights what is at stake in the inappropriate use of language, as well as the significance of its relationship to the sacrificial system. Unfulfilled oaths and interpersonal deception damage the entire community, not only because they defraud individuals, implicate YHWH, and diminish the character and integrity of the individual who perpetrates them. As we have seen, they also undermine a shared sense of what is real and true, threatening the social stability that comes from all parties being able to recognize and agree on basic facts and mutually affirm a shared experience of the world. Deception is a real threat to the created order, unleashing social, religious, and psychological destabilization.

In contrast, confession brings everything out into the open as a public acknowledgement of what the individual has done and his or her realization of the damage that it has caused. Confession reverses the environment of doubt and distrust that was created through either the neglect to fulfill one's oath or actively working to manipulate and deceive.

---

61. Douglas, *Leviticus as Literature*, 127.
62. Douglas, *Leviticus as Literature*, 131.

It restores a common ground of perception and truth-telling on which all relationships are built, reweaving the social fabric in order to ensure the survival and flourishing of the community. Both aspects of language—its power to destroy and its power to rebuild—are recognized within the sacrificial processes that are so central to forming the nation of Israel in good patterns of communication.

Discerning the Direction of Thought

The sacrificial system offers a unique perspective on how communication functions in mediating relationships and forming social structures. In each of the focal points we have explored, a view of discourse, broadly conceived as either verbal or non-verbal communication, has emerged as a force that alters reality. In Israel's experience, two primary realities are at stake: the relationship between YHWH and Israel, and, consequently, Israel's identity as a nation.

In the first part of this chapter, we focused primarily on *how* sacrifice functions as a mode of communication between YHWH and Israel to establish and maintain this vital relationship. We saw that the non-verbal character of sacrifice highlights important aspects of communication that are often overlooked in contemporary discourse, including the role of gift-giving, the unavoidability of proximity, and the significance of embodiment in the pursuit of communion. We observed that sacrifice provides a structure for establishing and maintaining the boundaries between self and other, but that the purpose of these boundaries is ultimately to enable healthy relationships in which mutual recognition does not threaten distinction. This stands in direct contrast to a notion of boundaries as impermeable barriers that provide safety by keeping things and people strictly separated. As it is expressed in the sacrificial system, the logic of boundaries is that they facilitate relationships rather than prohibit them.

We then turned to the two places in the sacrificial system where human language makes an appearance, affirming that in the priestly view of language, it is not only the divine word that has the power to create or destroy. Learning to communicate well is central to Israel's relationship with YHWH as well as their relationships with one another, and there is not always a clear line between these two spheres.

Along the way I have gestured toward several directions of thought that the text opens up that could fruitfully be followed through to new formats of significance in contemporary life. There is one in particular that I would like to return to here, and that is the question of what the language of sacrifice suggests about the role of language in shaping identity.

We have repeatedly seen how Israel's survival as a nation rests on their proximity to the divine presence, and consequently, their ability to learn appropriate forms of communication to nurture and sustain their relationship with YHWH. But there is more to this than pragmatically securing basic survival. Sacrifice is fundamental to Israel's formation in holiness, recreating them as a particular kind of people, with a particular character as the people of YHWH. If sacrifice is indeed Israel's primary mode of discourse with the divine, then it follows that discourse plays a key role in Israel's formation in holiness. Two particular aspects of what we have observed from the language of sacrifice bring this element of identity-formation into clearer focus.

First, it became clear from the narrative leading up to Leviticus 1 that new patterns of communication were required in the new situation of Israel's formation as a nation. Israel needed to be able to respond to the divine initiative in order to pledge their acceptance of the covenant and their commitment to being identified as the people of YHWH, with its concomitant responsibilities and world-shaping habits of life. Verbal affirmation was not enough to solidify this mutual recognition (Exod 19:8; cf. 24:3–7). Instead, bringing their offerings to the altar gave Israel the chance to respond by giving back what they had received from YHWH, an essential stage in the process of human maturity and development. Jonathan Sacks observes that Israel's total dependence on God and on Moses as their go-between had, until this point, "infantilized" the people.[63] The inauguration of a rhythm of responding to YHWH by regularly bringing their offerings to the altar marked the beginning of a new stage in Israel's development, serving to establish their identity as a covenant partner and enabling them to express their gratitude and respect so that they, too, might be worthy of respect.[64] The sacrificial system provided Israel with the dignity of returning the generosity that YHWH had extended to them.

---

63. Sacks, *Leviticus*, 20.
64. Hénaff, *The Price of Truth*, 396.

Second, this ongoing mutual exchange provides the foundation for Israel's formation in holiness that will continue as the book of Leviticus unfolds, grounding them in patterns of communication that weave together the social fabric. Using language to generate and sustain life is a divine attribute, and in the priestly view of reality humans are not only created in the image of God (Gen 1:27), but also endowed with life by the divine breath (יִפַּח בְּאַפָּיו נִשְׁמַת חַיִּים Gen 2:7). Noting that Onkelos renders נֶפֶשׁ חַיָּה ("living being") as לְרוּחַ מְמַלְלָא ("speaking spirit"), Shai Held suggests that perhaps speech is not only a divine attribute, but also "constitutive of what it means to be human."[65] The question that Leviticus seeks to answer is whether human use of speech will reflect the divine image, as it was created and intended, or whether it will reflect that other human attribute of yielding to the capacity of language to deceive and destroy (Gen 3:12–13).

Viewing the sacrificial system in this light, we can see yet another way in which Mary Douglas was right to see in Leviticus the "real heart of religion" too often presumed "to be found in other parts of the Bible."[66] The power of the tongue to bring life or death is a theme that runs throughout the Torah, Prophets, and Writings (e.g., Num 12:1–13; Prov 18:21; Isa 55:11), and Leviticus is no exception.

This vision stands in stark contrast to the ways that language is often enacted in twenty-first century contexts. For contemporary readers, this priestly conception of the constitutive function of discourse affirms that the words and forms we use to communicate with one another matter. The shape that our discourse takes has the power to determine social structures and weave the fabric of civic life, but it is not only a tool that we utilize to the benefit or detriment of those around us. The ways that we enact language—in all its forms—profoundly affect our own identity as individuals and survival as a society, determining the kind of people we will be and the future we will have.

---

65. Held, *The Heart of Torah*, 47–48.
66. Douglas, *Leviticus as Literature*, 1.

5

Dangerous Discourse, Divine Discernment
Leviticus 24:10–31

לֹא תִשָּׂא אֶת־שֵׁם־יְהוָה אֱלֹהֶיךָ לַשָּׁוְא כִּי לֹא יְנַקֶּה יְהוָה אֵת אֲשֶׁר־יִשָּׂא אֶת־שְׁמוֹ לַשָּׁוְא

—*Exodus 20:7*

"Words can be like X-rays if you use them properly—they'll go through anything. You read and you're pierced."

—*Aldous Huxley*

Why the Blasphemy Narrative?

THE MOST EXPLICIT TREATMENT of human speech in the book of Leviticus comes late in the book, in the so-called narrative of the blasphemer that appears in 24:10–23. This brief passage develops and vividly illustrates the priestly view of speech that we explored in chapter 4, namely that human speech is a powerful force capable of altering reality for good or for ill. Where Leviticus 5 dealt with inappropriate speech in the form of inadvertent offenses, however, the stakes have been raised: here we encounter a case in which speech seems to be wielded for deliberately destructive purposes, and results in the gravest of consequences.

Our interest in this pericope extends beyond its treatment of speech as a direct form of encounter with the divine, however. Closer inspection reveals that this perplexing passage is actually a story within a story that condenses and encapsulates the most important message of the book: Israel's total dependence on YHWH for continued existence, and the capacity of individuals to threaten this relationship. The central role of speech in a narrative that deals with the most important themes of the book suggests that this narrative is particularly fertile soil for generating new forms of life in the discourse between text and reader.

While Lev 24:10–23 presents the interpreter with many intriguing puzzles, a common thread that connects and explains many of them has received surprisingly little sustained attention from interpreters: the prominently featured names, both human and divine. In this chapter we will explore this theme of names as a window into the larger meaning of the narrative, focusing on two related aspects: the literary function of human names to point to the theological significance of the divine Name. I will argue that two particularly puzzling ambiguities—the precise nature of the offense against the Name, and the relationship of this offense to the doctrine of equivalence expressed in the talion laws of vv. 17–22—fall into place when the divine Name is viewed as the ultimate protective covering that holds Israel in life, defining the border between order versus chaos, and existence versus non-existence. Significantly, human speech is the vehicle through which the integrity of this covering can be breached.

Setting the Stage

Overview of the Narrative

The narrative itself is brief and to the point. The unnamed son of an Israelite woman—Shelomith, daughter of Dibri, of the tribe of Dan—goes out (presumably from his tent)[1] among the Israelites and gets into a brawl with an also unnamed, but fully Israelite man, as we read in v. 10: וַיֵּצֵא

---

1. The ambiguity of וַיֵּצֵא in v. 10 has not escaped the attention of interpreters, who have suggested that it implies that because the man was of mixed parentage, he would have been living among the "mixed multitude" mentioned in Num 11:14 (see also Num 2:34). For discussion see Milgrom, *Leviticus 23–27*, 2106. Alternatively, Origen suggests that this first mention of "going out" indicates the man's spiritual departure "from good purpose and right judgment," before any offense had even been committed. He had, in other words, already separated himself from the "fellowship and concord of the faithful." Origen of Alexandria, *Homilies on Leviticus 1–16*, §14.2.

בֶּן־אִשָּׁה יִשְׂרְאֵלִית וְהוּא בֶּן־אִישׁ מִצְרִי בְּתוֹךְ בְּנֵי יִשְׂרָאֵל וַיִּנָּצוּ בַּמַּחֲנֶה בֶּן הַיִּשְׂרְאֵלִית וְאִישׁ הַיִּשְׂרְאֵלִי. In the heat of the conflict, וַיִּקֹּב בֶּן־הָאִשָּׁה הַיִּשְׂרְאֵלִית אֶת־הַשֵּׁם וַיְקַלֵּל—that is, he commits some sort of verbal trespass against the divine Name. The witnesses to the incident (we assume) apprehend the offender and bring him to Moses, where they settle him down in custody to await a decision about what should be done next.

In narrative time, YHWH immediately replies that the man—known from v. 14 on as הַמְקַלֵּל (*ha-meqallel*)—is to be taken outside the camp, where everyone who heard (כָּל־הַשֹּׁמְעִים) is to lay their hands on his head and the entire congregation is to pelt/stone (רגם) him. Here the frame widens from YHWH's address to Moses to include all Israel. It is as if the entire congregation had been waiting to hear the divine decision while the man was in custody, with everything suspended in time. So Moses turns to address the crowd:[2]

> Anyone—yes, anyone!—when he (יְקַלֵּל) his god shall bear his sin. And the one who (נֹקֵב) the Name of YHWH is to be put-to-death; the entire congregation is to pelt, yes, pelt him; as the sojourner, so the native: (בְּנָקְבוֹ) the Name, he is to be put-to-death. Anyone who strikes-down any human life: he is to be put-to-death, yes, death. One who strikes-down the life of an animal is to make-it-good, life in place of life. Anyone who causes a defect in his fellow: as he has done, so it shall be done to him. Fracture for fracture, eye for eye, tooth for tooth: as he has rendered a defect in a human being, so it shall be rendered to him. One who strikes-down an animal shall make-it-good, and one who strikes-down a human being shall be put-to-death. One standard will there be for you: as the sojourner, so shall the native be: for I, YHWH, am your God (24:15b–22).

With this, the narrative concludes: the Israelites take the מקלל outside the camp and pelt him with stones, "just as YHWH had commanded Moses."

Major Interpretive Questions: Where Shall We Begin?

As the summary above illustrates, the narrative details of the pericope leave much to the imagination. The situation is summarized in a mere three verses, with the divine decision, talion laws, and summary/conclusion comprising the remaining ten. As Gerstenberger has aptly observed,

---

2. The words in parentheses are intentionally left untranslated here, as what follows hinges on the interpretation of their meaning.

"the anecdote is not really developed,"³ which gives rise to a number of questions.

To begin with, the immediately surrounding literary context provides few clues that could help fill in the sparsely sketched narrative outline. 24:10–23 erupts onto the scene in the middle of an extended section on instructions for festivals and calendrical items that began in chapter 23 and resumes in 25:1. This literary placement has long baffled interpreters,⁴ although various explanations have been suggested.⁵ The most compelling solution calls for a broader perspective that takes in the overall structure of the book as Mary Douglas has demonstrated. As we have seen in Douglas's schema, the book of Leviticus is structured as a series of rings that form a "tripartite projection of the tabernacle," with the two narratives in chapters 8–10 and 24:10–23 functioning as two "screens" that mark major conceptual and spatial transitions in the book. In this light, "the narrative interrupts the movement through the laws as the two screens interrupt the movement through the tabernacle and divide it into three sections."⁶ Douglas's argument is well known and need not be fully rehearsed here,⁷ save to flag an important detail that comes to light when viewing the two narratives as "screens." Each of the narratives deals with one of the two major ways that the Israelites could commit sacrilege: either against sancta (chs. 8–10), or against the divine Name (24:20–23).⁸ In this reading, the literary placement of the narratives underscores their theological message: the stories are about boundary

---

3. Gerstenberger, *Leviticus*, 361.

4. Wenham observes, for example, that "commentators have been unable to discern any obvious connection between the material in this chapter and what precedes and follows it." Wenham, *Leviticus*, 307–13.

5. Leigh Trevaskis has argued, for example, that a symbolic interpretation of 24:1–9 is the key to understanding the literary unity of chs. 23–25; see Trevaskis, "The Purpose of Leviticus 24," 295–312. Alternatively, Wilfried Warning suggests that chs. 19–24 "exhibit an ascending progression of holiness terminating with the inner sanctum (24:1–9) and the inner sanctum (i.e., the name of God; 24:10–23); see Warning, *Literary Artistry*, 94.

6. Douglas, *Leviticus as Literature*, 195.

7. Douglas's theory has been met with wide acceptance, including Milgrom, *Leviticus 23–27*, 2082; Balentine, *The Torah's Vision of Worship*, 191–93; and especially Rendsburg, "The Two Screens," 175–89. For dissenting views on the basis of quite different methodological approaches from Douglas's, see Watts, *Ritual and Rhetoric*, 20–21; and especially Nihan, *From Priestly Torah to Pentateuch*, 78–94.

8. For further discussion see Milgrom, *Leviticus 23–27*, 2141; and *Leviticus 1–16*, 320.

violations. Accordingly, the first screen addresses inappropriate priestly approach to the sanctum, while the second screen expands the frame of reference to deal with situations in which anyone in the community, including a גר, may commit a major boundary violation.[9] We will return to a closer examination of what that boundary is and how it is conceived in the priestly logic below, in order to probe its broader significance.

A second major focus of scholarly attention involves the ambiguity surrounding the meaning and syntax of the operative verbs נקב and קלל. The problem is that, while these words are associated with verbal assaults in the semantic range of something like "blasphemy" or "cursing," they carry other connotations that cloud the precise nature of the man's offense. Furthermore, the first report of the incident in v. 11 does not clearly identify the object of קלל, stating only that וַיִּקֹּב בֶּן־הָאִשָּׁה הַיִּשְׂרְאֵלִית אֶת־הַשֵּׁם וַיְקַלֵּל. Are two distinct actions in view, or one that is related to the other in consequence, manner, or otherwise? Again, a more detailed discussion of this question will be necessary below.

Related to these questions about the precise nature of the offense, the correlation between the talion laws in vv. 17–22 and the surrounding narrative has also generated a great deal of debate. The following outline illustrates the basic structure of the pericope:

1. Narrative Summary of the Situation (vv. 10–12)
   The Divine Decision (v. 13)

2. Address to the Congregation (vv. 15–22)

   One standard of Judgment: Trespass against the Name (v. 15b–16)
   Trespass against human life (v. 17)
   Trespass against animal life (v. 18)
   a. Maiming for maiming (v. 19)

---

9. The larger context for this extension from priests to laity and sanctum to מחנה is that 24:10–23 is found in the section of the book widely recognized as H, presenting a counterpart to P's narrative (9:23—10:2) "in line with H's larger program of supplementation and re-emphasis with regard to P." Milgrom, *Leviticus 23–27*, 2141. While the distinction between P and H can provide valuable interpretive insight, it is peripheral to my interest in the literary shape of the text as it stands. For further discussion of H's narrative as the mirror to P's, see especially Nihan, *From Priestly Torah to Pentateuch*, 512–20 and Bibb, *Ritual Words*, 153–56.

Fracture for fracture, eye for eye, tooth for tooth (v. 20a)

b. Injury for injury (v. 20b)

Trespass against animal life (v. 21a)

Trespass against human life (v. 21b)

One standard of Judgment: כִּי אֲנִי יְהוָה אֱלֹהֵיכֶם (v. 22)

3. Narrative Conclusion (v. 23)

While it is generally recognized that the laws have been carefully integrated into the surrounding narrative as evidenced by the careful chiastic structure, it is not immediately apparent why—that is, how the narrative is related thematically or theologically to talion.[10] First, the subject of the narrative appears to be the law about the blasphemy of the גר (ger); why, then, are the talion laws with their central message of equivalence at the center of the narrative structure?[11] Second, if equivalence is indeed the deeper message of the story, meant to illumine the narrative, why is the מקלל put to death—is stoning really commensurate with blasphemy? Milgrom puts it bluntly: "the story of the blasphemer is inexact,"[12] so what does it have to do with talion?

Finally, the identity of the מקלל and the significance of his mixed ancestry to the larger themes of the narrative cannot be overlooked. Chelcent Fuad has recently argued, for example, that the central ambiguity of the narrative that required divine counsel was not the crime or the required punishment (these, he posits, would have been clear to the Israelites), but rather the ambiguous identity of the blasphemer: should he be considered an Israelite, or a גר?[13] In other words, do the laws for the Israelites apply equally to everyone in the community regardless of ancestry, or do crimes involving non-Israelites call for a different response—and what? This narrative would thus be about the question of the status and legal culpability of sojourners within the community,[14] an interpretive lens that

---

10. For various treatments of the chiastic structure and redaction history of the pericope, see Milgrom, *Leviticus 23–27*, 2130; Balentine, *The Torah's Vision of Worship*, 188–90; Nihan, *From Priestly Torah to Pentateuch*, 517; and Fuad, "The Curious Case of the Blasphemer," 65.

11. Milgrom, *Leviticus: A Continental Commentary*, 297.

12. Milgrom, *Leviticus: A Continental Commentary*, 294.

13. Fuad, "The Curious Case of the Blasphemer."

14. Trevaskis, "The Purpose of Leviticus 24," 309; Vroom, "Recasting Mishpatim," 27–44; and Schwartz, "Leviticus," 254.

makes sense in light of the fact that the structure of the narrative follows a set formula that parallels three other cases in which the lack of legal precedent required a divine decision.[15] The narrative of the מקלל thus provides a window into legal development in ancient Israel and carries important implications for our understanding of the formation of the Pentateuch.[16]

These questions have been met with compelling treatments that illumine the historical significance of the narrative and certain aspects of its literary function and theological message, but scholarship has struggled to integrate these historical and literary considerations within a unified overarching theme. This may be partly due to the fact that some of the key features remain perplexing in and of themselves: As we have seen, no clear consensus has emerged concerning either the exact nature of the offense or the relationship of the narrative to the talion laws in vv. 17–22. Perhaps in part because of these lingering questions, the narrative's direction of thought has rarely been identified in such a way that it can be followed through to generative applications in contemporary contexts, beyond the obvious takeaway about the seriousness of "taking the Lord's name in vain." Indeed, it is difficult to imagine how this narrative, tersely prescribing stoning in return for blasphemy, could have much more to say in contemporary discourse.

If improper use of the divine Name provides the basic storyline for the narrative, then careful attention to this theme would suggest a promising entry point for deciphering the narrative's theological direction of thought, both within and beyond its literary context. But while most interpreters recognize the obvious centrality of the Name—Nihan writes, for example, that "[YHWH's] sacred name . . . lies at the heart of this story"[17]—its meaning and significance as articulated in this narrative have not been fully developed. In a study examining the notion of a "Name" theology in the priestly literature more broadly, Tamara Kamionkowski confirms this surprising lacuna, writing that "the question of what it means to desecrate God's name" has been met with relative silence compared to the attention that has been devoted to "the holiness and profanation of people, objects, and places."[18] This, I suggest, is where we

---

15. i.e., Num. 9:1–14; 15:32–36; and 27:1–11.

16. For the preeminent articulation of these parallels and discussion of their significance, see Fishbane, *Biblical Interpretation*, especially 98–102.

17. Nihan, *From Priestly Torah to Pentateuch*, 513.

18. Kamionkowski, "האם היתה לכוהנים תאולוגיה של 'שם'? / Did the Priests Have a 'Name' Theology?," 17. Emphasis mine.

should begin: What does this narrative reveal about the priestly notion of the significance of names, both human and divine? And how does the centrality of speech in the story function to illumine the significance of the Name—that is, what does it mean to trespass against the Name?

A Story about Names: Literary Function and Theological Significance

Two aspects concerning names require investigation: the literary function of human names within this narrative, and the theological significance of the divine Name as informed by the broader context of Leviticus.

Pointing beyond Themselves:
The Literary Function of the Human Names

One of the most striking features of this story is the sudden appearance of a cluster of unfamiliar character names: "Shelomith, daughter of Dibri, of the tribe of Dan" (v. 11). In the book of Leviticus there are at most a total of twenty proper names, and only in chapter 10 is there a higher concentration of named individuals.[19] Other than the patriarchs and non-human names (i.e., Azazel and Molech), the only characters in the entire book who are not of priestly lineage are the three mentioned here. Even more striking is the fact that other than Moses and Aaron, these three are the only humans identified in H by name, and Shelomith is the only woman.[20]

Furthermore, the function of these characters in the narrative is not at all clear. They say nothing and do nothing; the significance of their mention is not explained; and no one else says anything to or about them. Syntactically, the names are spliced into the middle of a sentence as if in a narrative voice-over, interrupting the flow of the action in vv. 11–12 in the strangest way possible:

---

19. The numbering of twenty proper names includes the tetragrammaton, collectives such as "Levites" and "Israelites," and references to non-human beings Azazel and Molech. Stephen Sherwood offers an interesting discussion of names throughout the book, although his enumeration differs slightly from mine; see Sherwood, *Leviticus, Numbers, Deuteronomy*, 11, 20.

20. Dupont, "Women and the Concept of Holiness," 174.

וַיִּקֹּב בֶּן־הָאִשָּׁה הַיִּשְׂרְאֵלִית אֶת־הַשֵּׁם וַיְקַלֵּל וַיָּבִיאוּ אֹתוֹ אֶל־מֹשֶׁה וְשֵׁם
אִמּוֹ שְׁלֹמִית בַּת־דִּבְרִי לְמַטֵּה־דָן
וַיַּנִּיחֻהוּ בַּמִּשְׁמָר לִפְרֹשׁ לָהֶם עַל־פִּי יְהוָה:

> "Now the son of the Israelite woman reviled the Name, and insulted, so they brought him to Moshe—now the name of his mother (was) Shelomith daughter of Divri, of the tribe of Dan—and they put him under guard, to clarify it for them by order of YHWH."

The awkward word order is reflected in most English translations, which bracket the names in parentheses; a few of them rearrange the verse altogether to include the names with the first mention of the mother in v. 10.[21] While Martin Noth simply concludes that the reason for interposing the mother's name in this precise location "remains obscure" and "must be supposed to be a later addition,"[22] this does nothing to explain why anyone would have added it here. The reason does indeed remain obscure, save for the way that the interjection is doubly jarring. These unusual names appear out of nowhere, arresting the reader's attention at the exact moment that the מקלל finds himself being taken into custody. The question is: why?

Many commentators have observed that the genealogy of the מקלל is significant to the narrative because it reflects the extension of the law to include foreigners, as we have noted, and that the inclusion of the names has something to do with this, highlighting or clarifying his mixed ancestry. But the names of the man's mother, grandfather, and tribe are not necessary to this basic point—the comment that his mother was Israelite while his father was Egyptian would have been sufficient. This has led interpreters to wonder if there is particular significance to the meaning of the names themselves. The most thorough attempt to connect the dots has been Douglas's suggestion that Shelomit carries some resonance with the idea of "retribution," that Dibri suggests "lawsuit," and that the tribe of Dan is associated with "judgement," according to Gen 49:16: "Dan shall judge his people as one of the tribes of Israel."[23] So Douglas suggests that the names would function to underscore a theme of judgment and equivalence, and she paraphrases the passage to read:

---

21. i.e., the Good News Translation and New English Bible.

22. Noth, *Leviticus*, 180.

23. Douglas, *Leviticus as Literature*, 207; for variations following Douglas's lead, see also Sherwood, *Leviticus, Numbers, Deuteronomy*, 27; and Turner, *Leviticus*, 73.

Once there was a man (with no name), son of Shelomith-Retribution, grandson of Dibri-Lawsuit, from the house of Dan-judgement, and he pelted insults at the Name ... and the Lord said 'He shall die, he pelted my Name, he shall be pelted to death.[24]

While these meanings for the names are admittedly conjectural, there is little evidence to contradict them, either, so Milgrom accepted the gist of the idea with a minor amendment of Shelomit-Retribution to "Requital."[25] Others have suggested different conjectural meanings. Joanne Dupont draws on the root of Dibri, דבר, to propose an emphasis on the fact that the offense was committed through speech; few other commentators have addressed the name at all, as it is unattested elsewhere.[26] Most assume that the mention of Dan was intended to cast the מקלל in a negative light, as the tribe was associated with the northern cult and considered illegitimate by the Jerusalemite priesthood.[27]

Extending this idea, there has been a great deal of speculation about what the names imply about the man's genealogy more generally. Gerstenberger optimistically reads Shelomit as "peaceful," wondering if this reflects an effort on the part of the narrator "to remove the burden [of her son's quarrelsome nature] from both her and thus also the Israelites," but ultimately concludes that "a blemish seems to attach to the perpetrator, since otherwise his lineage would not have been mentioned."[28] Dupont also highlighted the triliteral root underlying the woman's name (שלם), asking whether it suggests anything about her union with an Egyptian: "Could [Shelomit] be considered one who had attempted, whether consciously or not, a peacemaking alliance, in this case marriage, between the hated Egyptians and Israel?"[29] As imaginatively generous as this is, the narrative nevertheless seems to feature the ultimate futility of

---

24. Douglas, *Leviticus as Literature*, 207.
25. On the basis of Deut 7:10; Milgrom, *Leviticus 23–27*, 2110.
26. Dupont, "Women and the Concept of Holiness," 175.
27. Levine, *Leviticus*, 166; Milgrom, *Leviticus 23–27*, 2110; Gerstenberger, *Leviticus*, 361. Dupont adds that the charge of apostasy against the Danites originates from Judges 18:30, and also suggests the possibility that "since the Danite priesthood claimed descent from Moses," the provenance of the narrative itself may have been the priests at Dan; see Dupont, "Women and the Concept of Holiness," 175–76.
28. Gerstenberger, *Leviticus*, 361.
29. Dupont, "Women and the Concept of Holiness," 177. Dupont also emphasizes the fact that the periodic references to Egypt that appear throughout H are unfavorable; see especially Lev 18:3.

Shelomit's efforts. Finally, some interpreters have looked beyond the context of the Hebrew Bible to suggest possible connections between the name Shelomit and the Canaanite god Shalem, implying apostasy not only in the family's lineage but also within their immediate household.[30] Others have seen an allusion to a "queen mother formula" in the compound construct בת דברי, suggesting that the name Shelomit may a coded reference to Bathsheba and that the מקלל is Solomon, her son.[31] Of all these suggestions, the significance of the fact that the protagonist himself is not named is mentioned only in passing, even in studies devoted entirely to the ambiguity of the man's identity.[32]

The swirl of speculation surrounding these names is unlikely to be met with more concrete evidence, which supports Douglas's conclusion that it is not the meaning of the names themselves that is important, but rather why they are included here at all. Her sensitivity to the function of the names as a literary device was stimulated by Moshe Garsiel's study of puns, especially puns upon names, in the Hebrew Bible. Garsiel demonstrated that names are often used as "a significant literary device to enrich and intensify the plot through a correspondence between names and themes." This does not mean that the names were "intended for the purpose of punning," Garsiel cautioned, or that the narratives were invented to make use of the puns in historical names. It does, however, suggest that the phenomenon of a correspondence between names and themes may well be "an outcome of a punning technique widely used by the biblical authors, who had the artistry to fit the connotative sense of names into the stories."[33] But if the meanings of the names in Leviticus 24 have no connotative sense, or at least any that is discernible to contemporary readers, do they in fact contribute to enriching and intensifying the plot?

Though she admitted that her suggestions for what the names might mean was necessarily speculative, Douglas still relied on some connection between meaning and plot for her interpretation of the narrative, suggesting that "the punning on names draws attention to the punning

---

30. Sherwood, *Leviticus, Numbers, Deuteronomy*, 27.

31. Leuchter, "Ambiguous Details," 437–40.

32. Curiously, though Fuad's thesis is that the central ambiguity of the narrative is the identity of the מקלל, he never mentions the man's namelessness. Fuad, "The Curious Case of the Blasphemer."

33. Garsiel, "Puns," 386.

about the punishment."[34] Pointing to other narratives in the Hebrew Bible in which puns on names figure prominently, Douglas argued that names signal a "tale within a tale" that condenses and vividly illustrates the main theme of the book. In Leviticus 10, for example, Nadav and Avihu's inappropriate fire is met with fire from YHWH, "fire for fire" that metes out poetic justice.[35] In Numbers 25:1–15, Zimri "the fornicator is speared through" in "an obvious case of the punishment fitting the crime."[36] Drawing a connection between the meaning of the names and the meaning of the narrative is not necessary to her larger point, however, which was that each of these interludes draws attention to something more important at stake in the narrative by employing gratuitous names and exaggerated correspondences between crime and punishment. If we set aside the notion that the names in Leviticus mean anything significant in and of themselves (as this has proven impossible to determine), we can imagine them functioning literarily as something like street signs: the important thing is to follow the direction toward which they point, rather than asking why a given street is named one thing instead of another. The courtroom metaphor accentuating themes of justice and retribution that Douglas saw in the names would lose some of its force. In its place, the startling juxtaposition of an unnamed protagonist with a series of gratuitous names (tracing his own lineage, no less) comes to the fore. The story within a story that these names would then alert us to is less a story about justice and retribution—though it is that, to a degree—and more a story about names. Specifically, it is a story about THE Name, and its significance for everyone within the Israelite community. Later on, we will explore how this shift of emphasis away from retribution and toward the significance of the divine Name reframes the notion of equivalence, but first we need to examine what this narrative suggests about how the divine Name is conceived in the priestly logic.

The Ultimate Covering:
The Theological Significance of the Divine Name

The question posed earlier—what does it mean to trespass against the name?—is inextricable from a basic understanding of how the divine

---

34. Douglas, *Leviticus as Literature*, 208.
35. Douglas, *Leviticus as Literature*, 200–205.
36. Douglas, *Leviticus as Literature*, 208.

Name is conceived in the book of Leviticus. I suggest that the logic of Lev 24:10–23 is that the divine Name is considered the ultimate protective "covering" for the Israelite community, the ultimate boundary between a life of flourishing and the non-existence of chaos and disorder. If this is true, then continuity can be demonstrated between two features of the narrative that have long baffled interpreters: the precise nature of the offense itself, and the relationship between the talion laws in vv. 17–22 and the surrounding narrative. Three focal points form the basis for this proposal: 1) a careful examination of the language used to describe the offense in Leviticus 24; 2) the priestly notion that YHWH's name is equivalent to the sanctum; and 3) Douglas's treatment of the logic that explains the problem with "eruptions" from bodies, skin, or houses.

As we observed earlier, the meaning of the operative verbs that describe the offense against the Name leaves a great deal of ambiguity concerning what the man actually did and why it was so bad. The unadorned statement of the incident reads, וַיִּקֹּב בֶּן־הָאִשָּׁה הַיִּשְׂרְאֵלִית אֶת־הַשֵּׁם וַיְקַלֵּל (v. 11a). The object of the first verb, וַיִּקֹּב, is clear: something has been done to the Name. But what? Translations variously render the word "blaspheme" (NRSV, KJV, ESV) or "pronounce" (NJPS, Milgrom), but these are not synonymous terms. The choice of "blaspheme" may have something to do with debate about whether the root should be read as קבב, a bi-form of נקב that is unquestionably associated with cursing, rather than root נקב itself, which includes something like cursing within its semantic range (particularly when its object is השם) but is more strongly associated with an action of "piercing or marking." נקב can mean "to bore through, to pierce," or "to denote, establish, designate;"[37] hence the more descriptive translation favored by Milgrom and others: "to pronounce."[38] Furthermore, the reappearance of the root נקב in v. 16 (בְּנָקְבוֹ־שֵׁם ... וְנֹקֵב) leaves no doubt that the root in v. 11 is also נקב, the most common usage of which is simply "to pronounce, designate, invoke." On this reading נקב could denote simply pronouncing the Name, a neutral action that would indicate that the second verb, קלל, is what caused the problem.[39]

---

37. Koehler and Baumgartner, *HALOT*, s.v. "נקב."

38. Furthermore, Milgrom observes that the root קבב never occurs with the object שם. Milgrom, *Leviticus 23–27*, 2108; see also Weingreen, who unequivocally concludes that the word has "no implications beyond the sense of uttering the Name of God," Weingreen, "The Case of the Blasphemer," 119; and Hutton, "The Case of the Blasphemer Revisited," 535.

39. Weingreen, "The Case of the Blasphemer," 119.

But this reading overlooks the direct syntactic relationship between נקב and disastrous consequences in v. 16: וְנֹקֵב שֵׁם־יְהוָה מוֹת יוּמָת ("But whoever reviles the name of YHWH is to be put-to-death, yes, death"). Rodney Hutton argues that נקב cannot be fully cleared of its negative implications, and must mean invoking the divine Name in an illegitimate way.[40] The root's derivation from a more literal sense of inscribing or engraving supports the idea that when it is used to describe a speech-act, it carries connotations of pronouncing something in a forceful, violent manner—in a way that leaves a mark, so to speak. So several interpreters describe the offense as a "volley of insults" borne of "verbal aggression" that "pierces" and "bores through" the Name.[41]

The second verb, קלל, presents two questions: what does it mean, specifically in this context, and how is it related to נקב? As with נקב, the semantic range of קלל can include "to curse, declare accursed," but far more common are extensions of the root's basic meaning of ("to be light"), such as "to be small, insignificant; to treat with contempt, despise, consider trivial; to demean, belittle."[42] The root is used in three places in Leviticus, in reference to the deaf (19:14), parents (20:9), or the divine Name (24:11, 16). In all instances it involves speech, and in the latter two cases it constitutes a capital crime—interestingly, all capital crimes in Leviticus constitute some sort of boundary violation, whether literally or metaphorically.[43] But besides these three instances involving קלל, all other behaviors that implicate the Name use a different verb, חלל ("to profane, make common") which appears to have a broader application. Other things besides the Name may be made חלל (the sanctum, 21:12; priests or their family members, 19:8, 29; etc.), and it can result from a range of actions not limited to speech (defilement, 21:6; inappropriate marriage, 21:13–15; etc.).[44]

---

40. Hutton, "The Case of the Blasphemer Revisited," 535.

41. Gerstenberger, *Leviticus*, 362; Kamionkowski, *Leviticus*, 264–65; Douglas, *Leviticus as Literature*, 207.

42. Koehler and Baumgartner, *HALOT*, s.v., "קלל."

43. In addition to the instances cited above, these include trespass against the sanctuary (chapter 10), sacrificing children to Molech (20:2), sexual sin (20:10), murder (24:17), and regulations concerning individuals under the ban (28:29).

44. While only קלל and חלל are used in conjunction with שם, I agree with Milgrom that חלל is H's equivalent to מעל in P, i.e., the "trespass (מעל) against YHWH" that occurs as a result of unfulfilled oaths in 5:20–26. See Milgrom, *Leviticus 1–16*, 345–56; and *Leviticus 17–22*, 1635. קלל is thus, in my view, closely connected but more limited in range than מעל/חלל.

In other words, קלל may have a specific connotation of causing harm to another individual through speech; in Leviticus, קלל always has a personal being as its object, either someone who should be protected, or someone who should be esteemed. Other interpreters have arrived at similar conclusions. Kamionkowski surveys uses of קלל outside of Leviticus (Jud 9:27; Neh 13:25, etc.) to observe that "the common thread in all of these cases is that the root קלל indicates a stance of disrespect that impacts the social order."[45] Similarly, Hutton provides further support by observing that קלל is the antonym of the word כבד ("to be heavy, honored"), thus suggesting that "the primary meaning relates to the 'belittling' or 'dishonoring' (thus 'degrading') of the deity."[46] While Milgrom acknowledges that the precise meaning of קלל is unclear, he points to ample evidence in which it clearly means "to curse," arguing especially that the equivalent law in Exod 22:27 holds קלל and ארר to be parallel, which "tips the balance in favor of the view that cursing God, not reviling him, is the case under discussion."[47] There are two problems with this conclusion, however: if "cursing" implies invoking the deity's name against another, as we saw in our discussion of Lev 5:1, 4 in the previous chapter, how is "cursing" God not oxymoronic?[48] Furthermore, ארר and קלל cannot be exact synonyms, as ארר is used exclusively in the context of cursing and carries none of the neutral connotations of "making light" that קלל does. In their discussion of קלל, Jenni and Westermann specifically distinguish between the two verbs, in fact: while ארר is exclusively declarative, קלל (*piel*) is simultaneously declarative and factitive, so that "to declare someone 'light' i.e., despicable, insignificant, meaningless, means nothing other than to make the person despicable . . . Word and deed are entirely identical."[49] The best translation for קלל, then, is the most obvious one: "to make insignificant, to belittle, to make of no account." "To curse" is a derived sense from this primary meaning, and while it is clearly appropriate in some cases, Lev 24:11 is not one of them, as we shall see in the syntax of the verse.

---

45. Kamionkowski, *Leviticus*, 264.

46. Hutton, "The Case of the Blasphemer Revisited," 539; see also Milgrom, *Leviticus 23–27*, 2109; and Jenni and Westermann *TLOT*, s.v., "קלל."

47. Milgrom, *Leviticus 23–27*, 2109.

48. For a more detailed discussion of this problem, see both Hutton, "The Case of the Blasphemer Revisited," 538; and Kamionkowski, *Leviticus*, 264.

49. Jenni and Westermann, *TLOT*, s.v., "קלל."

Having determined that the best rendering for the two verbs in v. 11 is something like "he pierced" and "made light, insubstantial, insignificant," we are now in a better position to discuss the syntax of the verse. The primary question is whether the two verbs denote two distinct actions—implying that pronouncing the Name is, in and of itself, a crime—or two aspects of a single action. Most commentators have settled on the latter, taking קלל as the adverbial modifier of נקב. The Name was thus articulated (נקב) in an offensive or inappropriate way (קלל). In the clearest and most comprehensive discussion of the grammatical difficulties at play in this verse, Hutton agrees that a single action seems most likely, but he also points out that there are least four different ways that these two verbs could be understood to describe a single action, a fact that is generally overlooked while one of the options is simply assumed. The possibilities include:

- Adverbial modification: (he did A in a B manner)
- Resultative coordination: (he did A with the result that B happened)
- Inverse resultative coordination (A happened when he did B)
- Synonymous equation (he did A; that is to say, he did B)[50]

Hutton supports the conclusion that resultative coordination makes the most sense on the basis of both what we understand these verbs to mean, and the syntactical priority of נקב both in v. 11 and v. 16.[51] So there is one action in view, that involves both נקב and קלל: נקב is the main verb (cause), with the result that קלל happens (effect). While this is the only instance in which נקב is used in Leviticus, this cause/effect relationship would mirror other situations involving capital punishment in which X (cause) results in חלל (effect). It is thus reasonable to conclude that נקב is considered the verbal equivalent of other actions that constitute grave boundary violations, as noted above: sanctuary trespass, sacrificing children to Molech, sexual sins, and murder.

The grammatical evidence thus suggests that for both נקב and קלל, "blasphemy" and "cursing" are abstractions of the most obvious, more common, and far more descriptive meanings of the words. This has obscured not only the nature of the offense that occurs in this narrative, but how the divine Name is construed in the priestly imagination as

---

50. Hutton, "The Case of the Blasphemer Revisited," 533–34.
51. Hutton, "The Case of the Blasphemer Revisited," 539–40.

something that can be "pierced" and "made light, trivial, insubstantial." There are two further areas that we need to examine in order for this understanding of the Name to make sense: the notion that the Name is equivalent to the sanctum, and the priestly logic of "coverings."

The notion that, for the priestly writers, the divine Name is equivalent to sancta is evident in the fact that sacrilege may be committed either against the sanctuary and its appurtenances (including priests and those of the priestly line; 19:8; 21:12), or against the Name (5:21; 19:11–12; 22:32). Accordingly, there are two ways that YHWH may be approached: either physically or verbally.[52] As we saw in the previous chapter, the gift-giving structures of sacrifice provide an avenue through which humans can safely approach the divine, non-verbally communicating reciprocation and good will while also demonstrating an appropriate respect for the boundary between human and divine. The gift mediates this boundary but does so in a way that maintains its essential integrity, enabling the kind of approach that cultivates relationship rather than the kind that disregards the fundamental difference between self and Other. The sacrificial regulations conclude with a narrative warning in chapter 10 about the disastrous consequences of approaching the holy place without these essential safeguards in place: Nadav and Avihu breach the boundary, and they cease to exist.

As the literary counterpart to chapter 10, the narrative in 24:10–23 vividly illustrates the second way that the divine can be approached, but in many ways it simply expands the treatment of speech that began in chapter 5. In both chapters, the force that a speech-act may carry is depicted through association with some kind of physical contact, either as the equivalent of corpse contamination through touch (נגע, 5:1–5) or accompanying the physical assault against another human (נצה, 24:10). Both treatments acknowledge that speech is available to virtually anyone in the community, Israelite or גר, so that it is not only priests in relation to the holy space but anyone, at any time, who may approach the sanctity of the Name. No location is specified in chapter 5, indicating that oaths have consequences regardless of where or when they are spoken, and chapter 24 explicitly states that the incident occurs out among all the people (וַיֵּצֵא ... בְּתוֹךְ בְּנֵי יִשְׂרָאֵל; v. 10) and need not be connected to the sanctuary to constitute a grave offense. Further, in both treatments inappropriate speech is understood to constitute a trespass that is sacrilege,

---

52. Milgrom, *Leviticus 23–27*, 2140–45; Balentine, *Leviticus*, 192.

an "incursion into the divine sphere [that] reduces God's realm of holiness, desanctifying or desecrating it."[53] The primary difference in these two treatments is that in chapter 5 the trespass occurs inadvertently and is eligible for expiation, whereas in chapter 24 it appears to have been committed with intention and is immediately recognized as problematic by the entire community, a point to which we will return below.

The conceptual symmetry between these narratives has long been observed: one illustrates trespass of sacred space, while the other illustrates trespass against the holy Name (i.e., 20:3; 22:2, 32).[54] Douglas's notion of a literary symmetry in which the two narratives are the counterparts to the two screens in the tabernacle underscores this parallel between holy space and the holiness of the Name, demonstrating that in both cases sacrilege is understood to be a breach of a boundary. The sanctity of the Name is not just an idea to be respected; it is a sphere that can be encroached upon. This suggests another subtle nuance in the way that the Name is conceived; it is not exactly synonymous with the divine but is the approachable "boundary" that separates between human and divine, the boundary that protects humans from the pure, unmediated holiness of the divine Presence. This is why the Name can be assaulted, damaged even, without implying a theology in which actual deicide is possible.[55]

One further aspect of the logic of Leviticus illumines this notion of the Name as the ultimate boundary that can be breached. By themselves, the language of "piercing" and "making light" of the Name as a sphere of holiness could simply be understood as a graphic depiction of disrespect. But considered in light of the significance of other "coverings" in Leviticus, the seriousness of the crime and its outcome come into clearer focus.

Douglas has argued that the rules governing reproductive processes and צרעת of skin, clothing, or houses in Leviticus 12–15 are held together by a logic of sacred contagion, "whereby any contact with the polluted thing will transmit the pollution just as virulently, and on, and on, indefinitely, from contact to contact. The line of dangerous contacts will eventually impinge on sacred food or place."[56] In each of these cases, the source of the impurity is a breach of the body's limits, the outermost

---

53. Milgrom, *Leviticus 17–22*, 1635.

54. For further discussion, see Milgrom, *Leviticus 23–27*, 2082, 2141.

55. The suggestion that deicide is the true intent of blasphemy, thus illustrating the seriousness of apostasy, was suggested by Simeon Chavel, as discussed in Milgrom, *Leviticus 23–27*, 2141.

56. Douglas, *Leviticus as Literature*, 187.

boundary that separates what is inside the body from what is outside, in a series of concentric circles of covering that include body, garment and house. The problem with these breaches of limits is that they create "exposed and risk-prone conditions" that constitute "threats to the integrity of the living being."[57] Douglas explains that,

> the breach of the body's containing walls evidenced by escape of vital fluids and the failure of its skin cover are vulnerable states which go counter to God's creative action when he set up separating boundaries in the beginning ... Everything in creation is arranged in order; each thing on a lower rank to be kept apart from one above, contact between them to be mediated by sacred powers given for the purpose.

If these separations fail to maintain their integrity, however, it is as if the order of creation is undone:

> The body's skin erupting with burgeoning pustules, then the affliction with the same name erupting upon the garment upon the skin, then the leprous house that is upon the garment that is upon the skin that is upon the body ... If there is no cure, the incurably defiled house must be destroyed (Lev 14:39–42), as also the incurable leprous garment (Lev 13:52), and eventually the incurable leper can expect to be destroyed by the disease.[58]

The series of analogies of צרעת in body, garment, and house, Douglas argues, converges with the doctrine of atonement described for the tabernacle in chapter 16; the body is the microcosm of the tabernacle.[59] But when the holiness that is associated with the tabernacle is extended to the entire land, what then? Do the gradations of holiness that mirror the order of creation and enable Israel's ongoing sanctification (21:8, 15; 22:32) cease to exist? Israel has been separated from the nations in her creation as a new nation and tasked with participating in the patterns of holiness that distinguish YHWH's holy people (11:44–45; 19:2; 20:26), but is the distinction between human and divine thus no longer operative? What is the ultimate covering at the far edges of the priestly writers' "microcosms of the world"?[60] The answer to this points us back to the equivalence between the holy space and the holy Name.

---

57. Douglas, *Leviticus as Literature*, 189–90.
58. Douglas, *Leviticus as Literature*, 191.
59. Douglas, *Leviticus as Literature*, 191.
60. Douglas, *Leviticus as Literature*, 180.

The logic that equates intact coverings with purity, and porous boundaries with impurity—that is, a logic in which a blurring of boundaries produces a decreative, chaotic state—is thus analogous to the basic logic of sacrilege. Sacrilege constitutes a loss of distinction between degrees of holiness, as we have seen in the close association of the verbs חלל, מעל, and קלל. Taking them all in view, מעל, P's term for sacrilege that we encountered in chapter 5 as a result of false oaths, is essentially an act that causes a change in the status of the object in question, reducing its holiness.⁶¹ H's synonymous term, חלל, more vividly depicts the range of things that are vulnerable to this reduction in status; in short, anything that has been offered or dedicated to YHWH (19:8; 21:4; 21:23), in addition to the Name (18:21; 19:11–12; 21:6; etc.), can be profaned.⁶² The sanctity of the name, furthermore, is vulnerable to this reduction in "status" in exactly the same way as are other holy things, as Tamar Kamionkowski has shown. The phrase לחלל את שם in the Holiness writings is not a euphemism meaning that YHWH's "reputation" has been damaged, Kamionkowski argues, but should literally be understood as "to desecrate, that is, 'to reduce the sacredness of'" the divine Name.⁶³ In this thought-world of sacrilege as a change in status, the use of קלל in chapter 24, in connection with a verbal assault that pierces the Name, makes perfect sense. The Name—the covering that protects Israel, separating between human and divine—is damaged, punctured, and made "lighter." The sacrilege of blasphemy, properly understood, is thus a verbal eruption that does damage to the covering defining the ultimate boundary between human and divine, understood by the priestly writers as the Name of YHWH. When this boundary is breached, analogous to all other breaches of boundaries, the community is exposed to risk-prone conditions that threaten the integrity of the community—quite literally, that threaten the community's existence. So blasphemy is intrinsically a deconstructive act, as we shall see. Blasphemy enacts non-being, triggering a liminal state of disorder and chaos.

To summarize: the literary function of the human names in our narrative is to point beyond themselves, indicating that the story is really

---

61. Cf. 5:20; 26:40; Milgrom, *Leviticus 1–16*, 351.

62. Milgrom, *Leviticus 17–22*, 1635.

63. Kamionkowski argues that the notion of "reputation" is post-biblical and has been interpreted through the lens of Ezekiel, but does not accurately reflect the priestly theology of Leviticus. Kamionkowski, "שם' של תאולוגיה לכוהנים היתה 'האם? / Did the Priests Have a 'Name' Theology?," 28.

about the divine Name and the seriousness of breaching its integrity as the protective covering that holds Israel in the appropriate place in the created order, a place of human flourishing and formation in holiness. The breach of the divine Name through the words of the מקלל—words that pierced the covering, rendering it permeable and insubstantial—resulted in the death of the מקלל through stoning. In violating the divine Name, the ultimate boundary between life and death, the man with no name literally ceases to exist.

The Divine Name: Connecting Literary and Theological Equivalence

In her careful attention to the sophisticated literary construction of the narrative, Douglas observed a poetic equivalence between the crime of the מקלל and his punishment, a sort of "grim playfulness" on the part of the priestly writers; because "the blasphemer has hurled insults at the name of God, let him die by stones hurled at him."[64] Douglas thus saw the inclusion of the talion laws in the pericope as having a certain literary continuity, underscoring a theme of justice and equivalence through both law and narrative. Milgrom also argued that the talion laws were carefully and artfully integrated into their narrative frame, observing that "all seven laws that emanate from this single case of blasphemy (vv. 15–22), even though they are general in form, can never be dissociated from the narrative framework in which they are [chiastically] embedded (vv. 10–14, 23)."[65]

Literary vs. Theological Equivalence

While arguing for the coherence of the passage at the literary level, however, both Douglas and Milgrom struggled to understand how the punishment of the blasphemer expresses a deeper theological equivalence. The crux of the difficulty is that the punishment of death seems disproportionate to the crime of blasphemy. Douglas wrote about this passage in two places: first in an essay that sought to extend the logic of the purity laws to the biblical laws of retaliation, grounding them both in the idea of reciprocity; and again a few years later in her literary

---

64. Douglas, *Leviticus as Literature*, 207.
65. Milgrom, *Leviticus 23–27*, 2102.

treatment of Leviticus that we have thus far been referencing.⁶⁶ While her interpretation in *Leviticus as Literature* is more fully developed and introduces some altogether new ideas than were represented in her earlier essay, her basic conclusion in both treatments is that the laws of talion should not be taken literally; rather they are poetic illustrations of a general principle about balance and justice within an ordered universe that runs on reciprocity. They cannot be taken literally, she reasons, because the penalty of death for blasphemy depicted in the narrative is a "poor fit" for matching punishment to crime: "Death by hurling stones and sin by hurling insults have a weak literary match, but apart from the pun there is no matching of the punishment with the crime."⁶⁷ Besides her difficulty to find true equivalence between the crime and the punishment of the מקלל, Douglas's view of the nature of talion was that a universe that runs on reciprocity must, unfortunately, include both the good and the bad. At least, she argued, "Exodus 21.23 and Leviticus 24 where the negative retaliations occur are balanced with positive laws; both positive and negative should be read in the spirit of generosity . . . the Bible is retaliatory in a perfectly proper sense of requiring reciprocity."⁶⁸ Apart from the discomfort of settling on a conclusion that offers no real resolution to the enigma of the relationship between the narrative and talion, it is truly difficult to square this conclusion with Douglas's conviction that "the doctrine of divine compassion" expressed in the purity rules should be the interpretive principle for the book.⁶⁹

Milgrom, on the other hand, argued both that there is a theological equivalence between the talion laws and the punishment for blasphemy in the logic of the priestly writers, and that literal talion is intended in the

---

66. Douglas, "Sacred Contagion," 86–106; Douglas, *Leviticus as Literature*, 205–15.

67. Douglas, *Leviticus as Literature*, 212. Here, Douglas also floated the idea that perhaps the "jingly form" of the narrative frame, along with its unclear fit with the talion laws, suggested a subtle attempt on the part of the priestly writers to "test the universal validity of the principle of retribution." Like the book of Job, she suggested, the seemingly imprecise analogy between the narrative and talion may have been intended to "bring into the spotlight logical fallacies that have attached themselves to the doctrine," thus spurring more careful reflection on the true balance of equanimity and justice. Her attempt to make sense of the puzzling inner logic of the passage is worth citing for her determination to unravel the tangle of the priestly logic, but the theory itself is only shakily supported and has generally been ignored by commentators. For further discussion, see Nihan, *From Priestly Torah to Pentateuch*, 519 n. 490.

68. Douglas, "Sacred Contagion," 87.

69. Douglas, "Sacred Contagion," 88.

laws of Leviticus.⁷⁰ To demonstrate the theological rationale for the punishment for blasphemy, Milgrom builds his case on the complex chiastic structure of 24:13–23 in which vv. 19–20 form the heart of the message:

> If anyone maims (מום) another, as he has done so shall it be done to him: fracture for fracture, eye for eye, tooth for tooth.
> The injury (מום) he has inflicted on the person shall be inflicted on him.⁷¹

He then observes that H uses the same word here for "maim," מום, as the "blemish" that disqualifies a person for service at the altar as described in 21:16–23 and 22:19–25. Because humans are created in the image of God (Gen 1:26–27; 9:6b), causing physical injury to another person is thus equivalent to disfiguring the image of God. Milgrom similarly concluded that it is precisely this association that forms the common thread between the laws and the narrative in 24:10–23: "A theological message emerges here: He who injures a person has disfigured 'the image of God.' For the priestly legist, this is blasphemy, and so he applies the law of talion to the case of the blasphemer."⁷² Disfigurement for disfigurement; pelting for pelting.

An obvious difficulty remains, however: even if blasphemy is understood to be the equivalent of doing physical harm to another, injury is not the same as murder. So why must the מקלל be put to death? How is this punishment commensurate with the crime?

Milgrom concludes that the point of the narrative is not to extend and illustrate the doctrine of talion at all. Instead, the narrative deals with a different topic that is only loosely associated with the talion laws through the common thread of sacrilege, that is, doing harm to the *imago Dei*. On its own the narrative reflects a notion of speech as a contagion that causes impurity (and thus sacrilege), Milgrom contends, so the death of the מקלל was the necessary intervention to contain the destructive force of impurity that his verbal eruption had released within the community. "If the community had not put the blasphemer to death," Milgrom writes, "the inexpiable impurity generated by the curse would have caused the destruction of the community. Thus one might even say that the community had to kill the blasphemer in self-defense."⁷³ He also observes, as we have noted, that this treatment of speech in Lev 24:10–23

---

70. Milgrom, *Leviticus: A Continental Commentary*, 297.
71. Milgrom, *Leviticus 23–27*, 2128–29.
72. Milgrom, *Leviticus: A Continental Commentary*, 297.
73. Milgrom, *Leviticus: A Continental Commentary*, 294.

is the counterpart to the inadvertent or unwitting desecrations caused by unfulfilled oaths in 5:1–6, 20–26. Whereas those offenses are expiable by sacrifice, the "advertent, brazen desecration [caused by the מקלל] is punishable by death."[74] So he concludes that literal talion is intended in vv. 17–22, but the relationship between the laws and narrative is not literally equivalent. There was a close enough resonance that these two sections were brought together, and "talion is frequently but a literary figure for the purpose of vividly emphasizing that God's justice is uncompromisingly inexorable."[75] If there is any lingering discomfort on the part of the reader with the apparent imbalance between blasphemy and the penalty of death, Milgrom simply observes that "YHWH's talion need not always be precise."[76]

Douglas and Milgrom are not alone in their struggle to understand how the logic of equivalence in the talion laws is related to the theme of the narrative frame, while ultimately concluding that the fit is inexact. I have carefully engaged their treatments of the passage, singling them out among a wide field of interpreters, because their work has done more than most to illumine various aspects of this difficult text and influence contemporary commentary. It is their work, in fact, that makes it possible to see the one missing piece of the puzzle that creates a seamless whole: the notion of the divine Name as the protective covering between life and death, order and chaos, existence and non-existence. There is deep literary and theological coherence between the narrative and talion that comes to light with this in view. If the integrity of the Name is the ultimate boundary on which Israel's existence depends, and if damage to boundaries creates an "exposed and risk-prone condition," then the destructive eruption, the impurity, that is released through blasphemous speech exposes the community to life-threatening conditions. Doing verbal damage to the Name is thus precisely equivalent to death, insofar as it destroys the conditions in which life can flourish.

From this perspective, the narrative functions to reframe—literarily and conceptually—the notion of equivalence expressed in the talion laws in two significant ways: punishment is reframed as containment, and the outcome of the trespass is conceived as inseparable from and intrinsic to the crime itself.

74. Milgrom, *Leviticus 23–27*, 2106.

75. Milgrom, *Leviticus: A Continental Commentary*, 294.

76. Milgrom, *Leviticus: A Continental Commentary*, 294; Milgrom, *Leviticus 23–27*, 2138.

Containment, not Punishment: Arresting Speech

The analogy between corrupt speech and צרעת as destructive forces that "erupt" and do damage to the integrity of protective coverings is key to understanding YHWH's verdict regarding what should be done with the מקלל. In several ways, the depiction of the incident portrays a process of damage control much like the procedures that are to be followed when צרעת is discovered. If this analogy holds true, then it is possible to read the response to blasphemy less as "punishment" and more as a process of containment. The operative metaphor is not the courtroom as much as it is the emergency protocol for managing an epidemic. Like a highly contagious disease, "anyone who cursed was a dangerous person," Gerstenberger explains; "maledictions brought misfortune upon the entire community because evil words ... poisoned the atmosphere."[77] A destructive force had been unleashed and had to be contained in order to prevent further damage within the community.

Before taking a closer look at the response to the מקלל through this lens of damage control, an important nuance that Douglas brought to light in her study of defilement may help to loosen the firm grip that the notion of punishment holds on our understanding of the death penalty. Douglas argued that in Leviticus, defilement from disease or bodily conditions was understood as an inevitable fact of life. In contrast to other occurrences of contagion in the narrative books, defilement in Leviticus is not the result of punishment for sin but a natural condition that, if untreated, could evoke consequences.[78] Approaching sacred space while ritually impure, for example, would be to take one's life in one's hands; staying away until the appropriate purification procedures have been fulfilled, however, incurs no punishment or moral opprobrium. So the logic of the procedures for dealing with naturally occurring defilement through quarantine, expiation, et cetera, is that of containing contagion and protecting the individual, rather than punishing him or her. As a result, Douglas explained, "misfortunes are effectively decoupled from sins."[79] Defilement sets in motion a process for limiting the effects of defilement and restoring the individual to full function within the

---

77. Gerstenberger, *Leviticus*, 362.

78. Douglas points to 1 Kings 5:25–27 and 2 Kings 15:1–5 as situations involving contagion that contrast to the logic expressed in Leviticus. "Sacred Contagion," 95.

79. Douglas, "Sacred Contagion," 96–97.

community, ultimately resuming the rhythms of offerings that maintained communication with YHWH.

There are some clear discontinuities between defilement from צרעת and the case of the מקלל. Most glaringly, the person with צרעת bears no responsibility for the defilement that inheres, whereas defilement caused by speech is a voluntary and avoidable crime. It is generally accepted among interpreters that the offense of the מקלל was a brazen, intentional sin, and that this is why it was ineligible for expiation.[80] But was it intentional? The portrayal of the offense provides no commentary on the man's intent. On the contrary, it relays a series of "eruptions" loosely imagined, in quick succession; the man "comes out" in public (וַיֵּצֵא), a fight "breaks out" in the camp (וַיִּנָּצוּ), and words burst out of his mouth (וַיִּקֹּב . . . וַיְקַלֵּל). Does the evidence suggest a purposeful attack, or a series of rash missteps, the thoughtless lapses of a person with a possibly volatile nature? The analogy to צרעת may be closer than it appears at first glance.[81]

Regardless of whether or not the offense was intentional, the procedure for containing explosive speech does bear a strong resemblance to the procedures for handling צרעת. The man is immediately brought to Moses—no details are given to describe how he is apprehended and by whom, whether he comes willingly or under duress—and placed in confinement; literally, they "settle him down" or "calm him down" under watch (וַיַּנִּיחֻהוּ בַּמִּשְׁמָר).[82] Similarly, the person with a suspicious blemish or scab or anomaly of the skin is to be brought to Aaron (וְהוּבָא אֶל־אַהֲרֹן הַכֹּהֵן) or one of his sons (13:2). The priest is to examine the blemish, and make a pronouncement: if the blemish has penetrated the skin, the person is טמא; if it has not, the person is to be placed in confinement (סגר) to see how it progresses—that is, whether it appears to be spreading or not (13:3–6). In the case of the מקלל, the man is not brought for Moses's inspection, but YHWH's, לִפְרֹשׁ לָהֶם עַל־פִּי יְהוָה (24:12). What is the extent of the damage? How deep was the penetration? Since there is no visible blemish for the priest to examine the circumstances require divine discernment, so the man is confined until it can be made clear.

The person who is found to have a disruption in the skin's integrity is טמא. If the mark does not heal, the person must live alone outside the camp for as long as it continues, warding off any who would approach

---

80. Milgrom, *Leviticus 23–27*, 2106.

81. JPS translates וַיֵּצֵא as "a fight broke out," which nicely resonates with the notion of a verbal eruption analogous to צרעת. See Levine, *Leviticus*, 166.

82. Jenni and Westermann, *TLOT*, s.v. "נוח."

(13:45–46). The מקלל is also to be taken מִחוּץ לַמַּחֲנֶה, but the analogy appears to break down here at the point of diagnosis. Rather than avoiding all physical contact with the individual, everyone who heard the outburst (כָּל־הַשֹּׁמְעִים) is to place their hands on the head of the מקלל, and the entire community is to stone him (24:14). This would seem to challenge the notion that what is occurring here is fundamentally a procedure of containing a dangerous and contagious force; should the man not be ostracized and avoided, rather than touched? The fact that it is those who were within earshot of the incident are the ones who are implicated is significant; they have already been affected by what they heard. They are already "contaminated." The placement of their hands on the man, in this reading, could be understood as symbolically directing the destructive element (i.e., the verbal outburst) back to its source, thus "containing" it and restoring things to order.

There is some debate whether this gesture signifies transference or identification. Is physical contact meant to convey the impurity back to the מקלל, or to identify him as the source of the impurity? In his classic study of the meaning of the gesture of hand placement in the Hebrew Bible in its ancient Near Eastern context, for example, David Wright argues that the latter interpretation is correct: the laying on of hands is "a means whereby the witnesses designate the blasphemer as guilty of the crime and worthy of death. By it the witnesses symbolically confirm their testimony to the community and also acknowledge their responsibility in the death of the criminal."[83] Because there is no exact parallel to this procedure as it is described in 24:14, 23, Wright supports his position by analogy to similar situations, and by his view that there is no evidence elsewhere in the Bible that blasphemy causes pollution.[84] Milgrom's conclusion is the opposite; precisely because there are no identical parallels, the appearance of the procedure in the context of a book that deals so extensively with ritual impurity and the processes for its purification support the notion that the laying on of hands "serves a transference function: to convey the pollution generated by the blasphemy back to its producer."[85] The notion of speech as an eruption, which finds support on multiple fronts, tips the balance heavily in favor of a logic of transference. Nonetheless, it is also possible that both functions may be

83. Wright, "The Gesture of Hand Placement," 435.

84. i.e., the execution of apostates in Deuteronomy (17:7; 13:10) and the case of Susanna (Sus 34; Dan 13:34 LXX). See Wright, "The Gesture of Hand Placement," 435.

85. Milgrom, *Leviticus 23–27*, 2113.

in view here; there is no compelling evidence to suggest that transference and identification could not both be understood to occur simultaneously within a single symbolic gesture.

So the threat is contained; the damage is directed back to its source. It is the outcome of this reversal, however, that makes it truly difficult to separate the notion of containment from that of punishment. In the final stage of the process, returning the destructive force back to its source destroys the source itself.

A Crime Too Great to Bear: Reversing Destruction

The logic is clear enough. A trespass so violent, so powerful that it is capable of piercing the integrity of the Name exposes the community to a vulnerable, liminal state between order and chaos, life and death. It is the opposite of the ultimate life-giving, creative force of divine speech, and when it is returned to its source the result is literally non-existence. Blasphemy is intrinsically de-creative. This logic is consistent with other trespasses in the book that are punishable by death: each instance is a boundary violation that threatens the distinction between the קדש and the חל, the sacred and the profane, whether of persons, places, or things. At the national level, Israel may also lose her "distinction" by doing any of the things that are like the nations or unlike the *imago Dei* (18:1–5), effectively ceasing to exist as a nation (18:24–30; 26:33). As damage to the divine Name is inseparable from its effects on the מקלל, Israel's self-destructive behavior cannot but implicate YHWH. If Israel ceases to exist, then YHWH's presence in the world is diminished; YHWH's capacity to be bodied forth through the people who are called to be holy as YHWH is holy (10:3; 11:44; 19:2; 20:26; 21:8) is limited.[86]

On the face of it the distinction is subtle, but this internal logic of containing a verbal force-field is radically different than a concept of equivalence as a quid-pro-quo mirroring of destructive behaviors with destruction in kind. Such a simplistic understanding of equivalence is difficult to reconcile with the complex priestly vision of cultivating habits of life in which humans can learn to live—and flourish—in proximity to the divine. In the logic of the text, the procedures that result in the death of the מקלל are not simply retribution in kind, as if there were a two-stage process of crime and punishment. The outcome is both intrinsic

---

86. Balentine, *Leviticus*, 189–90. See also Josh 7:8–9 and Ezek 20:14, 22.

to and inseparable from the deed done. The notion of equivalence that comes into view through this narrative, seen in the larger context of the priestly logic, is thus neither incongruous nor disproportionate, but the inevitable outcome of destructive and decreative behaviors.

Discerning the Direction of Thought

The elegance of this literary and logical symmetry does not erase the theologically troubling nature of the narrative's plain meaning, however. Even if we understand the logic of equivalence as containment, even if we understand that the crime was so serious as to threaten the existence of the community, and that, once returned to their source, there are destructive forces too great for a human to bear, the fact remains that the community takes up stones in their own hands to put a man to death. Can we accept a logic of equivalence that, in its practical application, requires violence to maintain order and balance?

This discomfort has long been felt by interpreters. Baruch Levine reports that the earliest interpretations by the sages sought to demonstrate that the talion of Torah was intended to lay the groundwork for substituting monetary compensation in place of retaliatory physical injury. "The broad scope of the Talmudic discussion," Levine writes, "reflects an intense polemical effort on the part of the rabbis to demonstrate the milder intent of biblical law."[87] This effort has never really dissipated; Douglas's treatment of contagion begins by reflecting on the twentieth-century work of Raphael Draï, who forcefully argued that talion has widely been misunderstood in a way that is "antipathetic to the spirit of Torah, which enjoins forgiveness and compassion."[88] Other attempts to mitigate misinterpretation have highlighted the law's intent to provide an upper limit on retaliation in order to guard against excessive vengeance, suggested that it is a metaphorical or literary device to teach a general principle of justice and equanimity, or concluded that regardless of its intent, talion in cases involving physical injury was likely never enforced.[89] Noticing the repetition within the divine speech in 24:15b–16a, Origin even suggested that two consequences are delineated for the distinction between נקב and קלל: death and eternal damnation. The man's death should thus

---

87. Levine, *Leviticus*, 268–70.
88. Douglas's paraphrase, from "Sacred Contagion," 86.
89. For all of these possibilities, see Milgrom's discussion, *Leviticus 23–27*, 2133–38.

not be viewed negatively at all, but is, in fact, the mechanism for the man's atonement, releasing him from eternally bearing the weight of his sin both here and in the afterlife.[90]

None of these proposals satisfactorily ameliorate the gruesome reality of a story in which the community is actively involved in putting a man to death—but perhaps this is exactly the point. Regardless of whether the narrative was "meant" to be taken literally or metaphorically, and regardless of whether its principles were ever enacted or enforced, the response of generations of faithful and careful readers who have struggled to come to terms with this narrative suggests that perhaps the discomfort itself is worth considering: Why is it still disturbing even when it "makes sense"?

There are two related questions at the heart of the difficulty: First, why is this offense—why are any offenses—not expiable? There is precedent for the possibility of reparation in other situations involving inappropriate and damaging speech, as in the unfulfilled oaths of Leviticus 5. In fact, the analogy with the logic of contagion makes the absence of a restorative process for the מקלל even more glaring; whereas the purity rules include procedures for both containment and the individual's restoration to the community, there is no such allowance here. Even if a person with צרעת remains unwell, he is allowed to live beyond the borders of the community. In the case of the מקלל there is no restoration, but complete annihilation. What are we to make of this?

To set the problem in its full literary and theological scope: How we are to reconcile a logic that supports the enforcement of death for destructive behaviors with the priestly vision of establishing patterns of life conducive to human flourishing? Setting procedures in place to repair the inevitable damage that human sin will cause is central to the priestly vision of life, but in this case there is not only the absence of reparation; the requirements of containment result in even more loss of life. Limiting the extent of the damage to protect the broader community is clearly the goal, but the fundamental question persists: Why is this trespass not eligible for confession and expiation?

Rather than attempting to resolve these questions head-on, it may ultimately be more fruitful to ask how they function in the discourse between text and reader. What if we were to approach this snag in the weave of the narrative as a true tactical difficulty, a strategically located roadblock that redirects the attention, compelling us to pursue a different

---

90. Origen of Alexandria, *Homilies on Leviticus 1–16*, Homily 14, §4.2.

direction of thought? What if the absence of a process of expiation and reintegration, jarring as it is in the context of the priestly rhythms of life, could be read as an extended and inconclusive reflection on what it means to discern truly—and rightly—the shape of reparative justice in changing contexts? Fidelity to the text requires that we apply ourselves to understanding the text's own logic, as indeed we have; but as we have learned from Steiner's study of difficulty, this fidelity also means following the text's direction of thought into new formats of significance and translating its logic into generative conversation with the readerly context. The challenge presented by the disorienting and destabilizing parts of this particular text is to read them as a reflection on what it means to be called upon to exercise and participate in divine discernment as the entire congregation of Israel is called upon to do. The gap that leaves the possibility of the offender's restoration and reintegration into the community unaddressed could be an invitation to discern the shape of justice and equanimity in the readerly context.

Several aspects of this text do, in fact, point to a central theme of discernment—most notably, the fact that a key moment in the narrative is the community's instinctive response to bring the מקלל to Moses לִפְרֹשׁ לָהֶם עַל־פִּי יְהוָה, "to make it clear for them by the mouth of YHWH" (v. 12). What the man actually did does not seem to be the primary interest of the priestly writer, as is evident from the laconic description of the offense. The ambiguity has occupied the imaginations of interpreters for centuries and may never be fully resolved; all we are told is that an eruption occurred, before the focus immediately shifts to the process for handling it.

There is an unmistakable echo here of the parallel trespass in Leviticus 10 that resulted in the deaths of Nadav and Avihu. We know that it was an inappropriate boundary crossing, but it is not clear what they did wrong. We are told only that an eruption occurred, before the focus shifts to the process for dealing with its aftermath. Both of these situations mirror the weight of emphasis in the purity rules for dealing with the discovery of צרעת, as Douglas has observed: "the interest is not upon the cause of the condition," but on the procedures that must be followed once it has been noticed.[91]

From all of this it would be logical to conclude that focusing primarily on the element of the story that has to do with cause and effect or

---

91. Douglas, "Sacred Contagion," 97.

crime and punishment is to miss the larger point. If these examples were intended as cautionary tales or hortatory examples of "what not to do" they are certainly not very good ones, leaving so much confusion about the precise nature of the "cause" in each situation. In the face of such ambiguity, readers would be left to cut a wide berth around anything that might come close, constantly guessing whether some inadvertent misstep may evoke divine punishment.

Instead, the weight of emphasis suggests that perhaps the point of the stories is to provide instructions for what should be done in the aftermath of tragedy or disaster rather than to focus unhealthily on what could have been done to avoid it in the first place. One important part of formation in holiness would thus be knowing how to contain the damage when disorder cannot be avoided, a theme that we will examine more closely in the following chapter. For contemporary readers, the narrative would thus serve as a reminder that cause and intent are usually not the most important things to focus on when circumstances have gone terribly awry; things will inevitably go wrong, and there may be times when reasons are not discernible at all. The health of the community is maintained by the capacity of its members to respond appropriately in ways that limit the extent of the damage, not by their propensity to belabor blame.

A faithful reading of this text—informed by the context of the priestly vision of life and Torah's overarching interest in what it means to be human in relation to God—might thus animate the reading community to discern a kind of justice that goes beyond "damage control" to actively enact reparation for damage that has been done to the fabric of social life through speech that attacks and makes light of the values that ground public discourse and civility—that is, the values that enable us to live together in safety and flourishing.

The text sets us in the right direction with the few details that describe the processes of containment. As soon as the eruption occurs, the man is apprehended—how or by whom does not seem to matter—set apart, and settled down. Everyone who heard (הַשֹּׁמְעִים) plays a part in acknowledging that something has gone terribly wrong, that this is the source, and that they were affected. What is our own role in identifying the things, people, or behaviors that unleash chaos in the relationships that structure our communities? What are the breaches in the fabric of our own existence? The active role taken by those who were affected suggests the importance of reclaiming agency when we have been affected by violence that is outside of our control, recovering the power to turn things in a different direction. The involvement of not only those who heard, but everyone in the community, points to the ripple effect that dangerous speech and destructive behaviors have. None of us are immune; once damage has been done, we are all compelled to participate in repairing the breach.

The direction of thought that the narrative of the מקלל generates ultimately invites readers "to reach out towards more delicate orderings of perception," discerning the shape of both justice and reparation in situations of unprecedented destruction and instability, when the health of the community hangs in the balance.[92] In the following chapter, we will take a closer look at another situation in which ambiguity and discernment take center stage.

---

92. Steiner, *On Difficulty*, 40.

6

Developmental Discourse
Leviticus 10

"Understanding is patiently won, and, at all times, provisional."
—GEORGE STEINER[1]

"'Now' is the moment when change erupts."
—ANNE CARSON[2]

Why Leviticus 10?

OUR STUDY BEGAN WITH the observation that Leviticus portrays an event of discourse: YHWH speaks to Israel through Moses, generating a vision for their new life as a nation capable of hosting the presence of the divine. Literarily, this portrayal includes the reader in the "audience" addressed by the divine discourse, inviting us to imagine ourselves a part of the wilderness community. We then asked whether the discourse of Leviticus, as it is literarily addressed to the reader, may be generative in a way that is analogous to the priestly notion of speech as generative and creative of the Israelite community: What happens—or could happen—when we

---

1. Steiner, *Real Presences*, 176.
2. Carson, *Eros the Bittersweet*, 150.

read this book? What does Leviticus *do*? To answer this question, we have sketched out a notion of interpretation as a process of learning to understand a text's direction of thought in order to identify areas where it may challenge, inspire, or expand our own ways of thinking and the categories that we have come to accept as defining the human experience. Interpretation, maximally conceived, can open up new possibilities when a text's direction of thought is followed through from its originating context into new applications. The catch, of course, is that this is often difficult and always provisional.

Because Leviticus is literarily presented as an event of discourse, our entry point for testing this notion of interpretation has been to probe the function of speech in the priestly writers' portrayal of life in the wilderness community. What is the role of language? What does it do? How does it generate, support, or threaten the community's flourishing? And how might this understanding of the power of speech speak to contemporary concerns?

We now turn to a chapter in which all of these elements converge to bring our study full circle. In a narrative literarily driven by speech and portraying an enigmatic incident that has puzzled interpreters for centuries, Leviticus 10 discloses the priestly writers' own reflections on the inherent difficulty of interpretation—what is involved, what is at stake, and what it does. Significantly, it has recently been proposed that Leviticus 10 is the product of a final post-priestly redaction, "composed with the prospect of editorially *closing* the book of Leviticus."[3] If this is true, then Leviticus does not just happen to offer insight into the challenges and difficulty of interpretation, but does so quite intentionally, flagging the issues that will inevitably arise in attempts to read and interpret the book for generations to come.

This chapter will examine how Leviticus 10 directly engages the difficulties of interpretation through its literary portrayal of Aaron in the aftermath of the deaths of his sons, Nadav and Avihu. Our investigation will proceed in four parts:

First, we will find our footing by reviewing the literary context and basic content of the narrative, highlighting the major interpretive questions that it raises. Observing the tendency of scholars to focus too

---

3. This argument has been thoroughly set forth by Christophe Nihan, who follows and amends the thesis of R. Achenbach in *Die Vollendung*. Nihan's treatment is found in *From Priestly Torah to Pentateuch*, 148–50 and 576–607. Italics in the original, from p. 604.

narrowly on the account of Nadav and Avihu in vv. 1–2, I will suggest that chapter 10 is a complete narrative unit that must be read as a literary whole. Focusing excessively on vv. 1–2, 1–7, or any other discrete section within the whole renders the narrative's direction of thought incoherent.

Second, we will turn to an examination of how speech (the particular interest that has shaped each of our exegetical probes) functions as a prominent feature of Leviticus 10. I will suggest that careful attention to the literary function of speech reveals that it 1) drives the movement and development of the narrative; 2) highlights YHWH's speech to Aaron in vv. 8–11 as the centerpiece, condensing and distilling the larger point of the narrative; and 3) signals important developments in Moses and Aaron as literary characters and a rebalancing of their relationship, with the result that Aaron emerges as the key figure of the narrative.

To understand how Leviticus 10 functions in the literary development of Aaron's character, however, our third move will be to look beyond this chapter to the broader pentateuchal narrative as it relates to Aaron. The events that are portrayed here are part of a larger narrative arc, stretching throughout Moses and Aaron's history. Further, they bear a direct relation to what is arguably the most significant moment in their shared history: the episode of the golden calf in Exodus 32. Reading these two events in conjunction with one another, we will discover that Leviticus 10 marks an important moment in Aaron's literary development, in which he is given a second chance to exercise sensible leadership at a moment of high stakes encounter with the divine. Significantly, this moment is portrayed as interpreting discourse in the context of a particular event, so that Aaron's literary rehabilitation is effected through his formation as a wise and discerning interpreter of the received word.

Finally, we will explore how this reading of Leviticus 10 opens up a substantive reflection on the challenges and requirements of interpretation in broader contexts. The priestly writers understand interpretation to be situational, unavoidable, and potentially perilous. Even more importantly, the ability to interpret well is a primary job requirement for priests, who facilitate and oversee the day-to-day life of the Israelite community. In the priestly vision of life, interpretation is essential to human flourishing. How might this awareness translate into contemporary contexts, both within and beyond communities of faith?

Setting the Stage

Literary Context and Overview of the Narrative

The chapters leading up to Leviticus 10 have taken us through the construction of the wilderness tabernacle (Exod 35–40), the consecration and installation of Aaron and his sons (Lev 8), and the public inaugural ceremony (Lev 9) that climaxes with the long-awaited moment when the glory of YHWH, the כְּבוֹד יְהוָה, appears "to all the people" (9:23). "Fire came out from YHWH (וַתֵּצֵא אֵשׁ מִלִּפְנֵי יְהוָה)," the text concludes, "and consumed (וַתֹּאכַל) the burnt offering and the fat on the altar; and when all the people saw it, they shouted and fell on their faces" (9:24). Abruptly the scene narrows in on Nadav and Avihu, and in a few short phrases the same fire that had consumed the offerings has consumed them (וַתֵּצֵא אֵשׁ מִלִּפְנֵי יְהוָה וַתֹּאכַל, 10:2).

This sequence of events forms the backdrop for the enigmatic and seemingly disjointed narrative that follows, as Moses, Aaron, and Aaron's sons scramble to deal with the aftermath of the priestly deaths and make sense what has happened and how to proceed. After dispensing his interpretation of what just happened (v. 3), Moses quickly moves into a mode of damage-control, giving instructions for the removal of the corpses from the sacred precinct and instructing the priests not to begin formal mourning rituals, not to leave the tent of meeting, and not to deviate from the procedures for completing the offerings that had been so violently interrupted. Meanwhile, YHWH addresses Aaron directly, with puzzling instructions about fulfilling priestly duties that do not seem to have anything to do with the situation at hand (vv. 8–11). As if it had been taking place simultaneously on another stage, the narrative then returns to Moses's instructions for completing the last of the offerings. Finding that one of them has not been handled as he expected, he bursts into a fit of rage. The narrative concludes with a third enigmatic address as Aaron states his rationale for the aberration, and Moses is seemingly appeased (vv. 19–20).

Major Interpretive Questions: Where Shall We Begin?

A number of questions immediately arise which have generally coalesced into two primary interpretive foci: 1) Did Nadav and Avihu do something wrong, and what? Or 2) What does the rest of the chapter reveal about larger priestly concerns that may have given rise to the episode with Nadav and Avihu?

The first set of questions has occupied the vast majority of interpretive attention to Leviticus 10, focusing on the deaths of Nadav and Avihu as the crucial event of the narrative. Bursting unexpectedly onto the scene of orderly ritual instructions and the long-awaited inauguration of the sacrificial system, this account of death by divine fire naturally upsets readerly expectations and casts a pall over the narrative that follows. Before the heat of the divine fire had even subsided, Moses immediately turns to Aaron with the first theory about what had happened. Thus he himself anticipates the long history of attempts to answer the question: Why did Nadav and Avihu die?

The answer has not been forthcoming. Ancient interpreters largely sought to justify the deaths, proposing a number of possible errors that Nadav and Avihu could have committed in the manner or intent of their approach to sacred space. The rabbis proposed no fewer than twelve theories as to what the men did wrong, including various kinds of arrogance or presumption, procedural errors such as bringing an improper offering, being inappropriately dressed, not having properly washed, bringing the wrong kind of fire, being drunk, encroaching further into the sacred space than they should have, or even failing to have fathered children before assuming their priestly duties.[4] Alternatively, a few interpreters sought to exonerate Nadav and Avihu by reading their deaths not as punishment but as a sign of divine favor. Most notably, Philo suggested that they became "the complete and perfect offering [as] they were resolved into ethereal rays of life."[5] On this reading, YHWH recognizes the men's desire to draw near to the presence of the divine—emphasized in the triple repetition of לִפְנֵי יְהוָה in vv. 1–2—and accepts their enthusiastic offering of themselves as a crowning moment in the inaugural sacrificial ceremony.[6] Milgrom attributes Philo's treatment of the narrative to the positive view of the incident that surfaces in rabbinic literature, namely

---

4. For further discussion of the rabbinic treatment of Lev 10, see especially Kirschner, "Rabbinic and Philonic Exegeses, 375–93; along with Milgrom, *Leviticus 1–16*, 633–35; and Levine, *Leviticus*, 58–59.

5. From Philo, *De somniis* II.6–7, cited in Begg, "The Death of Nadab and Abihu," 163; see also Milgrom, *Leviticus 1–16*, 634–35.

6. Thus Bryan Bibb's observation that "From the beginning of the story, the key movement of the action is toward פני יהוה. The presence of God is the chief problem and complicating factor in the narrative. The initial characters are motivated by their desire to be in the presence of God." See Bibb, "Nadab and Abihu," 84–85.

that "Nadab and Abihu consecrated the Tabernacle by their deaths and thereby sanctified the divine name."[7] More recently, Tamar Kamionkowski has experimented with expanding Philo's reading "through a queer reading lens," suggesting that Nadav and Avihu "choose to risk all the cultural norms and legal prescriptions of their generation in order to merge with this ultimate male figure." In response,

> God accepts the men and takes them into his innermost sanctum, and he consumes them in an act of burning passion. There is no indication that God is angry with them; in fact one could argue the opposite. God's verbal response is, "I am made holy through those that come close to me." Thus, God's holiness is supported and even enhanced by the acts of Nadav and Avihu.[8]

A common theme among all of these explanations is the assumption that the ambiguities surrounding Nadav and Avihu are contingent difficulties. Their deaths are not random, irrational, or unfair, in other words, and could be explained given time and worlds enough. Underlying this assumption are questions of theodicy: Is YHWH just? Is the ritual system flawed? The only certainty about why the men died is what the text itself says: "They brought outside fire (אֵשׁ זָרָה), which he had not commanded them" (v. 1), a striking variation following the eight repetitions of the phrase כַּאֲשֶׁר צִוָּה יְהוָה that had appeared in chs. 8–9.[9] But this puzzling rationale raises more questions than it resolves, and the text itself does not elaborate. So Milgrom concedes that "the hypotheses thus far proposed are unadulterated speculation and . . . the historical background remains a mystery."[10]

In light of this, interpretive attention has more recently shifted away from its preoccupation with Nadav and Avihu and toward what the rest of the chapter indicates about what may have given rise to their deaths, essentially taking the incident as a literary foil for a broader agenda on the part of the priestly writers. These approaches roughly coalesce into

---

7. Milgrom, *Leviticus 1–16*, 635; see also Kirschner, 382–83, for further discussion of positive rabbinic treatments.

8. Kamionkowski, *Leviticus*, 72.

9. i.e., Lev 8:4, 9, 13, 17, 21, 29, 31, 34, 35, 36; 9:6, 7, 10, and 21. For discussion of the significance of this repetition, see Kamionkowski, *Leviticus*, 57; as well as Watts, *Ritual and Rhetoric in Leviticus*, 106–7.

10. Milgrom, *Leviticus 1–16*, 628. For a similar conclusion, see also Bibb, *Ritual Words*, 120.

two groups, framing the narrative through either a historical/political or a literary/theological lens.

The first stream of thought sees the narrative as reflecting a power struggle between various groups, either between Moses and Aaron or between Aaron and other priestly groups. Kamionkowski highlights, for example, the vulnerability and liminality of establishing a new power system.[11] In chs. 8–9, Moses has temporarily stepped into the role of priest to perform the ordination rites. The conflict that arises between Moses and Aaron in vv. 16–20 underscores the transfer of power that is taking place as Aaron and his sons assume full ritual authority, and the incident with Nadav and Avihu was thus the pretext for that conflict. In a similar vein, some have seen the conflict between Moses and Aaron as a working out of the priestly prerogative to be interpreters of the law in their own right rather than merely instruments of its performance, while others interpret YHWH's address to Aaron in vv. 8–11 as in fact "subordinating the priestly class to the supervision of Moses."[12] Milgrom splits the difference, articulating the distinction between Moses's role in the reception of the law and the priestly commission to transmit it that is specified in 10:11.[13] We will return to the dynamic between Moses and Aaron in the following section.

Others have focused less on the dynamic between Moses and Aaron than on the subtle clues that may suggest an internal power struggle between the descendants of Aaron and other priestly groups. These approaches are aptly summarized by Noth's observation that "behind the narrative of the first part there stood in the far background internal disputes between different priestly groups, about which we have no further knowledge."[14] Notwithstanding, many attempts have been made to see through the historical fog, tracing complex arguments through connections to other texts such as Ezek 44:10–27, which reflects a negative view of the descendants of Aaron in favor of the Zadokites.[15] Many have also

---

11. Kamionkowski, *Leviticus*, 63–65.

12. Gerstenberger, *Leviticus*, 125. Regarding the priestly prerogative of interpretation, Mark Leuchter suggests, for example, that Leviticus 1–16 may reflect a "polemical valence against the Mosaic teaching of Deuteronomy ... for Leviticus presents Moses as deferring to Aaron's pedagogical authority." Leuchter, "The Politics of Ritual Rhetoric," 349.

13. Milgrom, *Leviticus 1–16*, 617.

14. Noth, *Leviticus*, 84.

15. A useful summary of the major arguments surrounding this thesis as debated by Achenbach, Nihan, and Otto is presented by Meyer, "Getting Bad Publicity."

observed that the challenge to the stratification of priestly authority by Korah and his followers recounted in Num 16:1—17:15 resonates strongly with the Nadav and Avihu incident. In this story, an ordeal takes place at the behest of Korah and his assembly—two hundred and fifty well-known men and leaders in the community—to determine who would be the "holy one" qualified to approach YHWH (Num 16:5). Gerstenberger notes, among other things, that Mishael and Elzaphan would have been cousins of Korah (Exod 6:21), "suggesting perhaps that in Lev 10:1f. the Korah motif was transferred to Nadab and Abihu."[16] In contrast to these negative readings of the Aaronides, some argue that Aaron is portrayed favorably, supporting and affirming the authority of his descendants. Watts, for example, reads Leviticus 10 as priestly rhetoric affirming the power of the priesthood generally, but the Aaronides specifically, who he argues dominated the Second Temple period: "The fact that the reader/hearer cannot understand either the nature of the danger in 10:1-3 or the logic of the Aaron's ruling in 10:16-20 only increases the mystique of the priestly office. Summarized in a more modern idiom, the message from the Aaronide priests to the congregation of Israel in Leviticus 10 is this: 'We are professionals doing a necessary and dangerous job, and only we can do it right.'"[17]

While the roles of Mishael and Elzaphan, deaths of Nadav and Avihu, and the conflict between Moses and Aaron are indeed suggestive, approaches that probe the narrative for priestly power dynamics have examined the same limited information to arrive at completely opposite conclusions. Some find the narrative to be pro-Aaron, some find it to be anti-Aaron. These differences are unlikely to be definitively resolved since, as Blenkinsopp has observed, "anyone attempting to understand the Judean priesthood in its historical development has to take seriously the fact that, apart from Priestly material (P) and Chronicles, our sources are silent both on Aaronide priests and on Aaron as their priestly eponym."[18] There is simply no extra-textual evidence to tip the scales

---

16. Gerstenberger, *Leviticus*, 120. See also Nihan for a detailed discussion of the points of resonance between the two passages, where he concludes that "the story of Nadab and Abihu in Lev 10:1-2 appears therefore as a kind of digest of the ordeal between Aaron and the 250 chieftains in Num 15." *From Priestly Torah to Pentateuch*, 584. Other accounts that read Lev 10 as reflecting poorly on Aaron include Damrosch, "Law and Narrative," 266–69; and Houston, "Tragedy in the Courts of the Lord," 31–39. Both Damrosch and Houston's arguments will be discussed at greater length below.

17. Watts, *Ritual and Rhetoric*, 129.

18. Blenkinsopp, "The Judaean Priesthood," 37; as well as Meyer, "Getting Bad Publicity," 5.

toward any particular hypothesis about priestly power struggles that may lie behind this text, so the endeavor must remain, as Milgrom concluded, "sheer speculation."[19]

Recognizing these tenuous grounds for building a historical background for the narrative, other approaches have focused more closely on the theological concerns that the text highlights within its literary context. These approaches foreground the priestly instructions in vv. 8–11 to view the surrounding narrative as a vivid illustration of the importance of correct observance in cultic matters. Attention to the interplay of law and narrative shows that the two are integrally related and serve mutually illuminating purposes, both here and elsewhere in the Hebrew Bible.[20] So Milgrom observes that Lev 10:1–7 is "a good example of law in story form" which "generally has a greater effect upon hearers and readers than apodictic, casuistic, or other legal forms."[21] The question, then, is how the narrative portion about Nadav and Avihu illustrates and illuminates YHWH's address to Aaron. What is the connection between them, and what is the effect?

Resonances between Leviticus 10 and 24:10–23, the only two narrative passages in the book, may help illumine the larger function that the integration of law and narrative in Leviticus 10 works to emphasize.[22] As we have earlier observed, Douglas accounted for the literary placement of the two narratives by locating them as two screens structuring the literary projection of the tabernacle, marking important theological and literary transitions in the book.[23] This placement of Leviticus 10 would thus underscore the narrative's warning about encroaching on sacred space. Milgrom agreed, building on and refining Douglas's analysis by noting that the two narratives spotlight the two primary ways that sacrilege can

19. Milgrom, *Leviticus 1–16*, 604.

20. Most notably, Damrosch, *Narrative Covenant*; Carmichael, *Illuminating Leviticus;*; and Milgrom's discussion with additional bibliography in *Leviticus 23–27*, 2102–2104. For a treatment of Leviticus 10 sensitive to the interplay of law and narrative but narrowing in more closely on the concept of *ritual* law, see Eliasen, "Aaron's War Within," 81–98.

21. Milgrom, *Leviticus 1–16*, 632.

22. Others have added Leviticus 16 to this list, or include chs. 8–9 along with ch. 10 as part of a longer narrative unit; see especially Smith, "The Literary Structure of Leviticus." While it is true that those chapters differ in form from the instructions that characterize the rest of the book, they are more akin to description of an event than a narrative that includes multiple characters, dialogue, and some sort of plot development as in chs. 10 and 24:10–23; see also Milgrom, *Leviticus 23–27*, 2102.

23. Douglas, *Leviticus as Literature*, 195–200.

be committed in Leviticus, "the Name defiled balancing the Holy Place defiled."[24]

In the context of the ordination events that began in chapter 8, then, the priestly trespass of vv. 1–2, in conjunction with the emphasis on priestly responsibilities within the divine address, seems to suggest that the overarching point of Leviticus 10 is to convey the importance of right procedure. The juxtaposition of law and narrative underscores the "necessity of complete observance of [YHWH's] laws, as well as the consequences of disobedience."[25] But if the primary message of Leviticus 10 is a warning about "what not to do," we end up back where we began with the problem of the narrative's extreme concision in portraying the trespass: what, exactly, is not to be done? Why was Nadav and Avihu's error not more clearly articulated, and why does it not receive greater emphasis, occupying only the first two verses of the pericope? These questions point to a different weight of emphasis, as we will discover.

In sum, most treatments of Leviticus 10 gravitate toward one of two focal points: 1) The disturbing intrusion of human death into the orderly progression of chapters 1–9 and the many questions that the incident raises about a system ordained by YHWH to facilitate human safety and flourishing in the presence of the divine; or 2) What other aspects of the chapter may reveal about larger priestly concerns, political or theological. In both of these focal points, the common thread is attention to the world behind the text or what readers perceive as missing from the narrative account—that is, what the text does not say. In fact, Bryan Bibb argues that this interpretive propensity arises from the text itself to suggest that "this story does not merely *have* gaps that need to be filled; this story is itself *about* gap-filling and its attendant danger and frustration," such that "the real problem for Nadab and Abihu is the absence of [YHWH's] word or command."[26] Bibb thus reads the narrative as a reflection on the inevitable gap between human and divine, and the limitations of human knowledge and understanding, a story that "exposes our need to fill in gaps of understanding," Bibb writes, "and reveals the inherent fragility of our attempts to do so."[27] This is an intriguing notion, but it concedes that Nadav and Avihu could not have known what their error was, a theologically troubling notion that Bibb does not fully resolve. Another solution

---

24. Milgrom, *Leviticus 1–16*, 345–56; *Leviticus 23–27*, 2106.
25. Nihan, *From Priestly Torah to Pentateuch*, 586; Levine, *Leviticus*, 38.
26. Bibb, "Nadab and Abihu," 117, 122. Italics in the original.
27. Bibb, "Nadab and Abihu," 84.

is possible, in which the narrative does reveal the inevitable gap between human and divine while exposing the limitations of human knowledge, but not in a way that is callously illustrated through the irrational loss of human life. We will return to this shortly. While these studies provide a wealth of insight into various features and possible functions of Leviticus 10, this focus on the world behind the text has ultimately proven inconclusive. In fact, as we saw above, Watts argues that the ambiguities of the text cannot be resolved because they are rhetorically crafted to cast the priesthood in a mysterious aura of cultic authority.[28]

The overwhelming majority of approaches have also tended to atomize certain features of the narrative to the exclusion of others, offering interpretations that focus either on the incident with Nadav and Avihu or various features of its aftermath. What has not been thoroughly examined is the relationship between these two aspects of the chapter: Is one simply a pretext for the other?

This neglect has been justified by an assumption that the chapter is not a coherent literary unit, but the result of multiple layers of composition and redaction. Gerstenberger writes, for example, that "even a cursory reading reveals that Leviticus 10 has been put together by different tradents and groups. The chapter lacks any thematic or stylistic unity, and we everywhere notice breaks, gaps, and doubling."[29] More recently, this view has fallen out of vogue in favor of compelling arguments that the chapter is not, in fact, composite, but stems in its entirety from the hand of the final redactor of the book and constitutes the "founding legend of priestly exegesis," as cogently argued by Nihan.[30] Regardless of whether or not Nihan's late date for the chapter is found to be persuasive, his demonstration of the literary coherence and thematic unity of the chapter lays the groundwork for fresh readings of Leviticus 10 as a narrative whole.

Focusing on what may lie behind the text, along with a piece-meal approach to various aspects of the chapter, has left two crucial gaps in our understanding: First, what does the narrative accomplish in its literary context? Second, what is the direction of thought that the narrative opens up in front of the text? In light of this, our point of entry will be a careful analysis of the literary structure of the chapter as a complete unit, in order to form the basis for a fresh reading of its literary function. We will

28. Watts, *Ritual and Rhetoric*, 117.
29. Gerstenberger, *Leviticus*, 115.
30. For this argument and a comprehensive discussion of the compositional history of Leviticus 10, see Nihan, *From Priestly Torah to Pentateuch*, 148–50 and 576–607.

then be in a better position to evaluate how the text's direction of thought may give rise to a new event of discourse in the text/reader relationship.

What the Text "Says": Speech as a Structuring Device and Interpretive Key

Our point of departure from attention to the ambiguities and silences of the text and toward what it does say—and how it says it—will be careful attention to the literary function of speech. In Leviticus 10, speech is the catalyst that 1) drives the development of the narrative; 2) frames YHWH's speech to Aaron in vv. 8–11 as the centerpiece that condenses and summarizes the larger point of the narrative; and 3) signals an important shift taking place in the literary development of Moses and Aaron as characters, namely, a rebalancing of their relationship, through which Aaron emerges as the key figure of the narrative.

A Narrative Shaped by Speech

The first two verses quickly sketch the backdrop against which the rest of the story plays out. Nadav and Avihu's actions and demise are stated concisely, without elaboration or development: readers are afforded no insight into their intentions or motives, there is no explicit statement about whether or not what they did was wrong, and there is no deliberation about what the consequences should be.[31] X was done, with the result that Y happened, End of Scene. There is no further discussion of what Nadav and Avihu did and they are not named again, here or ever again in the book.[32] Observing this extreme lack of detail, Gerstenberger comments that the portrayal of what we would expect to be the focal point of the story—the deaths of Nadav and Avihu—is strangely terse: "It is as if the author merely wants to allude, for the congregation, to some [other] occurrence. He seems to presuppose the significance of any priestly transgression."[33] This may be true, but it may also indicate

---

31. Interestingly, this lack of deliberation is one striking point of difference between Lev 10 and the narrative of the מקלל in 24:10–23. The trespass occurs and is met with immediate consequences, rather than a period of waiting, a divine decision, and the community's participation in restoring order.

32. Though "the death of Aaron's sons" is referred to in Lev 16:1, their names are not specified.

33. Gerstenberger, *Leviticus*, 115.

that the priestly transgression, if it is that, was simply not the author's main interest. Verses 1–2 are the necessary "prologue" to contextualize vv. 3–20, but they are not substantive enough to constitute the main act.

Immediately after this, Moses begins to speak. First he turns to Aaron with an enigmatic interpretation of what has just been witnessed (v. 3) before launching into a rapid-fire succession of directives for dealing with the corpses (vv. 4–5) in order to keep the situation from further deteriorating into chaos (vv. 6–7), and to ensure that the sacrificial procedures that had been interrupted (vv. 12–15) are successfully completed. He speaks first, and he speaks the most, with the goal of restoring order to what has become a disordered and unprecedented event.

The main driver of this flurry of activity is speech. There is nothing intrinsically unusual about the use of speech here in comparison to other patterns of biblical narrative and it would be easy to overlook its significance, except for the fact that it creates such a striking stylistic contrast to the preceding chapters. Up to this point in the book there has been no dialogue. Save for a brief change of address in 8:5 ("Moses said to the congregation . . .") and two short sets of instructions in the form of a direct address from Moses to Aaron in 8:31–35 and 9:2–7, there has been an uninterrupted flow of "Then YHWH spoke to Moses . . ." followed by a long section of instructions (1:1; 4:1; 5:14; 6:1, 8, 19, 24; 7:22, 28; 8:1), or summary compliance reports of Moses's fulfillment of those instructions (8:4, etc.).

The progression of chapter 10 runs against this flow. Every few verses begin with a direct address to either Aaron or his sons in place of the opening phrase וַיְדַבֵּר יְהוָה אֶל־מֹשֶׁה, which we have come to expect. Further, the dominant voice we hear is no longer YHWH's but Moses's. With this divergence, the reader is warned: pay attention to who is speaking.

"And YHWH Spoke to Aaron": Commissioned to Interpret

Following the prologue of vv. 1–2, there are seven sections of direct address. Of these, six are spoken by either Moses or Aaron, with YHWH's address to Aaron in verses 8–11 chiastically forming the center of the narrative:[34]

---

34. Others have also observed a chiastic structure highlighting the divine speech, but on grounds other than the seven sections that begin with speech. Balentine, for example, notes three major sections: 1) an introduction (vv. 1–7), 2) the divine instructions (vv. 8–11), and 3) a conclusion (vv. 12–20). Balentine, *Leviticus*, 83. Nihan sees

(v. 3) וַיֹּאמֶר מֹשֶׁה
(v. 4) וַיֹּאמֶר מֹשֶׁה
(v. 6) וַיֹּאמֶר מֹשֶׁה

(v. 8) וַיְדַבֵּר יְהוָה

(v. 12) וַיְדַבֵּר מֹשֶׁה
(v. 16) דָּרֹשׁ דָּרַשׁ מֹשֶׁה
(v. 19) וַיְדַבֵּר אַהֲרֹן

The significance of highlighting YHWH's address to Aaron in this way goes beyond the fact that it is divine speech and might be expected to hold a prominent position for that reason alone. This structuring device contributes two specific things to our understanding of the narrative: First, it redirects the reader's attention. Verses 1–7 focused entirely on what had just taken place with Nadav and Avihu, and the urgency of what needed to happen in the aftermath. The divine speech interrupts this preoccupation to draw our attention away from Moses, the dominant figure in vv. 3–7, and beyond the situation immediately at hand. In addition to this, the divine word is not even addressed to Moses but to Aaron, who up to this point has been almost completely sidelined. Not only is this startling in the context of chapter 10, but it is almost unprecedented in the wilderness narrative up to this point and one of only three times that YHWH speaks directly to Aaron in the entire Hebrew Bible.[35] Of these, Exod 4:27 recounts only YHWH's brief directive for Aaron to go meet Moses in the wilderness, leaving Lev 10:9–11 and Num 18:1–24 as the only two instances in which Aaron is the recipient of a major divine address. Although its full significance is not yet entirely clear, the placement of the divine speech at this moment in the narrative briefly draws Aaron back into the main frame and signals to the reader that his role may be more central than has been evident.

Second, locating the divine speech at the center of the pericope functions as a clear statement of the narrative's main theme, which is the priestly responsibility to distinguish (לְהַבְדִּיל) and to teach (לְהוֹרֹת, vv. 10–11). As it is encountered synchronically the divine speech seems like

---

five sections: 1) transgression of cultic laws, sanctioned (vv. 1–5); 2) Instruction by Moses to Aaron (vv. 6–7); 3) Instruction by YHWH to Aaron (8–11); 4) Instruction by Moses to Aaron (vv. 12–15); and 5) transgression of cultic laws, not sanctioned (vv. 16–20). Nihan, *From Priestly Torah to Pentateuch*, 579.

35. Numbers 18 outlines the priestly responsibilities and their compensation.

an awkward intrusion, occurring outside of time and space and wedged into a sequence of events to which it does not appear to be directly related. How does YHWH speak to Aaron? From where? Does anyone else witness this happening? Most importantly, where is Moses while this is taking place? As the narrative progresses, however, we come to understand that the divine commission is not only deeply connected to its immediately surrounding context but is in fact the interpretive key for understanding the narrative as a whole. We might ask whether, prior to this event, Aaron truly understood the role that he was called to fulfill or the extent of his errors in his misguided attempt to respond to the people's voiced needs in Exod 32. If the story had ended there, we would have been left with only a one-dimensional picture of the priests as functionaries who follow orders, with each movement and gesture of their cultic routine preordained for them to execute. By the end of Lev 10, however, both Aaron and the reader realize that the charge to distinguish and to teach is in fact a unique charge to Aaron to step into his specific role as an interpreter of the received word—and we will also have learned something about what this involves.

"Then Aaron Spoke to Moses": Rebalancing a Relationship

The literary placement of the divine address as the center point of the narrative serves one further function, which is to initiate a recalibration of the narrative portrayal of Moses. At first subtle, this shift culminates in a complete reversal of the relational dynamic between Moses and Aaron that had existed at the beginning of the story—in fact, dynamics that had existed for quite some time in the narrative of the wilderness wanderings—so that Aaron emerges as the key character in Leviticus 10.

For the first time in verse 12, the narrator refers to Elazar and Itamar as Aaron's remaining sons (הַנּוֹתָרִים), effecting an immediate shift in tone from the detached crisis-management that had characterized verses 3–7 to a reminder of the tragedy that has just occurred. Right after this expression of "indescribable sadness,"[36] Moses echoes the same word in his instructions to Aaron for completing the procedure for the remainder of the מנחה: קְחוּ אֶת־הַמִּנְחָה הַנּוֹתֶרֶת מֵאִשֵּׁי יְהוָה וְאִכְלוּהָ מַצּוֹת אֵצֶל הַמִּזְבֵּחַ כִּי קֹדֶשׁ קָדָשִׁים הִוא ("Take the remaining minhah of the fire-offerings of YHWH and eat it unleavened beside the altar, for it is most-holy," Lev

---

36. Arnold Ehrlich, cited in Milgrom, *Leviticus 1–16*, 618.

10:12). From the reader's perspective the resonance is striking, but is it significant? Are we to hear in this an analogy between the remaining sons and the remainder of the offering, thus implying that the divine fire that consumed the first-born sons was not one of wrath—as Moses seems to have understood (vv. 6–7)—but of acceptance? Alternatively, does the use of this charged word on Moses's lips, spoken to a bereaved father, portray Moses's insensitivity and obliviousness to Aaron's situation? If these questions are not answerable, they are at least unavoidable.

After concluding his instructions for the מנחה, Moses turns to the last task in need of completion only to find that liberties have been taken without his knowledge: "About the goat of the חטאת Moses asked and asked, and look! it had already been burned" (10:16). His response is telling: "He-became-furious (וַיִּקְצֹף) with Elazar and Itamar, Aaron's remaining sons" (v. 16), and upbraided them for not having eaten the חטאת in the holy-place. The verbal resonance is striking: קצף had appeared earlier in v. 6, apparently referring to the wrath of YHWH, but now we realize that no clear subject was in fact articulated there.[37] The use of the same word (in similar prefixed forms) to describe both divine and human anger in such close proximity, combined with an ambiguous subject in verse 6, blurs the line between YHWH's commands and Moses's own interpretation and enforcement of them.[38] Whose wrath is actually in view—YHWH's, or Moses's? It is not surprising that Moses should be angered at what he understands to be a serious procedural error that puts the entire community at risk. We could even read this blurring of the line between divine and human wrath as an indication of Moses's intimate position as YHWH's representative, tasked with faithfully conveying the divine word: He is angered on behalf of, and in anticipation of, the greater wrath that he fears may be invoked.

Alternatively, we might also see Moses's rush to judgment as a sign that his complete command of both himself and the situation is not as

---

37. Curiously, the major translations and commentaries largely ignore the lack of a subject in relation to the verb קצף in v. 6, translating יִקְצֹף along the lines of "anger/wrath will strike the entire community" (NRSV, NJPS, Alter; along with, for example, Milgrom, Gerstenberger, and Kamionkowski), or assuming YHWH as the subject as in "he (YHWH) will be angry against all the community" (Noth, Nihan, Fox).

38. While focusing on a different aspect of Moses's anger over the חטאת—namely, that Moses adds a rationale (in 10:17b) for what should be done with the חטאת to his citation of the instructions from 6:19—Nihan observes that "Moses does not simply quote the law, he also comments upon it." Nihan, *From Priestly Torah to Pentateuch*, 599.

sure as it had seemed. He is either unable or unwilling to recognize the full scope of the situation: the חטאת has already been burned, and yet everything is fine. The divine wrath has not been evoked, so why should Moses's be?

The concluding phrase of Moses's censure of Elazar and Itamar further reinforces the reader's suspicion that Moses's perception of his role has become distorted. "Look, its blood was not brought into the interior of the holy-place—you were supposed to have eaten it in the holy-place, just as I commanded!" (10:18). If no doubts have thus far surfaced about Moses's handling of the situation, the words "just as I commanded" (כַּאֲשֶׁר צִוֵּיתִי) should bring the careful reader to a full stop: just as Moses commanded? This could be understood as an innocent slip of the tongue. Moses had already relayed this instruction to Aaron and his sons in 6:23, so he had, in fact, "commanded" them what should be done with the חטאת. Colloquially, his expression could be understood as something to the effect of "Didn't I just tell you about this?!"

In the context of Leviticus 10, however, the phrase seems less innocuous. The priestly consecration procedures that began in chapter 8 were introduced to the congregation with a public statement that, "This is what YHWH has commanded to be done" (8:5). As each stage of the process was completed, the assurance that what had been done was in compliance with the divine word was repeated no fewer than fourteen times, כַּאֲשֶׁר צִוָּה יְהוָה becoming a familiar idiom in the account of the cult's inauguration.[39] With chapter 10, however, the phrase is almost entirely absent. Instead we read that the priests remove the corpses of Nadav and Avihu and refrain from mourning their deaths "just as Moses had spoken" (10:5, 7). There is no notice of completion following the instructions for the מנחה in vv. 12–15, but only a reminder that this is what YHWH had commanded—the sole occurrence of the phrase in all of chapter 10. On Moses's lips, the phrase כַּאֲשֶׁר צִוֵּיתִי in v. 18 is thus a startling departure from the expected formulation.[40]

---

39. i.e., Lev 8:4, 9, 13, 17, 21, 29, 31, 34, 35, 36; 9:6, 7, 10, and 21. See Kamionkowski, *Leviticus*, 57.

40. It must be noted that the rendering of צוה as an active *piel* is not a foregone conclusion. Milgrom notes that "*Tg. Ps.-J.* and the Pesh. Read (or interpret) [it] 'as I was commanded' (cf. 8:31)" while the LXX retains the active verb but interpolates 'as the LORD commanded me'" (Milgrom, *Leviticus 1–16*, 626). Milgrom nonetheless retains the active verb, as do most translations. While the possibility that the verb should have been pointed as a *pual* is not out of the question, this seems unlikely as the *pual* צֻוֵּיתִי does, in fact, appear a few verses earlier in 10:13. The difficulty is real, but because the

These small details in how Moses's character and actions are portrayed in vv. 12–18 culminate in vv. 19–20 when, for the first time, Aaron speaks. Stepping up in response to Moses's censure of Elazar and Itamar—his remaining sons—Aaron takes responsibility for the liberties that were taken with the חטאת and states his rationale. In stark contrast to the rest of the narrative, "Moses listened, and it was good in his eyes" (10:20). It is a stunning plot twist for Aaron to have finally spoken up, resisting Moses's censure with an alternative perspective of the situation and leaving Moses with nothing else to say. This unexpected turn of events prompts a re-reading of the narrative that focuses more closely on Aaron and his role in the story.

Doing so, we see two important developments that have been interwoven in this complex account of Moses's behavior and the conflict that arises when he perceives that his authority has been disregarded. As we have already observed, Leviticus 10 is the culmination of a momentous transfer of power that has taken place with the inauguration of the cult and ordination of the priesthood. But chapter 10 reveals that this transfer of power does not come easily, and for good reason. Moses has borne the primary responsibility for Israel's leadership throughout the wilderness narrative, and particularly since Aaron's utter failure concerning the episode with the golden calf in Exodus 32. As Shai Held points out, this moment of Aaron's disregard for Moses's instructions, following on the heels of Nadav and Avihu's devastating deaths when so much is at stake, "must feel [to Moses] like déjà vu."[41] It is understandable that Moses should struggle to trust Aaron's judgment and feel as though things were once again spiraling out of control in his brief absence from the scene.[42] So another crucial development that is taking place at a deeper level in Leviticus 10 is the question of Aaron's character and ability to handle the responsibilities of the priesthood. I have suggested that Aaron emerges as the key figure in this chapter, but to understand the significance of this moment in the literary development of Aaron's character and his relationship to Moses we need to look beyond the immediate context to the broader pentateuchal narrative as it relates to Aaron. The events that are portrayed in Lev 10

---

blurring of a clear distinction between the word of YHWH and the word of Moses in ch. 10 rests on other grounds in addition to this single verbal form, I believe we are justified in following the Masoretic text as it appears.

41. Held, *The Heart of Torah*, 31–36.

42. Why does Moses not know what had happened to the חטאת? Where was he when its remains were being burned?

DEVELOPMENTAL DISCOURSE 171

presume the reader's knowledge of a larger narrative arc, in which there stands out another moment involving inappropriate fire and a high stakes encounter with the divine: the episode of the golden calf.

What the Text "Does": Aaron's Literary Rehabilitation

Recalling Exodus 32: Aaron Gets Another Chance

While Leviticus 8–9 has just detailed the ordination of the priesthood and the initiation of the cult, it is not at all apparent that Aaron is qualified and equipped to assume the role that he is being asked to take. In order for Aaron's position to make sense within the narrative itself and be convincing to readers, the weaknesses in his professional resumé must be addressed. Leviticus 10 consequently recalls his great failure at Sinai in order to construct an anti-narrative to Exodus 32 and thus literarily rehabilitate Aaron in this new moment in Israel's formation as a nation.

The parallels between Leviticus 10 and Exodus 32 begin with the fact that both stories are set in the context of a high stakes encounter with the divine. Exod 32 follows the long section of laws given to Moses in his encounter with YHWH at Sinai (Exod 19–31) and the giving of the tablets of the covenant (Exod 31:18), while Lev 10 follows the sacrificial laws of chapters 1–7. Both narratives involve rituals of ordination (מִלְאוּ יֶדְכֶם in Exod 32:29 and יְמַלֵּא אֶת־יֶדְכֶם in Lev 8:33). Both narratives are preceded by a consequential moment of sight: in Exod 32:1 the people see (וַיַּרְא הָעָם) that Moses has taken longer to return than expected, and in Lev 9:23–24 the כְּבוֹד יְהוָה appears to all the people and they see (וַיַּרְא כָּל־הָעָם) the fire of YHWH consume the offerings. Both narratives also involve inappropriate fire, appearing in Exod 32 as the instrument of Israel's idolatry (vv. 6, 24) and in Lev 10:1 as the אֵשׁ זָרָה of Nadav and Avihu's incense offering. In both narratives the highly unusual verb פרע also appears. In Exod 32:25 Moses "saw the people, that they were running wild—for Aaron had let them run wild (וַיַּרְא מֹשֶׁה אֶת־הָעָם כִּי פָרֻעַ הוּא כִּי־פְרָעֹה אַהֲרֹן)", and in Lev 10:6 he warns the priests against letting their hair be "let loose/disheveled (תִּפְרָעוּ)." This verbal form appears a mere fifteen times: six times in the Pentateuch, and only in these two moments in Aaron's history, where it appears as a sort of hyperlink to take readers from one moment back to the other.

While these similarities are intriguing, they are not necessarily significant. Other parallels, however, help to illumine some otherwise inexplicable features of Leviticus 10. Both narratives involve some form of inappropriate drinking: in Exod 32:6, 18 the people "sat down to eat and drink and rose up to revel" after presenting their offerings to the calf. When Moses returns to the camp, he grinds the calf into powder, scatters it in the water, and makes the Israelites drink it instead, in what Douglas suggests "sounds like a drinking ordeal" to identify the idolaters that would be struck down in the ensuing fight and plague of punishment (Exod 32:26–35).[43] When placed side by side, Douglas observes, this drinking ordeal is structurally parallel to the mention of strong drink (יַיִן וְשֵׁכָר) in Lev 10:8, where it had appeared out of the blue and is otherwise "quite unrelated to this context."[44] The "warning to Aaron not to take strong drink is [thus] a vital part of the story about unholy fire," she argues, flagging not only the parallel to Exod 32 but also the fact that Lev 10 substitutes a warning, which we assume Aaron heeded, in place of a drinking ordeal and punishment.[45] This deviation lets the reader know that the second story is "about something new" that is now taking place.[46] Douglas does not fully develop this claim—although we can infer from what follows that she probably meant the provisions for atonement described in Lev 16—but her comment is perceptive. There is indeed "something new" taking place in Lev 10 that we see as it develops parallel to Exod 32.

Two further similarities are significant in developing the alternative course that Lev 10 charts. First, both episodes involve Aaron acting independently of Moses in situations for which there was no precedent. In Exod 32, Moses had been on Mt. Sinai receiving the covenant when the Israelites panicked at his extended absence (Exod 32:1). Aaron later refers to this absence in v. 23 as an excuse for what had happened, essentially arguing, "What was I to do?! You know what these people are like, and you left me here with them alone." In Lev 10 we have noted that Moses is similarly absent, but in a strangely disconnected way. They were all to have remained in the temple precinct as instructed in v. 7, but where was Moses when YHWH spoke to Aaron? And where was he when the חטאת was being burned? It does not make logical sense that Aaron would have had the opportunity to act on his own initiative without Moses's knowledge, but this is what the narrative reports.

43. Douglas, *Leviticus as Literature*, 204.
44. Noth, *Leviticus*, 86.
45. Douglas, *Leviticus as Literature*, 204.
46. Douglas, *Leviticus as Literature*, 204.

Second, these are the only two instances that involve a confrontation between Moses and Aaron. In fact, these are the only two places in the entire biblical account where there is an actual dialogue between Moses and Aaron. In every other instance their exchanges consist simply of Moses giving a command and Aaron silently complying, just as he does in 10:3. It is notable that both exchanges where there is dialogue between them record a moment of conflict: both accounts are preceded by Moses's anger (Exod 32:19; Lev 10:16), and in both accounts his words take the form of a sharp-edged question: "What did this people do to you that you have brought so great a sin upon them?" (Exod 32:21); and "Why did you not eat the חטאת in the holy place?" (Lev 10:17).

It is also remarkable that Exod 32:24 was the last time in the Pentateuchal narrative in which Aaron has spoken. Prior to that, Aaron had appeared in the biblical account only in conjunction with Moses, as his facilitator and sidekick. He was first introduced to us as Moses's spokesperson, enlisted by God to speak on Moses's behalf (Exod 4:10–17), and he dutifully fulfilled the role of mouthpiece and prophet (Exod 7:1–2). Throughout the book of Exodus Aaron speaks only with or on behalf of Moses, and his words are not his own. The first time Aaron is said to have spoken of his own accord was in Exod 32:2–6, when he instructed the people to bring their jewelry, presented it to them in the form of a calf, and instituted a festival in celebration. It was, to put it mildly, a disaster. Confronted by Moses's rebuke, Aaron then abdicated any responsibility for his part in the debacle, blaming the Israelites and claiming that the calf practically made itself in a turn of phrase that would be comical were it not so appalling. From that point on Aaron largely retreats from the scene until his appearance in the ordination offerings of Lev 8. Aside from the mention of his blessing the people in 9:22, he does not speak again until his response to Moses in Lev 10:19. For a man who can "speak well" (Exod 4:14) Aaron's silence up to this point is remarkable. Even more astonishing is the moment in Lev 10:19 when we come to the words "Then Aaron spoke to Moses," flagging a moment that is truly worth paying attention to.

Taken together, how do these connections with Exod 32 illuminate Lev 10? Many commentators have observed at least some similarities between the two accounts, with various suggestions about their significance. Observing the parallel theophanies, Milgrom concludes that, "clearly, Nadab and Abihu's heresy (and hence, the heresy of those who followed their example) was deliberately equated in the mind of the

Priestly writer with the heresy of Israel at Sinai," so there is no question in his mind that Nadav and Avihu committed a grave error and that their deaths were divine punishment.[47] Similarly viewing both moments as instances of priestly overstep and failure, David Damrosch sees the incident as Aaron's punishment for the forging of the golden calf, reading Lev 10 as also parallel to the story of Jeroboam and his sons in I Kings 14–15, both of which he claims are reworkings of the Sinai story.[48] Damrosch's treatment of Lev 10 has had a wide readership, but his conclusion that the parallels support a negative reading of Nadav and Avihu that extends to Aaron is not persuasive. Without expounding, Douglas commented that it fails to explain why "Moses consistently treats Aaron as the revered head of the cult."[49] Two other factors also problematize Damrosch's thesis. First, Exod 32:35 explicitly details the divine punishment that YHWH metes out against the people in sending a plague, "because they made the calf–the one that Aaron made." There is no pending doom hanging overhead; justice has been met, and the case is closed. Second, even if it were to be argued that this punishment of plague deals only with the sins of the people and leaves Aaron's punishment for his priestly failure to a future date, it seems unlikely that Aaron would be punished through the death of his sons. Indeed, YHWH rejects Moses's own offer to bear punishment on behalf of the people, declaring that "whoever has sinned against me I will blot out of my book" (Exod 32:32–33). If Nadav and Avihu's deaths are understood as punishment, I find no justification for the claim that it was punishment for their father's sin and not their own errors, however elusive those errors remain. Furthermore, there is no indication in Lev 10 that these deaths are to be interpreted as Aaron's punishment. Moses's immediate rationale in Lev 10:3, while unclear, gives no hint of anything having to do with the golden calf.

The most literarily sensitive and sustained reading of the two narratives has been Mary Douglas's account in *Leviticus as Literature*. For Douglas, the most significant cues that Leviticus 10 recalls Exodus 32 are the strange fire that completes a sequence of three "fiery episodes" in 9:24, 10:1, and 10:2, the out-of-place reference to strong drink in v. 8, and most significantly, the names of Nadav and Avihu, which she renders as "willingness" and "he is my father." "This suggests that their deaths are a sequel to an earlier burning story in which their father was involved,"

47. Milgrom, *Leviticus 1–16*, 632.
48. Damrosch, *Narrative Covenant*, 266–69.
49. Douglas, *Leviticus as Literature*, 201.

Douglas perceives.⁵⁰ Her conclusion about the significance of these parallels is that Lev 10 is "a low-key inverted version of the story of the golden calf."⁵¹ She suggests that its presence in Lev 10 emphasizes continuity with Exodus in anticipation of Leviticus 16, the ultimate solution and correction to the illicit worship of the golden calf.⁵² Douglas thus sees Lev 10 as much more significant than a "neutral marker" functioning as the first screen in the plan of the book. It signals to the reader that she has arrived at an important moment of transition in the book, and further, it thematically supports the transition towards material that has to do with "the temple worship of the true God."⁵³

Douglas's reading of Leviticus 10 as not a parallel but rather an inversion of the episode of the golden calf is brilliant. She is right to see significance in the way Lev 10 establishes continuity with Exodus in order to emphasize a certain *dis*continuity that marks the dedication of the tabernacle as a new moment in Israel's process of learning the appropriate forms of worship. But where Douglas focuses on the culmination of this new moment in Lev 16—"the means which God in his mercy has given to the people of Israel for keeping his covenant"—the priestly writers recognized a more fundamental concern that needed to be addressed in preparation for the events of Leviticus 16. Curiously, the one "inversion" that Douglas neglects to tease out in her comparison of the two narratives is Aaron's response to Moses that takes place in Lev 10:19–20. While she rejects the idea that the story of Nadav and Avihu was intended to reflect badly on Aaron, Douglas pays little attention to Aaron as a literary character apart from the fact that he represents another aspect of the resonance between the two narratives.⁵⁴ Fleshing out this important aspect of the narrative builds on Douglas's work to clarify further the extent and sophistication of the inversion that takes place between Exod 32 and Lev 10.

---

50. Douglas, *Leviticus as Literature*, 202.
51. Douglas, *Leviticus as Literature*, 205.
52. Douglas, *Leviticus as Literature*, 205.
53. Douglas, *Leviticus as Literature*, 205.
54. Douglas, *Leviticus as Literature*, 201.

"Rewriting" Exodus 32: Constructing an Anti-Narrative

Picking up with the immediate aftermath of each narrative disaster, Douglas finds the following parallels:

Exodus	Leviticus
32:12–20 Moses restoring order, burns the calf, grinds up the gold	10:3 Moses restoring order, arranges for the bodies to be removed. Aaron and remaining sons to stay in the tent of meeting, 'lest you die' (10:7)
Scatters gold dust on the water, makes the people drink it	9 'Drink no strong drink'
21 Moses reproaches Aaron,	6–19 Moses reproaches Aaron
People are out of control, fighting ensues, Levites kill 3,000	
35 God sends plague	
33:7–12 Order is restored, pillar of cloud at the door of the tent of meeting.[55]	20 Moses accepts Aaron's response

Conspicuously absent from Douglas's summary of Exod 32:21 and Lev 10:16–19 as "Moses reproaches Aaron" are two major differences in Lev 10. First, Moses does not find that chaos has erupted, in contrast to the running wild that he found in Exod 31. In fact, there is no mention of anything being out of the ordinary, and so Moses's rage seems an absurd overreaction. The חטאת has already been burned, he must realize, and yet nothing drastic has happened. Second, in both narratives Aaron gets a chance to respond to Moses's reproach, but Lev 10:19–20 reveals a major plot twist. Instead of deflecting blame and making excuses as he had done in Exod 32:22–24, Aaron takes full responsibility and calmly—if cryptically—states his case. What is important to notice here is the fascinating dynamic between initiative and responsibility that surfaces when these two narrative moments are read side by side. In Exodus, Moses asks, "What did these people do to you?!" and Aaron's excuse is that the people brought their gold and "out came this calf!", when actually he had asked for their gold, melted it down, carved the calf himself, and orchestrated their idolatrous offerings (Exod 32:2–6). In Leviticus 10, however, Moses initially confronts not Aaron, but Elazar and Itamar, and Aaron voluntarily steps up and takes personal responsibility for something that

---

55. Douglas, *Leviticus as Literature*, 203.

could well have been Elazar and Itamar's fault.⁵⁶ There is no indication in the text itself that the initiative was Aaron's (although it is reasonable to assume that the sons would not have been so bold on such a day as this and were, in fact, working in concert with Aaron), and he does not even appeal to a collective responsibility by saying "such things have encountered us" or "should we have eaten it," but refers only to himself. This is remarkable. Rather than passively acceding to the people's whims (Exod 32:1–2), facilitating their idolatry (Exod 32:4–6), refusing to take responsibility (Exod 32:22–24), and precipitating sweeping devastation in the community (Exod 32:25–28), in Lev 10:3 Aaron was silent. In his silence, he hears YHWH speak to him alone, something that has not happened since his summoning to Moses's service in Exod 4:27. And this time, faced once again with an unprecedented situation that demanded his response and his alone, he demonstrates the wisdom and discernment fitting to his vocation as the high priest.

The surprises do not end here. Even more striking is the fact that Moses listens to Aaron, and is pacified. In no other place in the Pentateuch is Moses said to listen to Aaron, and only on one other occasion do we read of Moses listening to anyone at all, when he consults his father-in-law for advice in Exod 18:24. In fact, in all YHWH's speaking to Moses the word שמע is never used in reference to Moses, and on only two other occasions is Moses said to "listen" or "hear" (שמע), when he hears the people's weeping for meat in Num 11:10 and Korah's accusation in Num 16:4.

Milgrom reads Moses's acceptance of Aaron's reply as P's acknowledgment of "the superiority of the prophet (Moses) over the priest (Aaron)," assuming that "the ministration of Aaron and his sons required the approval not only of God but of Moses."⁵⁷ But the narrative does not actually confirm that Aaron's procedural divergence was approved by either YHWH or Moses. We assume from the fact that all parties are alive to dispute it that burning the חטאת did not violate the divine requirements. But from Moses's response we can only conclude with certainty that what was "good in his eyes" was Aaron's *un*certainty about the best way to proceed: "Would it have been good in the eyes of YHWH?" Aaron asks. Moses is persuaded by this logic, and the fact that he says nothing recalls the opening exchange of the narrative in v. 3. In response to Moses's

---

56. Rashi's suggestion that this was out of respect to Aaron cannot be accepted, since Moses had no problem berating Aaron in Exod 32. See Milgrom, *Leviticus 1–16*, 622.

57. Milgrom, *Leviticus 1–16*, 627.

"interpretation" of Nadav and Avihu's deaths, Aaron was enigmatically silent—we do not know if it is in acceptance of Moses's statement, or whether he has not yet either summoned the fortitude or formulated the words to dispute Moses's reading of the situation. But by the close of the story, Aaron has something to say: he reclaims his place in the interpretive conversation, and now Moses listens. The tables have been turned.

The Priestly Vocation: Interpreting Discourse in Changing Situations

I have been arguing that Leviticus 10 runs along two tracks simultaneously, doing double literary duty. Most obviously, it portrays the ordination of the priesthood and provides the definitive statement of the requirements of the priestly calling. At the same time, it works to restore Aaron's image and reputation in the mind of the reader to prove that he is qualified for this job. It is not surprising, then, that Aaron's rehabilitation takes place specifically through an act of interpretation.

While the resonances with Exodus 32 are crucial to fully understanding the significance of what takes place in Leviticus 10, they should not overshadow the most obvious function that Leviticus 10 plays in its immediate literary context. Coming as it does during the account of the dedication of the tabernacle and installation of the priesthood, it defines the role of the priests in this new stage of Israel's life with YHWH, asserting that interpretation is the core of the priestly vocation. The central theme of the narrative, chiastically highlighted in YHWH's address to Aaron in vv. 8–11, holds together both the ability "to distinguish between the holy and between the common; and between the unclean and between the clean" along with teaching the Israelites "all of the statutes that I have spoken to them through the hand of Moses." In his handling of the חטאת and exchange with Moses in vv. 19–20 Aaron immediately exercises both of these callings. Leviticus 10 might thus be viewed as "the founding legend of priestly exegesis" as Nihan has compellingly argued.[58] The ordination of the priesthood also marks a new moment in the community's formation. Having received, through Moses, the divine blueprint of their new life lived as the people of YHWH, it is now time to put that word into practice in the ongoing life of the community. Rather than viewing the rebalancing that takes place between Moses and Aaron as a power struggle or transfer of authority in which Aaron comes out on

---

58. Nihan, *From Priestly Torah to Pentateuch*, 602.

top, a better characterization of this exchange is a transition into Israel's different kind of life with YHWH. While their journey out of Egypt and nascent stages of life as a new nation had been characterized by the person and leadership of Moses, Israel's constant, quotidian life with YHWH will now be characterized by the steady, embedded presence and service of the priesthood, sustained not by the drama of Mt. Sinai or the burning bush, but by the daily rhythms of the tabernacle and the נר תמיד (*ner tamid*) (Exod 27:20; Lev 24:2).[59] So Milgrom is right to observe that the divine commission to Aaron is not a "new" word, but a confirmation of Aaron's role in implementing it. "The priests ... carry no new instruction; they transmit the old," Milgrom writes.[60] But the question is: how?

The priestly writers recognize that YHWH's commission to Aaron involves more than rote transmission of the received word. Aaron receives the definitive statement of his calling in the context of a narrative in which he will immediately need to discern and to teach, which suggests that the task of instructing the community will take the form of enacting wise discernment in concrete situations. The interweaving of law and narrative here thus accomplishes more than having a greater effect on the reader through "law in story form."[61] It reflects a priestly view of interpretation as fundamentally situational, much as Ricoeur suggests: Interpretation is an event in which discourse comes to life with particular immediacy.[62]

Because the priestly commission to discern and to teach is also the moment that affirms Aaron's qualification for the job and completes his transformation into a wise and discerning leader, Aaron is called upon to exercise his new responsibilities not in just any situation, but in one that involves him in a deeply personal and existential way. The "pathos"

---

59. Mark Leuchter makes much of this contrast between Moses and Aaron, writing that "In contrast to his exegetical role within Deuteronomy and despite his status as receiver of YHWH's laws, Moses engages in no interpretation within the chapters of Leviticus. He becomes a literary *topos* in the service of authenticity, but one whose personality or consciousness leaves no imprint whatsoever upon the ideology of the legislation. Interpretive authority in relation to society at large is left in the hand of the Aaronides." See Leuchter, "The Politics of Ritual Rhetoric," 345–65. While the gist of this is on track, it is not exactly true that Moses engages in *no* interpretation in the book of Leviticus, as evident from his interpretation of Nadav and Avihu's deaths in 10:2. See also Nihan, *From Priestly Pentateuch to Torah*, 598–601, on Moses's interpretation concerning the חטאת.

60. Milgrom, *Leviticus 1–16*, 616.

61. Milgrom, *Leviticus 1–16*, 632.

62. See especially Ricoeur, *Interpretation Theory*, 92–95.

of Aaron's situation was flagged at the very beginning of the narrative, with the explicit reference to Nadav and Avihu as Aaron's sons and the highly suggestive meaning of their names as "willingness" and "he is my father."[63] The impact of their deaths as a father's loss of his two eldest sons is momentarily overshadowed by Moses's frantic rush to restore order in vv. 4–11, but resurfaces in v. 12 and again in v. 16, where we encounter the phrase "his remaining sons." Here we begin to realize that this is not just any tragedy slotted in as a warning about the dangers of priestly service, it is a tragedy that has happened to Aaron. Whether or not we understand Nadav and Avihu's deaths as divine punishment, it is clear that the characters within the narrative itself are deeply disturbed. Moses's handling of the situation aims to avoid any more death (v. 7), which also confirms that Moses, at least, has read YHWH's consuming fire as punishment rather than acceptance (v. 6). We are also aware that the event is understood as cause for mourning "the burning that YHWH has burned" (v. 6). All of this suggests that Aaron's silence in v. 3 is less likely "shame," or "piety," than the shock of "a father, stunned into numbness by the unthinkable."[64]

Humanizing Aaron in this way—as a father rather than solely the high priest—does not only cast Aaron's character in a softer, more compassionate light, or serve as a clue that something significant is happening to him. If we are paying careful attention, it also fundamentally reorients our perspective on the deaths of the sons. Focusing carefully on Aaron and his perspective makes it difficult to see Nadav and Avihu merely as literary foils or a "pretext" for some other priestly agenda, as so many interpreters have understood their function in the narrative.[65] What they

63. Josephus was the first to observe the pathos of Aaron's situation, as discussed by Christopher T. Begg, "The Death of Nadab and Abihu," 162. On the meaning of their names, see again Douglas, *Leviticus as Literature*, 201. Finally, it is worth noting that Walter Houston has also suggested a sympathetic reading of Aaron as a "tragic hero," but because he largely follows Damrosch in accepting the men's deaths as reflecting badly on Aaron—a "disgrace of the father trope," he argues—it is unclear how he ultimately understands the function of Aaron's character in Lev 10. See Houston, "Tragedy in the Courts of the Lord," 36–37.

64. Shai Held's beautifully compassionate reading of this passage follows Abravanel while providing a useful overview of how Aaron's silence has been interpreted among Jewish commentators more broadly. See *The Heart of Torah*, 33. Reading Aaron's silence negatively as shame, see, for example, Noth, *Leviticus*, 85. Finally, for a discussion of the possibility that דמם may not indicate silence at all but the moaning of grief, see Levine, "Silence," 89–106. Notably, Levine here reverses his acceptance of the traditional reading of דמם as "silence" that he had articulated earlier in *Leviticus*, 60.

65. Nihan writes that "In the remainder of Lev 10, the death of Nadab and Abihu

did and what happens to them is not the main focus, but neither is it interchangeable with any other incident: it is integral to Aaron's transformation. Without this precise scenario, we do not have this Aaron.

Furthermore, Aaron's personal relationship to the situation is not a liability, but a catalyst. Rather than disqualifying him from the responsibilities of his calling, rendering him unable to exercise sound judgment "to discern and to teach," it is precisely his experience that generates his reevaluation of the situation.[66] This is made explicit in the dénouement of vv. 19–20, where Aaron himself points to the events of the day as the crucial factor in his reading of the situation: "Look—today they brought their חטאת and their עלה before YHWH, and such things as these have encountered me" (הֵן הַיּוֹם הִקְרִיבוּ אֶת־חַטָּאתָם וְאֶת־עֹלָתָם לִפְנֵי יְהוָה וַתִּקְרֶאנָה אֹתִי כָּאֵלֶּה, 10:19).

What exactly Aaron means by this has long puzzled exegetes. It seems obvious that he must be referring to the deaths of Nadav and Avihu as "these things," but why this should necessitate a change in the sacrificial procedures is unclear. In what has been the most influential examination of the difficulty, Milgrom concludes that Aaron must have felt that the deaths of Nadav and Avihu had polluted the sanctuary, thus changing the status of the offering from an ordinary חטאת that should be eaten (i.e., as instructed in 6:17–23) to an anomalous situation in which the impurity absorbed by the חטאת was so great that it must be burned (see also Lev 4:3–21; 16:27).[67] The priestly writers of Leviticus 10 thus allowed the discrepancy to stand because there were two possible procedures for the disposal of the חטאת, and the death of anointed priests while in the vicinity of the sanctuary presents a "borderline case."[68] More

---

forms the pretext for a further series of instructions (v. 6–20), adding new rules for the priests (v. 6–7, 8–11) or demonstrating that they are in conformity with the law in one significant case, the disposal of sacrificial remains (v. 12–15, 16–20)." This is undoubtedly true, but it overlooks the fact that all of that could have been communicated through the "pretext" of any priestly death, while the tragedy of Lev 10 specifically involves Aaron's own sons. See Nihan, *From Priestly Torah to Pentateuch*, 603.

66. Karen Eliasen has similarly observed what she understands to be Aaron's "emotional experience," arguing that Aaron discovers his calling because "he is intellectually reoriented by means of an emotionally provocative ritual setting." While I am sympathetic to the idea that the particulars of the situation are what clarifies Aaron's understanding and acceptance of his calling, I do not locate the key element of the situation in Aaron's emotional experience but in his unique perspective of the event as both father and priest. See Eliasen, "Aaron's War Within."

67. Milgrom, *Leviticus 1–16*, 637.

68. Milgrom, *Leviticus 1–16*, 639.

recently, Nihan has rejected Milgrom's specific hypothesis that a change in the status of the חטאת could occur once it had been offered on the altar, but he agrees that Leviticus 10 "resolves" a discrepancy between Lev 6:23 and Lev 8–9 (along with Exod 29) by appealing to the "exceptional events" of Nadav and Avihu's deaths.[69] Both Milgrom and Nihan argue their hypotheses with the acknowledgement that the precise reasons for Aaron's departure from the instructions for the חטאת as given in 6:17–23, the instructions that Moses believes to be normative, are simply not specified in the narrative itself. They are in agreement on the basic point that the decisive factor is the particular situation in which Aaron and his sons find themselves.

The larger conclusion to be drawn from this is that our ability to discern the function of the dispute as it stands within the narrative does not hinge on fully elucidating the argument itself. Aaron's rationale for his innovation could simply be a contingent difficulty whose solution has been lost to history, understood by an ancient audience but inaccessible to modern readers. But the open-endedness of Aaron's response suggests that the difficulty readers encounter here may be of a different order altogether. His rationale is, in fact, a question: "If I had eaten the חטאת today, would it have been good in the eyes of YHWH?" (v. 19). The question resists a decisive answer, prompting readers to evaluate it for themselves. In this way it engages a different mode of thinking, a challenge to "think with" the world of the text in which interpretation inevitably carries a degree of provisionality and precariousness. To a certain degree, it may even rise to the level of a tactical difficulty, intentionally holding open a space in which the precise meaning of "such things as these" cannot be reduced and confined to the originating situation in which they encountered Aaron.

Finally, the notion that Aaron's experience is the decisive factor in his assessment of the situation is supported by the fact that Aaron's reading of the situation is portrayed in direct contrast to Moses. Moses's singular focus had been to restore order to chaos in order to resume and complete the sacrificial procedures as instructed. What he did not realize was that

---

69. Nihan's interpretation of the larger significance of the narrative is that the priestly authors portray Aaron as participating in a kind of legal interpretation that would later become characteristic of midrashic exegesis. The discrepancy between the instructions for the חטאת in Lev 6:17–23 and the account of what had actually been done with the חטאת in 9:22–15 is thus clarified in Lev 10 by appeal to a third point of reference, namely the unique situation created by the unprecedented events of the day. Nihan, *From Priestly Torah to Pentateuch*, 600–601.

the situation had been fundamentally altered. Aaron, acutely aware of the change that had been wrought, accurately reassessed the situation and, without waiting for Moses's approval, changed course to complete the offerings in accordance with the events that had just occurred. In a fundamentally different relationship to the events of the day than Aaron, Moses was unable to "read" the situation for what it was, clinging to a precedent that no longer served the events at hand.

Discerning the Direction of Thought

In Aaron's experience of learning to understand and interpret the direction of thought that the received word opens up, the priestly writers sketch an intriguing portrait of what they understand interpretation to be. It is first of all grounded in a particular event, in which the received text—written or unwritten—comes to light. Because of this, interpretation may often be provisional and improvisatory. When there is no precedent to resort to, interpretation requires discernment and initiative to determine the right approach.

We also find a view of interpretation that affirms the ability of the person most affected by a situation to discern wisely and exercise sound judgment. With clear parameters of text and context, this does not mean that interpretation is entirely subjective or relative; it is not "to each his own." Nevertheless, this portrait of Aaron as the one whose perspective of the situation was the most penetrating and nuanced is sobering. The divine word remained unchanged, yet the ground in which it was to take root had irrevocably shifted and Aaron alone was able to feel its full magnitude. Consequently, we also see a perspective of interpretation as a calling made unavoidable by both divine decree and situational necessity. As anointed priest, the prerogative to retreat and mourn his sons' death was unavailable to Aaron. The well-being of the larger community depended on his perspective and willingness to offer it, as both father and priest. The necessity of interpretation follows wherever there is potential for an event of discourse to dramatically alter the course of human existence.

Finally, we see the priestly writers wrestling with the recognition that there is always a certain degree of risk involved in taking the initiative to articulate and enact new understandings of the meaning of the divine word. Misinterpretation is always a possibility, and great pain and damage can be inflicted before we are able to correct course. The story concludes with Aaron's question ringing indefinitely: "Would it have been good in the eyes of YHWH?"

Taking all of this into consideration, in Leviticus 10 the priestly writers reflect a keen awareness that fidelity to the received word may mean different things at different times. The kind of world that this priestly portrayal of discourse projects is one in which the process of learning to live safely in the presence of YHWH—that is, the process of learning to cultivate a life of human flourishing—presents continual challenges as unprecedented events are encountered and new knowledges are discovered. Acting faithfully in accordance with the divine word thus calls for the wisdom to discern its direction of thought and continually evaluate whether we are acting in accordance with it. It is perhaps no accident that the words at the exact center of the Torah are דָּרֹשׁ דָּרַשׁ, "he carefully—urgently, insistently—inquired" (Lev 10:16).

It is one thing to identify the direction of thought that the priestly writers portrayed as their vision of what life lived in proximity to the divine could, and should, be. What is more difficult is to determine the specific points of contact between that world and our own, which this book has argued is the aim of interpretation. Leviticus 10, however, has emphasized the extraordinarily situational and contextual nature of interpretation, which should caution us against generalizations made in the abstract about particular points of contact between the text and the contexts that contemporary readers inhabit. Nevertheless, we can suggest some examples of ways that this particular vision of life may challenge readers to rethink the terms that have come to define certain aspects of our own world. How does this story, inhabiting a world so different from our own, disclose new possibilities or press us to "regestalt," as Taylor writes, the categories that we have come to accept as normal and inevitable?

At the most basic level, the notion that Leviticus 10 resists a view of fidelity to the law as rigid and unchanging necessitates a paradigm shift for many readers. As we saw at the beginning of this study, the caricature of Leviticus as the ultimate expression of legalistic religiosity is deeply rooted in popular perception, as well as in various streams of religious life. It is one thing for scholars to point out that this is a misreading of the priestly vision of life, but quite another to recognize that the priestly writers themselves wrestled with the potential danger of dogmatism in discerning correct applications of the divine word. This direction of thought could open up an entirely new view of the priestly literature for many contemporary readers, bringing to light aspects of these texts that have previously been obscured.

In broader applications, we might ask how a notion of fidelity as flexible and fluid within certain parameters challenges contemporary expectations of leadership in spheres of life apart from the sacred. In the current political climate, for example, public interest in tracing the history of a political candidate's stance on a given issue for signs of inconsistency borders on the obsessive. As portrayed in Leviticus 10, Moses would be the ideal candidate for public office. But is this the best metric for assessing a candidate's trustworthiness and ability to fulfill her responsibilities to ensure the public good? Leviticus 10 presents a different picture of wise leadership, in which fidelity to supporting the public good may mean changing one's position on a matter if the situation merits a change of course. It affirms a vision of leadership in which a cautious change of perspective based on new information, or a new understanding of the information at hand, may be a sign of hard-won maturity and humility rather than inconstancy or a blanket disqualification for service.

Finally, the priestly portrayal of Aaron's intimate relationship to the situation that ultimately affirms his qualifications for leadership may inform contemporary notions of objectivity as a desirable professional standard. Is it imaginable that there may be times when objectivity is not an asset, but rather an impediment to fulfilling one's professional responsibilities? What does it take to be able to read a situation accurately and determine the best course of action? When are empathy, vulnerability, and perhaps even inferiority precisely the qualities needed to determine the best course of action?

These are just a few directions of thought that Leviticus 10 opens up, suggesting that even more possibilities may be generated as the text is brought into conversation with specific interpretive contexts.

Conclusion

"That, when you come down to it, is the only kind of courage that is demanded of us: the courage for the oddest, the most unexpected, the most inexplicable things that we may encounter."

—Rainer Maria Rilke[1]

"Like Odysseus bound to the mast of his ship, a reader may titillate himself with the siren song of knowledge and sail past intact."

—Anne Carson[2]

In her dazzling debut essay *Eros the Bittersweet,* Canadian poet and classicist Anne Carson "follows the traces of an ancient analogy between knowledge and the wooing of love."[3] The analogy unfolds as Carson probes Plato's *Phaedrus,* a dialogue between Socrates and a young man who has fallen in love with a text. At the heart of the analogy is desire, and the paradox that to desire is to be in pursuit of something that exists in the flow of space and time and so can never truly be possessed as the object you imagine it to be. The space between lover and beloved, between philosopher and *sophia,* is unpredictable. It is a space of transience and flux, a space that cannot be foreseen or controlled. To be a lover, Carson observes, is to embark on a quest with an uncertain destination,

---

1. Rainer Maria Rilke, *Letters to a Young Poet,* 43.
2. Carson, *Eros the Bittersweet: An Essay,* 165.
3. Carson, *Eros the Bittersweet: An Essay,* 170.

and therefore to relinquish control over what happens to you on the way. Only "non-lovers are people who remain 'masters of themselves,'" anchored securely within the predictable borders of what is known.[4]

But Socrates fears that the act of writing, which is "an experience of temporal arrest and manipulation" of language, affords the reader a vantage point that is abstracted from the effects of time.[5] Readers may come and go from a text at will without a sense of encountering it in real time, in the lived experience of the here and now. This is the image that Carson conjures in Odysseus bound to the mast of his ship. He wants two things: to hear the song of the Sirens, and to continue on his journey, unaffected by their seduction. He sails past intact.

Our own study began with the observation that Leviticus also portrays a kind of encounter: an encounter between YHWH and Israel, mediated through discourse, that generates new forms of life for the wilderness community. It is a moment in time, anchored at Sinai, but it is also a discourse that blurs and extends the boundaries of time to address the reader: the text is an invitation to step into the world the text creates, to experience the constitutive force of the divine discourse. This study has been an attempt to understand what is on offer in that invitation.

We began by probing the notion of discourse as a way to open up a new understanding of the text/reader relationship. In conversation with Paul Ricoeur and George Steiner, I have suggested that Leviticus's self-presentation as discourse asks readers to approach the text as a potential conversation partner. This conversation takes place in each new encounter between text and reader, in the present moment. As readers across space and time learn to listen to what the text is saying we are brought into contact with new thoughts and ideas, new visions of life that illumine our own categories of thinking and the ways of being that we have come to accept as normal or even inevitable. When a text is encountered as a direction of thought opening out before us, the discourse between text and reader can indeed be generative and constitutive, just as the divine discourse at Sinai generated new forms of life and new ways of being in the world.

As attractive as this notion of interpretation is, however, engaging Leviticus in discourse is, and probably always has been, notoriously difficult. Leviticus asks readers to listen in ways that are unfamiliar and

---

4. Carson, *Eros the Bittersweet: An Essay*, 149.
5. Carson, *Eros the Bittersweet: An Essay*, 121.

uncomfortable—sometimes even unintelligible. And so whether or not this is a conversation that is even worth having was a question that needed to be addressed. To find traction, we first needed to gain a better sense of what it is that "holds against us," as Steiner puts it: what is the extent and character of the difficulty? Can it be overcome—and how? With Steiner's help we saw that although understanding may be hard won, it is not usually entirely out of reach. Still, the question of whether the pursuit is worth it persists. Does *this* text bring enough to the conversation to make the difficulty of understanding productive?

To find out, we needed to test the transferability of specific aspects of the vision of life that Leviticus projects, so we asked how the priestly understanding of the function of speech might provide insight into contemporary patterns of discourse. This is only one entry point among many that we could have taken, but it seemed appropriate to this study because of our larger interest in the generativity of discourse and because of the centrality of speech to the priestly vision of life. Another consideration recommending this choice was that the function of speech is a topic that has weighed heavily on current events during the writing of this manuscript. The post-truth political scene spreading across the globe has rapidly destabilized the norms of public discourse that have shaped modern society, and there is urgent need for alternative perspectives on what is at stake in discourse, especially its capacity to unite or divide those with perspectives so different as to render the possibility of understanding out of the question. Unlikely though it may (at first) seem, Leviticus has a valuable perspective to offer in the public square, on exactly this point. The priestly writers offer a vision of life in which the power of speech to unravel the social fabric is acknowledged, and the community's role in limiting its destructive potential is considered from multiple perspectives. In at least this one way, the difficulty of learning to think with Leviticus in order to bring it into conversation with contemporary concerns proves worthwhile.

The exegetical probes of chapters 4–6 have shown Leviticus to be a valuable conversation partner, but the priestly view of speech is only one aspect of the text's vision of life. Furthermore, this study has only gestured toward a few ways that the priestly notion of discourse may shed new light on contemporary concerns. One possibility for further study would be a more thorough exploration of the view of speech that the book reflects, expanding the scope of inquiry to include the parts of the book not addressed here.

CONCLUSION

One of the main pillars of the argument I have set forth here is that the aim of interpretation, maximally conceived, is to identify points of contact between the vision of life a text projects and the lived experience of its readers. While scholars have made great progress in recent years toward identifying aspects of the direction of thought that Leviticus projects—in large part due to Jacob Milgrom and Mary Douglas's redirection of the scholarly conversation—identifying specific points of contact between the text and contemporary life is an aspect of interpretation that has been neglected. I have attempted to move the conversation forward with this study, and establishing a theoretical grounding for a hermeneutic of discourse that takes the unique difficulties of Leviticus as its starting point was the necessary first step. The goal, however, is that this hermeneutic of discourse might motivate and support the more explicitly connective work of identifying points of contact between the text's vision of life and contemporary experience. While the exegetical probes have made a beginning at certain concrete conversations, they have not carried the discussion as far as it might go. Whether this work occurs in the scholarly discourse of interpreters working at a specific nexus of text and context, such as we saw in the pastoral and ecological readings of Leviticus demonstrated by Wiener and Hirschman and Davis, or in the practical conversations of lay reading communities willing to engage the text in discourse with their own unique interpretive locations, it is the most promising and pressing frontier for our generation of Leviticus studies.

In hopes of encouraging that work, I offer a final comment on the notion of difficulty. Since most readers' initial impression of Leviticus is that it is difficult, that is where this project began. Leviticus has long fascinated me precisely because it has always seemed to elude my grasp, hovering just outside the reach of mastery. At the same time, the vision of life that it projects is never fully concealed, revealed in glimpses that suggest that there is more to be seen if we are willing to look more carefully. So while it has ultimately become only one part of the study in its final form, this experience of the difficulty of bringing the text's vision of life fully into focus has generated and propelled this project.

While charting a path through the difficulties of Leviticus in the hope of enabling productive discourse, I have come to see that the attraction of difficulty is not that it presents something to be conquered or overcome. It is, instead, an invitation to become or to experience something more than what we now are, to reach out beyond the borders of the self and into that liminal space where transformation is possible. This is the attraction that grounds the analogy between lover and learner; both have been seduced by something "over there," something that sets the mind and heart in motion. We can, of course, sail by as voyeurs, as Odysseus did in his determination to remain fixed on course, hearing but not turning aside. The difficulties of Leviticus beckon us beyond ourselves to what lies outside of the known and familiar, and it is a "high-risk proposition," as Carson warns, "to reach for the difference between known and unknown."[6] But it is in this difficult space where new forms of life take root. The extent of difficulty is the extent of any text's capacity to make us better readers, thinkers, and human beings, and this alone is reason enough to make Leviticus worth reading. If the text's vision of life beckons, drawing us into new perspectives of what is humanly possible in our own lived experience, what better reason could there be to learn to hear what it has to say?

---

6. Carson, *Eros the Bittersweet: An Essay*, 173.

Bibliography

Achenbach, Reinhard. *Die Vollendung der Tora: Studien zur Redaktionsgeschichte des Numeribuches im Kontext von Hexateuch und Pentateuch*. Wiesbaden: Harrassowitz, 2003.
Adams, Samuel L. *Social and Economic Life in Second Temple Judea*. Louisville: Westminster John Knox, 2014.
Aguilar, Mario I., and Louise Joy Lawrence. *Anthropology and Biblical Studies: Avenues of Approach*. Leiden: Deo, 2004.
Albertz, Rainer. *Israel in Exile: The History and Literature of the Sixth Century B.C.E.* Translated by D. Green. Leiden: Brill, 2004.
———. "The History of Israelite Religion in the Post-Exilic Period." In *A History of Israelite Religion in the Old Testament Period*, Vol. 2, 438–533. Translated by John Bowden. Louisville: Westminster John Knox, 1994.
Alter, Robert. *The Five Books of Moses: A Translation with Commentary*. New York: Norton, 2004.
———. *The Art of Biblical Narrative*. New York: Basic, 2011.
———. *The Art of Biblical Poetry*. New York: Basic, 2011.
Alter, Robert, and Frank Kermode, eds. *The Literary Guide to the Bible*. Cambridge: Belknap, 1987.
Anderson, Gary A. *Sacrifices and Offerings in Ancient Israel: Studies in Their Social and Political Importance*. Harvard Semitic Monographs 41. Atlanta: Scholars, 1987.
Arnoff, Stephen Hazan. "Memory, Rhetoric, and Oral-Performance in Leviticus Rabbah." PhD diss., Jewish Theological Seminary, 2011.
Baden, Joel. *The Composition of the Pentateuch: Renewing the Documentary Hypothesis*. New Haven: Yale University Press, 2012.
Baker, David W. "Division Markers and the Structure of Leviticus 1–7." In *Studia Biblica 1978, 1: Papers on Old Testament and Related Themes*, 1–15. Sheffield: University of Sheffield, 1979.
Bakhtin, Mikhail M. *The Dialogic Imagination: Four Essays*. Translated by Caryl Emerson and Michael Holquist. Austin: University of Texas Press, 1981.
Balentine, Samuel E. *Leviticus*. Interpretation. Louisville: John Knox, 2002.
———. *The Torah's Vision of Worship*. Overtures to Biblical Theology. Minneapolis: Fortress, 1999.

Barstad, Han. *The Myth of the Empty Land: A Study of the History and Archaeology of Judah During the "Exilic" Period*. Symbolae Osloenses Fasc. Supp.l 28. Oslo: Scandinavian University Press, 1996.

Bauckham, Richard. *The Bible in the Contemporary World: Hermeneutical Ventures*. Grand Rapids: Eerdmans, 2015.

Bauckham, Richard, Daniel R. Driver, Trevor A. Hart, and Nathan MacDonald, eds. *The Epistle to the Hebrews in Christian Theology*. Grand Rapids: Eerdmans, 2009.

Beebee, Thomas O. *The Ideology of Genre: A Comparative Study of Generic Instability*. University Park: Pennsylvania State University, 1994.

Begg, Christopher T. "The Death of Nadab and Abihu According to Josephus." *Liber Annuus* 59 (2009) 155–67.

Bell, Catherine. *Ritual Theory, Ritual Practice*. Oxford: Oxford University Press, 1992.

Benjamin, Walter. "The Task of the Translator." In *Walter Benjamin: Selected Writings, Volume 1, 1913–1926*, edited by Marcus Bullock and Michael W. Jennings, 253–63. Cambridge: Belknap, 1996.

Bergen, Wesley J. *Reading Ritual: Leviticus in Postmodern Culture*. Journal for the Study of the Old Testament: Supplement Series 417. New York: T. & T. Clark, 2005.

Berlin, Adele. "Reading Biblical Poetry." In *The Jewish Study Bible*, edited by Adele Berlin and Marc Zvi Brettler, 2097–104. New York: Oxford University Press, 2004.

———. *The Dynamics of Biblical Parallelism*. Bloomington: Indiana University Press, 1985.

———. "Literary Approaches to the Bible." In *The Cambridge Companion to the Hebrew Bible/Old Testament*, edited by Stephen B. Chapman and Marvin A. Sweeney, 163–83. New York: Cambridge University Press, 2016.

Berquist, Jon L. *Judaism in Persia's Shadow: A Social and Historical Approach*. 1995. Reprint, Eugene, OR: Wipf & Stock, 2003.

Bibb, Bryan D. "Nadab and Abihu Attempt to Fill a Gap: Law and Narrative in Leviticus 10.1–7." *Journal for the Study of the Old Testament* 26.2 (2001) 83–99.

———. *Ritual Words and Narrative Worlds in the Book of Leviticus*. Library of Hebrew Bible/Old Testament Studies 480. New York: T. & T. Clark, 2009.

Blenkinsopp, Joseph. "An Assessment of the Alleged Pre-Exilic Date of the Priestly Material of the Pentateuch." *Zeitschrift für die alttestamentliche Wissenschaft* 108.4 (1996) 495–518.

———. "The Judaean Priesthood During the Neo-Babylonian and Achaemenid Periods: A Hypothetical Reconstruction." *The Catholic Biblical Quarterly*, 60 (1998) 25–43.

Boyarin, Daniel. *Intertextuality and the Reading of Midrash*. Indiana Studies in Biblical Literature. Bloomington: Indiana University Press, 1990.

Breed, Brennan W. *Nomadic Text: A Theory of Biblical Reception History*. Bloomington: Indiana University Press, 2014.

Briggs, Richard S. *Theological Hermeneutics and the Book of Numbers as Christian Scripture*. Reading the Scriptures. Notre Dame: University of Notre Dame Press, 2018.

Brown, William P. *A Handbook to Old Testament Exegesis*. Louisville: Westminster John Knox, 2017.

Brueggemann, Walter. *Theology of the Old Testament: Testimony, Dispute, Advocacy*. Minneapolis: Fortress, 1997.

Buber, Martin, and Franz Rosenzweig. *Scripture and Translation*. Translated by Lawrence Rosenwald and Everett Fox. Bloomington: Indiana University Press, 1994.

Buss, Martin J. "Dialogue in and Among Genres." In *Bakhtin and Genre Theory in Biblical Studies*, edited by Roland Boer, 9–18. Semeia Studies 63. Atlanta: SBL, 2007.

Carasik, Michael, ed. *The Commentators' Bible: Leviticus*. The Rubin JPS Miqra'ot Gedolot. Philadelphia: Jewish Publication Society, 2009.

Carmichael, Calum. *Illuminating Leviticus: A Study of Its Laws and Institutions in the Light of Biblical Narratives*. Baltimore: Johns Hopkins University Press, 2006.

Carr, David M. *Writing on the Tablet of the Heart: Origins of Scripture and Litera-ture*. New York: Oxford University Press, 2005.

Carson, Anne. *Eros the Bittersweet: An Essay*. Princeton: Princeton University Press, 1986.

Chancey, Mark A., Carol Meyers, and Eric M. Meyers, eds. *The Bible in the Public Square: Its Enduring Influence on American Life*. Society of Biblical Literature: Biblical Scholarship in North America 27. Atlanta: SBL, 2014.

Chapman, Stephen B. "Imaginative Readings of Scripture and Theological Imagination." In *Out of Egypt: Biblical Theology and Biblical Interpretation*, edited by Craig Bartholomew, 409–41. Grand Rapids: Zondervan, 2004.

Cheal, David. "Ritual: Communication in Action." *Sociological Analysis* 53 (1992) 363–74.

Childs, Brevard S. *Old Testament Theology in a Canonical Context*. Philadelphia: Fortress, 1985.

Citton, Yves. *Lire, Interpréter, Actualiser: Pourquoi Les Études Littéraires?* Paris: Éditions Amsterdam, 2007.

Clines, David J. A. "Biblical Hermeneutics in Theory and Practice." *Christian Brethren Review* 31.32 (1986) 65–76.

Collins, John J. *The Bible after Babel: Historical Criticism in a Postmodern Age*. Grand Rapids: Eerdmans, 2005.

———. "Epilogue: Genre Analysis and the Dead Sea Scrolls." *Dead Sea Discoveries* 17.3 (2010) 389–401.

Comrie, Bernard. *Aspect: An Introduction to the Study of Verbal Aspect and Related Problems*. New York: Cambridge University Press, 1976.

Cothey, Antony. "Ethics and Holiness in the Theology of Leviticus." *Journal for the Study of the Old Testament* 30 (2005) 131–51.

Crüsemann, Frank. *The Torah: Theology and Social History of Old Testament Law*. Translated by Allan W. Mahnke. Minneapolis: Fortress, 1996.

Culler, Jonathan. *Structuralist Poetics: Structuralism, Linguistics, and the Study of Literature*. Ithaca: Cornell University Pres, 1975.

Damrosch, David. "Leviticus." *The Literary Guide to the Bible*. Edited by Robert Alter and Frank Kermode. Cambridge: Belknap, 1987.

———. *The Narrative Covenant: Transformations of Genre in the Growth of Biblical Literature*. San Francisco: Harper & Row, 1987.

Davis, Ellen F. *Opening Israel's Scriptures*. New York: Oxford University Press, 2019.

———. *Preaching the Luminous Word: Biblical Sermons and Homiletical Essays*. Grand Rapids: Eerdmans, 2016.

———. "Reasoning with Scripture." *Anglican Theological Review* 90 (2008) 513–19.

———. *Scripture, Culture, and Agriculture: An Agrarian Reading of the Bible*. New York: Cambridge University Press, 2009.

———. *Swallowing the Scroll: Textuality and the Dynamics of Discourse in Ezekiel's Prophecy.* Journal for the Study of the Old Testament Supplement Series 78. Sheffield: JSOT Press, 1989.

———. *Wondrous Depth: Preaching the Old Testament.* Louisville: Westminster John Knox, 2005.

Davis, Ellen F., and Richard B. Hays. *The Art of Reading Scripture.* Grand Rapids: Eerdmans, 2003.

Davis, G. Scott. "Two Neglected Classics of Comparative Ethics." *Journal of Religious Ethics* 36 (2008) 375–403.

Dershowitz, Idan. "The Secret History of Leviticus." *The New York Times*, July 21, 2018; accessed April 10, 2024, https://www.nytimes.com/2018/07/21/opinion/sunday/bible-prohibit-gay-sex.html.

———. "Revealing Nakedness and Concealing Homosexual Intercourse: Legal and Lexical Evolution in Leviticus 18." *Hebrew Bible and Ancient Israel* 6 (2017) 510–26.

Devitt, Amy J. *Writing Genres.* Carbondale: Southern Illinois University Press, 2004.

Dornisch, Loretta. "Paul Ricoeur and Biblical Interpretation: A Selected Bibliography." *Semeia* 4 (1975) 23–26.

———. "Paul Ricoeur and Biblical Interpretation: A Selected Bibliography." *Semeia* 19 (1981) 23–29.

———. "Paul Ricoeur and Biblical Exegesis." *Studia Missionalia* 52 (2003) 207–28.

Douglas, Mary. "Atonement in Leviticus." *Jewish Studies Quarterly* 1 (1993) 109–30.

———. "A Feeling for Hierarchy." *Believing Scholars: Ten Catholic Intellectuals.* Edited by James L. Heft. New York: Fordham University Press, 2005.

———. "The Forbidden Animals in Leviticus." *Journal for the Study of the Old Testament* 18.59 (1993) 3–23.

———. "The Glorious Book of Numbers." *Jewish Studies Quarterly* 1 (1993) 193–216.

———. "Holy Joy: Rereading Leviticus: The Anthropologist and the Believer." *Conservative Judaism* 46.3 (1994) 3–14.

———. *Implicit Meanings: Selected Essays in Anthropology* 2nd ed. New York: Routledge, 1999.

———. *In the Wilderness: The Doctrine of Defilement in the Book of Numbers.* Journal for the Study of the Old Testament Supplements 158. Sheffield: JSOT, 1993.

———. *Jacob's Tears: The Priestly Work of Reconciliation.* New York: Oxford University Press, 2004.

———. *Leviticus as Literature.* New York: Oxford University Press, 1999.

———. *Natural Symbols: Explorations in Cosmology.* New York: Routledge, 2003.

———. *Purity and Danger: An Analysis of Concepts of Pollution and Taboo.* New York: Routledge, 2002.

———. "The Stranger in the Bible." *Archives Européenes do Sociologie* 35 (1994) 283–98.

———. *Thinking in Circles: An Essay on Ring Composition.* New Haven: Yale University Press, 2010.

———. "Why I Have to Learn Hebrew: The Doctrine of Sanctification." In *The Comity and Grace of Method: Essays in Honor of Edmund F. Perry*, 147–65. Evanston: Northwestern University Press, 2004.

Duff, David. *Modern Genre Theory.* New York: Longman, 2000.

Dupont, Joanne M. "Women and the Concept of Holiness in the 'Holiness Code' (Leviticus 17–26): Literary, Theological, and Historical Context." PhD diss., Marquette University, 1980.

Durkheim, Émile, and Marcel Mauss. *Primitive Classification*. Translated by Rodney Needham. Chicago: University of Chicago Press, 1963.

Eliasen, Karen C. "Aaron's War Within: Story and Ritual in Leviticus 10." *Proceedings* 20 (2000) 81–98.

Elliott, Mark W. *Engaging Leviticus: Reading Leviticus Theologically with Its Past Interpreters*. Eugene, OR: Cascade Books, 2012.

Empson, William. *The Structure of Complex Words*. Cambridge: Harvard University Press, 1989.

Farber, Martin, ed. *Philosophical Essays in Memory of Edmund Husserl*. Cambridge: Harvard University Press, 1940.

Fardon, Richard. *Mary Douglas: An Intellectual Biography*. New York: Routledge, 1999.

Faust, Abraham. *Judah in the Neo-Babylonian Period: The Archaeology of Desolation*. Archaeology and Biblical Studies 18. Atlanta: SBL, 2012.

Feldman, Louis H. "The Case of the Blasphemer (Lev. 24:10–16) According to Philo and Josephus." In *Heavenly Tablets: Interpretation, Identity and Tradition in Ancient Judaism*. Edited by Lynn R. LiDonnici and Andrea Lieber. Journal for the Study of Judaism Supplements 119. Leiden: Brill, 2007.

Felski, Rita. "Context Stinks!" *New Literary History* 42 (2011) 571–91.

———. *The Limits of Critique*. Chicago: University of Chicago Press, 2015.

Fishbane, Michael. *Biblical Interpretation in Ancient Israel*. New York: Oxford University Press, 1985.

———. *The Exegetical Imagination: On Jewish Thought and Theology*. Harvard University Press, 1998.

Fowler, Alastair. *Kinds of Literature: An Introduction to the Theory of Genres and Modes*. Cambridge: Harvard University Press, 1982.

Fox, Everett. *The Five Books of Moses: Genesis, Exodus, Leviticus, Numbers, Deuteronomy; A New Translation with Introductions, Commentary, and Notes*. Schocken Bible 1. New York: Schocken, 2000.

Fraade, Steven D. *From Tradition to Commentary: Torah and Its Interpretation in the Midrash Sifre to Deuteronomy*. Albany: State University of New York Press, 1991.

Frei, Hans W. *The Eclipse of Biblical Narrative: A Study in Eighteenth and Nineteenth Century Hermeneutics*. New Haven: Yale University Press, 1974.

Fuad, Chelcent. "The Curious Case of the Blasphemer: Ambiguity as Literary Device in Leviticus 24:10–23." *Horizons in Biblical Theology* 41 (2019) 51–70.

Gadamer, Hans-Georg. *Truth and Method*. Translated by Joel Weinsheimer and Donald G. Marshall. New York: Crossroad, 1989.

Gagnon, Robert A. J. *The Bible and Homosexual Practice: Texts and Hermeneutics*. Nashville: Abingdon, 2001.

Garsiel, Moshe. "Puns upon Names as a Literary Device in 1 Kings 1–2." *Biblica* 72 (1991) 379–86.

———. "Wordplays, Puns and Puns Upon Names: As a Literary and Rhetorical Device in the Book of Samuel / משחקי מלים, צימודים ודרשות שם כתכסיס ריטורי-ספרותי בספר שמואל." *Beit Mikra* (1998) 1–4.

Geller, Stephen A. "Blood Cult: Toward a Literary Theology of the Priestly Work of the Pentateuch." *Prooftexts* 12.2 (1992) 97–124.

Gerstenberger, Erhard S. *Israel in the Persian Period: The Fifth and Fourth Centuries BCE*. Translated by Siegfried S. Schatzmann. Biblical Encyclopedia 8. Atlanta: SBL, 2011.

———. *Leviticus: A Commentary*. Translated by Douglas W. Stott. Old Testament Library. Louisville: Westminster John Knox, 1996.

Gesenius, W., and E. Kautzsch. *Gesenius' Hebrew Grammar*. Translated by A. E. Cowley. 2nd English ed. New York: Oxford University Press, 1910.

Gilders, William K. *Blood Ritual in the Hebrew Bible: Meaning and Power*. Baltimore: The Johns Hopkins University Press, 2004.

Gorman, Frank H., Jr. *The Ideology of Ritual: Space, Time and Status in the Priestly Theology*. Journal for the Study of the Old Testament Supplements 91. Sheffield, Eng: JSOT, 1990.

Grabbe, Lester L. *A History of the Jews and Judaism in the Second Temple Period*. Library of Second Temple Studies 47. London: T. & T. Clark, 2004.

———. *An Introduction to Second Temple Judaism: History and Religion of the Jews in the Time of Nehemiah, the Maccabees, Hillel, and Jesus*. New York: T. & T. Clark, 2010.

Green, Garrett. *Imagining God: Theology and the Religious Imagination*. Grand Rapids: Eerdmans, 1989.

Gunkel, Hermann. *Genesis*. Handkommentar zum Alten Testament. Göttingen: Vandenhoeck & Ruprecht, 1901.

———. *Die Psalmen*. Göttinger Handkommentar zum Alten Testament 2. Abt., 2. Bd., 4. Aufl. Göttingen: Vandenhoeck & Ruprecht, 1926.

Halbertal, Moshe. *On Sacrifice*. Princeton: Oxford University Press, 2012.

Harris, Maurice D. *Leviticus: You Have No Idea*. Eugene, OR: Cascade Books, 2013.

Held, Rabbi Shai. *The Heart of Torah*. Vol. 2: *Essays on the Weekly Torah Portion; Leviticus, Numbers, and Deuteronomy*. Lincoln, NE: Jewish Publication Society, 2017.

Hénaff, Marcel. "Lévi-Strauss and the Question of Symbolism." In *The Cambridge Companion to Lévi-Strauss*, edited by Boris Wiseman, 177–95. Cambridge: Cambridge University Press, 2009.

———. *The Price of Truth: Gift, Money, and Philosophy*. Translated by Jean-Louis Morhange. Stanford: Stanford University Press, 2010.

Hendel, Ronald. "Mary Douglas and Anthropological Modernism." *Journal of Hebrew Scriptures* 8.8 (2008) 2–11.

Hendel, Ronald, and Saul M. Olyan. "Beyond Purity and Danger: Mary Douglas and The Hebrew Bible." *Journal of Hebrew Scriptures* 8.7 (2008) 2–4.

Holtz, Barry, ed. *Back to the Sources: Reading the Classic Jewish Texts*. New York: Simon & Schuster, 1984.

House, Paul R., ed. *Beyond Form Criticism: Essays in Old Testament Literary Criticism*. Winona Lake, IN: Eisenbrauns, 1992.

Houston, Walter J. "Tragedy in the Courts of the Lord: A Socio-Literary Reading of the Death of Nadab and Abihu." *Journal for the Study of the Old Testament* 25.90 (2000) 31–39.

Hubert, Henri, and Marcel Mauss. *Sacrifice: Its Nature and Function*. Translated by W. D. Halls. London: Cohen & West, 1964.

Hutton, Rodney R. "The Case of the Blasphemer Revisited." *Vetus Testamentum* 49 (1999) 532–41.

BIBLIOGRAPHY

Huxley, Aldous. *Brave New World*. London: Chatto & Windus, 1932.
Jacobs, A. J. *The Year of Living Biblically: One Man's Humble Quest to Follow the Bible as Literally as Possible*. New York: Simon & Schuster, 2008.
Jaffee, Martin S. *Torah in the Mouth: Writing and Oral Tradition in Palestinian Judaism 200 BCE–400 CE*. New York: Oxford University Press, 2001.
Jenni, Ernst, and Claus Westermann. *Theological Lexicon of the Old Testament*. Translated by Mark E. Biddle. Peabody, MA: Hendrickson, 1997.
Johnson, Christopher. "Before Babel: Lévi-Strauss and Language." In *The Cambridge Companion to Lévi-Strauss*, edited by Boris Wiseman, 237–54. Cambridge: Cambridge University Press, 2009.
Jones, Robert Alun. "Robertson Smith, Durkheim, and Sacrifice: An Historical Context for the Elementary Forms of the Religious Life." *Journal of the History of the Behavioral Sciences* 17.2 (1981) 184–205.
Joüon, Paul, and T. Muraoka. *A Grammar of Biblical Hebrew*. Rev. English ed. Subsidia Biblica 27. Rome: Editrice Pontificio Istituto biblico, 2006.
Kamionkowski, S. Tamar. *Leviticus*. Wisdom Commentary 3. Collegeville, MN: Liturgical, 2018.
———. "'שם' של תאולוגיה לכוהנים היתה ?האם / Did the Priests Have a 'Name' Theology?" *Iggud: Selected Essays in Jewish Studies* (2005) 21–38.
Kaufmann, Yehezkel. *The Religion of Israel: From Its Beginnings to the Babylonian Exile*. Translated and abridged by Moshe Greenberg. Chicago: University of Chicago Press, 1960.
Kearney, Richard. *Dialogues with Contemporary Continental Thinkers*. Manchester: Manchester University Press, 1984.
———. *On Paul Ricoeur: The Owl of Minerva*. New York: Routledge, 2004.
Keck, Frédéric. "The Limits of Classification: Claude Lévi-Strauss and Mary Douglas." In *The Cambridge Companion to Lévi-Strauss*, edited by Boris Wiseman, 139–55. Cambridge: Cambridge University Press, 2009.
Keen, Karen R. *Scripture, Ethics, and the Possibility of Same-Sex Relationships*. Grand Rapids: Eerdmans, 2018.
Kirk, G. S. "Some Methodological Pitfalls in the Study of Ancient Greek Sacrifice (In Particular)." In *Le Sacrifice dans l'Antiquité: Huit Exposés Suivis de Discussions: Vandœvres-Genève, 25–30 Août 1980*, edited by Jean-Pierre Vernant et al., 41–80. Entretiens Sur l'Antiquité Classique 27. Geneva: Fondation Hardt, 1981.
Kirschner, Robert. "The Rabbinic and Philonic Exegeses of the Nadab and Abihu Incident (Lev 10:1–6)." *Jewish Quarterly Review* 73 (1983) 375–93.
Klawans, Jonathan. *Purity, Sacrifice, and the Temple: Symbolism and Supersessionism in the Study of Ancient Judaism*. New York: Oxford University Press, 2006.
———. "Rethinking Leviticus and Rereading Purity and Danger." *Association for Jewish Studies. AJS Review; Cambridge* 27.1 (2003) 89–101.
Knohl, Israel. *The Sanctuary of Silence: The Priestly Torah and the Holiness School*. Minneapolis: Fortress, 1995.
Knoppers, Gary N., and Bernard M. Levinson. *The Pentateuch as Torah: New Models for Understanding Its Promulgation and Acceptance*. Winona Lake, IN: Eisenbrauns, 2007.
Koehler, Ludwig, and Walter Baumgartner. *The Hebrew and Aramaic Lexicon of the Old Testament*. Translated and edited by M. E. J. Richardson. 2 vols. Leiden: Brill, 2001.

Kugel, James L. *Midrash and Literature*. Edited by Geoffrey H. Hartman and Sanford Budick. New Haven: Yale University Press, 1986.

———. "Two Introductions to Midrash." *Prooftexts* 3 (1983) 131–55.

———. *The Idea of Biblical Poetry: Parallelism and Its History*. New Haven: Yale University Press, 1981.

LaCocque, André, and Paul Ricoeur. *Thinking Biblically: Exegetical and Hermeneutical Studies*. Translated by David Pellauer. Chicago: University of Chicago Press, 1998.

Lam, Joseph. "On the Etymology of Biblical Hebrew: A Contribution to the 'Sin Offering' vs. 'Purification Offering' Debate." *Journal of Semitic Studies* 65.2 (2020) 325–46.

Landy, Francis, Leigh M. Trevaskis, and Bryan D. Bibb, eds. *Text, Time, and Temple: Literary, Historical and Ritual Studies in Leviticus*. Hebrew Bible Monographs 64. Sheffield: Sheffield Phoenix, 2015.

Langer, Ruth. "From Study of Scripture to a Reenactment of Torah." *Worship* 72.1 (1998) 43–67.

Latour, Bruno. *Reassembling the Social: An Introduction to Actor-Network Theory*. Oxford: Oxford University Press, 2005.

Laughlin, John C. H. "The 'Strange Fire' of Nadab and Abihu." *Journal of Biblical Literature* 95 (1976) 559–65.

Lawrence, Louise J., and Mario I. Aguilar, eds. *Anthropology and Biblical Studies: Avenues of Approach*. Leiden: Deo, 2004.

Leach, E. R. *Culture and Communication: The Logic by Which Symbols Are Connected: An Introduction to the Use of Structuralist Analysis in Social Anthropology*. Themes in the Social Sciences. Cambridge: Cambridge University Press, 1976.

———. "The Structure of Symbolism." In *The Interpretation of Ritual: Essays in Honour of A. I. Richards*, edited by J. S. LaFontaine, 239–75. London: Tavistock, 1972.

Lemos, T. M. "The Universal and the Particular: Mary Douglas and the Politics of Impurity." *Journal of Religion* 89 (2009) 236–51.

Leuchter, Mark. "The Ambiguous Details in the Blasphemer Narrative: Sources and Redaction in Leviticus 24:10–23." *Journal of Biblical Literature* 130 (2011) 431–50.

———. "The Politics of Ritual Rhetoric: A Proposed Sociopolitical Context for the Redaction of Leviticus 1–16." *Vetus Testamentum* 60 (2010) 345–65.

Levenson, Jon D. *The Hebrew Bible, the Old Testament, and Historical Criticism: Jews and Christians in Biblical Studies*. Louisville: Westminster John Knox, 1993.

Levine, Baruch A. "Silence, Sound, and the Phenomenology of Mourning in Biblical Israel." *Journal of the Ancient Near Eastern Society* 22 (1993) 89–106.

———. *Leviticus*. JPS Torah Commentary. Philadelphia: Jewish Publication Society, 1989.

Lipschits, Oded. *The Fall and Rise of Jerusalem: Judah Under Babylonian Rule*. Winona Lake, IN: Eisenbrauns, 2005.

Lipschits, Oded et al., eds. *Judah and the Judeans in the Fourth Century BCE*. Winona Lake, IN: Eisenbrauns, 2007.

Liss, Hanna. "The Imaginary Sanctuary: The Priestly Code as an Example of Fictional Literature in the Hebrew Bible." In *Judah and the Judeans in the Persian Period*, edited by Oded Lipschits and Manfred Oeming, 663–89. Winona Lake, IN: Eisenbrauns, 2006.

Macé, Marielle. *Façons de Lire, Manières d'être*. Translated by Marlon Jones. Paris: Gallimard, 2011.

———. "Ways of Reading, Modes of Being." *New Literary History* 33 (2013) 213–29.
Magonet, Jonathan. "The Structure and Meaning of Leviticus 19." *Hebrew Annual Review* 7 (1983) 151–67.
Mann, Thomas W. *The Book of the Torah: The Narrative Integrity of the Pentateuch.* Atlanta: John Knox, 1988.
Marx, Alfred. "The Relationship between the Sacrificial Laws and the Other Laws in Leviticus 19." *The Journal of Hebrew Scriptures* 8 (2008). https://doi.org/10.5508/jhs.2008.v8.a9.
Mauss, Marcel. *The Gift.* Translated by Jane I. Guyer. Chicago: HAU, 2016.
Meyer, Esias E. "Getting Bad Publicity and Staying in Power: Leviticus 10 and Possible Priestly Power Struggles." *Hervormde Teologiese Studies* 69.1 (2013) 1–7.
Milgrom, Jacob. "A Prolegomenon to Leviticus 17:11." *Journal of Biblical Literature* 90 (1971) 149–56.
———. "Biblical Diet Laws as an Ethical System." *Interpretation* 17.3 (1963) 288–301.
———. *Cult and Conscience: The Asham and the Priestly Doctrine of Repentance.* Studies in Judaism in Late Antiquity 18. Leiden: Brill, 1976.
———. *Leviticus 1–16. A New Translation with Introduction and Commentary.* Anchor Yale Bible 3. New Haven: Yale University Press, 1991.
———. *Leviticus 17–22. A New Translation with Introduction and Commentary.* Anchor Yale Bible 3a. New Haven: Yale University Press, 2000.
———. *Leviticus 23–27. A New Translation with Introduction and Commentary.* Anchor Yale Bible 3b. New Haven: Yale University Press, 2001.
———. *Leviticus: A Book of Ritual and Ethics.* Continental Commentary. Minneapolis: Fortress, 2004.
Miller, Carolyn R. "Genre as Social Action." *Quarterly Journal of Speech* 70.2 (1984) 151–67.
Miller, Patrick D. *The Religion of Ancient Israel.* Library of Ancient Israel. Louisville: Westminster John Knox, 2000.
Moffitt, David M. *Atonement and the Logic of Resurrection in the Epistle to the Hebrews.* Novum Testamentum Supplements 141. Leiden: Brill, 2011.
Muilenburg, James. "Form Criticism and Beyond." *Journal of Biblical Literature* 88 (1969) 1–18.
Musser, Sarah Stokes. "Sacrifice, Sabbath, and the Restoration of Creation." PhD diss., Duke University, 2015.
Newsom, Carol A. "Pairing Research Questions and Theories of Genre: A Case Study of the Hodayot." *Dead Sea Discoveries* 17.3 (2010) 241–59.
———. "Rhetorical Criticism and the Reading of the Qumran Scrolls." In *The Oxford Handbook of the Dead Sea Scrolls*, edited by Timothy H. Lim and John J. Collins, 683–708. Oxford: Oxford University Press, 2010.
———. "Spying Out the Land: A Report from Genology." In *Bakhtin and Genre Theory in Biblical Studies*, edited by Roland Boer, 19–30. Semeia Studies 63. Atlanta: SBL Press, 2007.
Nihan, Christophe. *From Priestly Torah to Pentateuch: A Study in the Composition of the Book of Leviticus.* Forschungen zum Alten Testament 2/25. Tübingen: Mohr Siebeck, 2007.
Noth, Martin. *Leviticus: A Commentary.* Translated by J. S. Anderson. Old Testament Library. Philadelphia: Westminster John Knox, 1977.

Olyan, Saul M. "Mary Douglas's Holiness/Wholeness Paradigm: Its Potential for Insight and Its Limitations." *Journal of Hebrew Scriptures* 8.10 (2008) https://doi.org/10.5508/jhs.2008.v8.a10.

Origen of Alexandria. *Homilies on Leviticus: 1–16*. Translated by Gary Wayne Barkley. The Fathers of the Church: A New Translation 83. Washington, DC: Catholic University of America, 1990.

Paddison, Angus, and Neil Messer, eds. *The Bible: Culture, Community, Society*. New York: Bloomsbury T. & T. Clark, 2013.

Paltridge, Brian. *Genre, Frames, and Writing in Research Settings*. Philadelphia: Benjamins, 1997.

Paran, Meir. *Forms of the Priestly Style in the Pentateuch: Patterns, Linguistic Usages, Syntactic Structures*. Jerusalem: Magnes, 1989.

Patrick, Dale. *Old Testament Law*. 1985. Reprint, Eugene, OR: Wipf & Stock, 2011.

Patrick, Dale, and Allen Scult. *Rhetoric and Biblical Interpretation*. Journal for the Study of the Old Testament Supplements 82. Sheffield: Almond, 1990.

Petersen, David L., and Kent Harold Richards. *Interpreting Hebrew Poetry*. Guides to Biblical Scholarship: Old Testament Series. Minneapolis: Fortress, 1992.

Philo. *The Works of Philo: Complete and Unabridged*. Translated by C. D. Yonge. Peabody, MA: Hendrickson, 1993.

Polen, Nehemia. "Leviticus and Hebrews . . . and Leviticus." In *The Epistle to the Hebrews and Christian Theology*, edited by Richard Bauckham et al., 213–25. Grand Rapids: Eerdmans, 2009.

———. "Vayikra: Touches of Intimacy." In *A New Hasidism: Branches*, edited by Arthur Green and Ariel Evan Mayse, 41–72. Lincoln, NE: Jewish Publication Society, 2019.

Rendsburg, Gary. "The Two Screens: On Mary Douglas's Proposal for a Literary Structure to the Book of Leviticus." *Jewish Studies Quarterly* 15 (2008) 175–89.

Rendtorff, Rolf. *Problem of the Process of Transmission in the Pentateuch*. Translated by John J. Scullion. Journal for the Study of the Old Testament Supplements 89. Sheffield: JSOT, 1990.

Rendtorff, Rolf, and Robert A. Kugler, eds. *The Book of Leviticus: Composition and Reception*. Vetus Testamentum Supplements 93. Leiden: Brill, 2003.

Ricoeur, Paul. "Biblical Hermeneutics." *Semeia* 4 (1975) 29–148.

———. *The Conflict of Interpretations*. Edited by Don Ihde. Northwestern University Studies in Phenomenology & Existential Philosophy, Essays in Hermeneutics 1. Evanston: Northwestern University Press, 1974.

———. *Essays on Biblical Interpretation*. Edited by Lewis S. Mudge. Philadelphia: Fortress, 1980.

———. *Figuring the Sacred: Religion, Narrative, and Imagination*. Edited by Mark I. Wallace. Translated by David Pellauer. Minneapolis: Fortress, 1995.

———. *From Text to Action: Essays in Hermeneutics, II*. Translated by Kathleen Blamey and John B. Thompson. Northwestern University Studies in Phenomenology and Existential Philosophy. Evanston: Northwestern University Press, 1991.

———. *Hermeneutics and the Human Sciences*. Translated by John B. Thompson. Cambridge Philosophy Classics. Cambridge: Cambridge University Press, 2016.

———. *Interpretation Theory: Discourse and the Surplus of Meaning*. Fort Worth: Texas Christian University Press, 1976.

———. *A Ricoeur Reader: Reflection and Imagination*. Edited by Mario J. Valdés. Buffalo: University of Toronto Press, 1991.

———. *Time and Narrative*. Translated by Kathleen McLaughlin and David Pellauer. Chicago: University of Chicago Press, 1985.
Rilke, Rainer Maria. *Letters to a Young Poet*. London: Penguin Random House, 2016.
Rogerson, J. W., ed. *Leviticus in Practice*. Practice Interpretation 3. Blandford Forum, UK: Deo, 2014.
Sacks, Jonathan. *Leviticus: The Book of Holiness*. Covenant & Conversation: A Weekly Reading of the Jewish Bible. New Milford, CT: Maggid, 2015.
Sawyer, John F. A., and Mary Douglas, eds. *Reading Leviticus: A Conversation with Mary Douglas*. Journal for the Study of the Old Testament Supplements 227. Sheffield: Sheffield Academic, 1996.
Schmid, Konrad. *Genesis and the Moses Story: Israel's Dual Origins in the Hebrew Bible*. Winona Lake, IN: Eisenbrauns, 2010.
Schniedewind, William M. *How the Bible Became a Book: The Textualization of Ancient Israel*. New York: Cambridge University Press, 2004.
Schwartz, Baruch J. "Leviticus." In *The Jewish Study Bible*, edited by Adele Berlin and Marc Zvi Brettler, 203–6. Oxford: Oxford University Press, 2004.
Schwarzwalder, Rob. "The Bible's Teaching on Homosexuality: Clear, Final, and Sufficient." *The Christian Post*, March 25, 2015. https://www.christianpost.com/news/the-bibles-teaching-on-homosexuality-clear-final-and-sufficient-136339/
Sedgewick, Eve Kosofsky. *Touching Feeling: Affect, Pedagogy, Performativity*. Durham: Duke University Press, 2003.
Sherwood, Stephen K. *Leviticus, Numbers, Deuteronomy*. Berit Olam. Liturgical, 2002.
Ska, Jean-Louis, and Pascale Dominique. *Introduction to Reading the Pentateuch*. Winona Lake, IN: Eisenbrauns, 2006.
Smith, Christopher R. "The Literary Structure of Leviticus." *Journal for the Study of the Old Testament* 21.70 (1996) 17–32.
Smith, Jonathan Z. *To Take Place: Toward Theory in Ritual*. Chicago: University of Chicago Press, 1992.
Sommer, Benjamin D. *The Bodies of God and the World of Ancient Israel*. New York: Cambridge University Press, 2009.
Steiner, George. *After Babel: Aspects of Language and Translation*. 3rd ed. New York: Oxford University Press, 1998.
———. *George Steiner at The New Yorker*. Edited by Robert Boyers. New York: New Directions, 2009.
———. *Grammars of Creation*. New Haven: Yale University Press, 2001.
———. *On Difficulty: And Other Essays*. New York: Oxford University Press, 1978.
———. *Real Presences*. Chicago: University of Chicago Press, 1991.
Steiner, George, and Laurie Adler. *A Long Saturday: Conversations*. Translated by Teresa Lavender Fagan. Chicago: University of Chicago Press, 2017.
Stern, David S. *Midrash and Theory: Ancient Jewish Exegesis and Contemporary Literary Studies*. Evanston: Northwestern University Press, 1996.
Strack, Herman L., and Gunter Stemberger. *Introduction to the Talmud and Midrash*. Translated by Markus Bockmeuhl. Edinburgh: T. & T. Clark, 1991.
Taylor, Charles. *The Language Animal: The Full Shape of the Human Linguistic Capacity*. Cambridge: Belknap, 2016.
Trevaskis, Leigh M. "The Purpose of Leviticus 24 within Its Literary Context." *Vetus Testamentum* 59 (2009) 295–312.

Trible, Phyllis. *Rhetorical Criticism: Context, Method, and the Book of Jonah.* Overtures to Biblical Theology. Minneapolis: Fortress, 1994.

Turner, Wayne A. *Leviticus.* Collegeville Bible Commentary. Old Testament 4. Collegeville, MN: Liturgical, 1985.

Vanhoozer, Kevin J. *Biblical Narrative in the Philosophy of Paul Ricoeur: A Study in Hermeneutics and Theology.* Cambridge: Cambridge University Press, 1990.

Vis, Joshua M. "The Purification Offering of Leviticus and the Sacrificial Offering of Jesus." PhD diss., Duke University, 2012.

Volf, Miroslav, and Matthew Croasmun. *For the Life of the World: Theology That Makes a Difference.* Grand Rapids: Brazos, 2019.

Vroom, Jonathan. "Recasting *Mišpāṭîm*: Legal Innovation in Leviticus 24:10–23." *Journal of Biblical Literature* 131 (2012) 27–44.

Wagner, Roy. "Ritual as Communication: Order, Meaning, and Secrecy in Melanesian Initiation Rites." *Annual Review of Anthropology* 13 (1984) 143–55.

Waltke, Bruce K., and M. O'Connor. *An Introduction to Biblical Hebrew Syntax.* Winona Lake, IN: Eisenbrauns, 1990.

Warning, Wilfried. *Literary Artistry in Leviticus.* Biblical Interpretation Series 35. Leiden: Brill, 1999.

Watson, Duane F. and Alan J. Hauser. *Rhetorical Criticism of the Bible: A Comprehensive Bibliography with Notes on History and Method.* Biblical Interpretation Series 4. Leiden: Brill, 1994.

Watts, James W. *Ritual and Rhetoric in Leviticus: From Sacrifice to Scripture.* Cambridge: Cambridge University Press, 2007.

———. *Reading Law: The Rhetorical Shaping of the Pentateuch.* Biblical Seminar 59. Sheffield: Sheffield Academic, 1999.

Wedderburn, A. J. M. "Theologizing Dangerously *Ad Hebreos*." *Journal of Theological Studies* 56 (2005) 393–414.

Weingreen, J. "The Case of the Blasphemer (Leviticus XXIV 10 ff.)." *Vetus Testamentum* 22 (1972) 118–23.

Wellek, René, and Austin Warren. *Theory of Literature.* New York: Harcourt, Brace, 1945.

Wellhausen, Julius. *Prolegomena to the History of Israel.* Scholars Press Reprints and Translation Series. Atlanta: Scholars, 1994.

Wells, Bruce. "Punishments in the Torah and Their Rationale." *Journal for Ancient Near Eastern and Biblical Law* 22 (2016) 245–67.

Wenham, Gordon J. *The Book of Leviticus.* New International Commentary on the Old Testament. Grand Rapids: Eerdmans, 1979.

———. "The Old Testament and Homosexuality." In *Guarding the Gospel: Bible, Cross and Mission*, edited by Chris Green, 155–60. Grand Rapids: Zondervan, 2006.

———. "The Old Testament Attitude to Homosexuality." *Expository Times* 102.12 (1991) 359–63.

Whitekettle, Richard. "Leviticus 15.18 Reconsidered: Chiasm, Spatial Structure and the Body." *Journal for the Study of the Old Testament* 49 (1991) 31–45.

Wiener, Nancy H., and Jo Hirschmann. *Maps and Meaning: Levitical Models for Contemporary Care.* Minneapolis: Fortress, 2014.

Williams, Ronald J. *Williams' Hebrew Syntax.* 3rd ed. Toronto: University of Toronto Press, 2007.

Wright, David P. "Deciphering a Definition: The Syntagmatic Structural Analysis of Ritual in the Hebrew Bible." *Journal of Hebrew Scriptures* 8.12 (2008). https://doi.org/10.5508/jhs.2008.v8.a12.

———. "Holiness in Leviticus and Beyond." *Interpretation* 53 (1999) 351–64.

———. "The Gesture of Hand Placement in the Hebrew Bible and in Hittite Literature." *Journal of the American Oriental Society* 106 (1986) 433–46.

Zahn, Molly M. "Genre and Rewritten Scripture: A Reassessment." *Journal of Biblical Literature* 131 (2012) 271–88.

Index

Aaron, 95–96, 154–85
Achenbach, Reinhard, 154n3, 159n15
actor network theory, 45
address form, 36
allegorical interpretation, 14
Alter, Robert, 53n58, 57
ambiguity, 4, 32–35, 125, 150–52
analogy, 5, 17, 34–35, 49, 144–46
anger, 168–69, 173
animal taxonomy, 15–16, 19
anthropology, 12–13, 16, 26, 68, 72
antiritualism, 17–18
appropriation, 30, 44
Aristotle, 31
atomization, 9–10, 19–20, 163
atonement, 24, 74, 138, 149
authorial intent, 32–35, 41–45
Avihu. *See* Nadav and Avihu

Baker, David W., 30n92
Bakhtin, Mikhail, 36
Balentine, Samuel E., 81–82, 86
Bauckham, Richard, 8n9
Beebee, Thomas O., 28n81
Bell, Catherine, 94n2
Berlin, Adele, 23n61, 53n58, 56n67
Bernstein, Basil, 94
Berry, Wendell, 48
bias, 6–12, 16–19, 31, 34, 78
Bibb, Bryan, 30, 85–86, 162
Bildung, 40
blasphemer, narrative of the, xv, 120–52

blasphemy, 124, 132–35, 139–47
blemish, 129, 142, 145
Boer, Roland, 23n60
boundaries, 77, 102–4, 111–14, 137–39, 143–48. *See also* separations
Briggs, Richard S., 51–52
Buber, Martin, 98
Buss, Martin, 36–37

Cain and Abel, 95, 102
Carr, David M., 23n60
Carson, Anne, 153, 186–90
chaos, 107–11, 114, 132–39
character development, 170–71, 178–83
Chavel, Simeon, 137n55
chiasm, 24, 55–56, 140, 165–66
Christ event, 7
Citton, Yves, 45
classification
    animal, 15–16, 19
    system(s), 12–17
Collins, John J., 11n18, 28n83
communication,
    mediatory function of, 102–3
    mode(s) of, 28–36, 57, 74, 80
    non-verbal, 94–95, 100–105
    sacrifice as, 94–106
    symbolic, 26, 105–6
    See also genre
communicative function, 29–36, 85
community formation, 94, 178–79
comparative, 12–15, 72

205

complex words, 68–72
composite. *See* literary composition
composition history, 10, 25, 163n30
Comrie, Bernard, 84
conditional statements, 4, 83
confession, 109, 114–17, 149. *See also* repentance
connotation, 41, 65–66
contagion, 137–38, 144, 148–49
contamination, 136, 64–66, 146. *See also* pollution; שקץ / *sheqetz*; טמא / *tamei*
context(s)
  contemporary, 52
  historical, 31–37, 63–66
  interpretive, 12–16 passim, 41–46
  literary, 9, 76
  narrative, 95–97
  readerly, 48, 50, 62, 87–90, 189
courage, 186
covenant, 7–8, 72, 106, 175
covenantal justice, 18
coverings, 131–32, 137–40
creation, 26, 65–66, 82–83, 97, 138. *See also* order
creativity, xiii, 35, 40, 43–44, 106
Crüsemann, Frank, 27
Culler, Jonathan, 29n87
cultic legislation, 7–8, 83n77
curiosity, 78–79
cursing, 124, 132–35, 139–47

Damrosch, David, 27, 53, 85n85, 174
Darnahung, 99
Davis, Ellen F., 11, 48–50, 57, 78–79, 88
deconstructive, 139
decreative, 139, 148. *See also* chaos; sacrilege
defilement, 13–14, 24, 144–45. *See also* contamination; pollution
deicide, 137n55
Dershowitz, Idan, 76
descriptive, 26, 43, 80, 87, 100
desire, 50, 58, 157, 186. *See also* love
destructive
  interpretation, 77
  speech, 113, 120, 143–48 passim

development. *See* character development
developmentalism, 8–9, 17–18
Devitt, Amy J., 33n103
dialogical
  relationships, 36–37
  situation, 41
dialogue, 36–37, 41, 93, 165, 173
dietary laws, 12–19 passim
difficulty
  contingent, 62–73, 158, 182
  generativity of, 87–89, 187–90
  of interpretation, 60–61, 154
  modal, 73–79, 87–88
  tactical, 79–88, 148–52, 182
dignity, 104, 118
direction of thought, 43, 56–58, 79, 87, 187
dirt, 14–17 passim. *See also* impurity; pollution
discernment, 20–22, 148–52, 178–84
discourse
  alternative, 4, 89, 100–101
  biblical, 36–37
  contemporary, xii–xiv, 31–37, 51–52, 188–89
  definition of, 40–43, 100
  divine, 4, 52, 80, 165–67, 187
  event of, 3–5, 41–43, 50–51, 87
  generativity of, xiii, 5, 87–89, 106, 187
  mediatory function of, 4–5, 101–3, 187
  moral/ethical, xii–xiv. *See also* priestly vision
  poetic, 57, 74
  sacrifice as, 94–106
  literary presentation of, xiii–xv, 5, 74
disfigurement, 124, 142
distance, 75, 87–88, 186–90
distanciation of meaning, 42, 44, 88
distinction(s), priestly, 20, 64–66, 80, 139, 147
Dornisch, Loretta, 39n4
Douglas, Mary, 12–24 passim, 34–35, 55–56, 94–95, 137–41, 174–76
drinking ordeal, 172
Duff, David, 29n84

INDEX

Dupont, Joanne M., 127n20, 129
Durkheim, Émile, 13, 15

ecology, 20–21, 48–50, 67
Eliasen, Karen C., 161n20, 181n66
Elliott, Mark W., 10n17
embodiment, 74, 104–6
emotions, 99, 179–80, 181n66
encounter
  with difference, ix–xvi, 78, 186–87
  human and divine, 87–88, 98–99, 103–4
  reading as, xiv, 38, 43–46
  See also קרבן / *qorban*
enigma of the unnamed fish, 66–68
equivalence, 125, 140–43, 147–48. *See also* retribution; talion laws
Erklären, 42
eruptions, 137–40, 142–46 passim, 150–51
ethical/moral vision, 11–19 passim, 26, 49, 52. *See also* values
Evans-Pritchard, E. E., 13, 17
event of discourse, 3–5, 41–43, 50–51, 87
evolutionism, 8–9, 17–18

Felski, Rita, 44–46
final form, xv, 24–25, 55, 64
fire, outside 131, 156–58, 171–74
Fishbane, Michael, 126n16
flourishing, 21, 117, 140, 184
food laws, 12–19 passim
form criticism, 23
formation, community, 94, 178–79
Fowler, Alastair, 29n85
Fox, Everett, 54, 57, 96, 99, 108, 111
fragmentation, 9–10, 19–20, 163
Fuad, Chelcent, 125, 130n32

Gadamer, Hans Georg, 43n23, 45, 60n3
Gagnon, Robert A., 76
gaps, xiii, 40, 87, 162–63. *See also* distance; distanciation; silence, textual
Garsiel, Moshe, 130
Gattungen, 23
Gattungsforschung, 23

generativity
  of difficulty, 87–89, 187–90
  of speech, xiii, 5, 87–89, 106, 187
  See also creativity; difficulty
generosity, 118
genre(s)
  legal instruction, 25–28, 161–62
  of Leviticus, 23–30
  narrative, 27, 29
  poetry, 53–57, 74, 80
  prose, 4–5, 27, 52–53, 80–83
  theory, 23, 28–30, 33n103, 36–37
גר / *ger*, 124–25, 136
Gerstenberger, Erhard S., 6, 122, 160, 163–64
Gese, Hartmut, 70n34
gift exchange, 101–3
golden calf, 106, 155, 170–78
Gorman, Frank H., Jr., 26
grammar
  of Leviticus, 4–5, 79, 81, 84
  of sacrifice, 97–99, 103
grammatical tense, 4–5
Gunkel, Hermann, 23

Halbertal, Moshe, 97n8, 102–3
חטאת / *hattat*, 19, 68–72, 168–89
Hays, Richard B., 8n9
Hebrews, Letter to the, 7–9
Heidegger, Martin, 39, 45
Held, Shai, xi, 119, 170–80
Hénaff, Marcel, 97n8, 101–3
hermeneutical arc, 42–43
hermeneutic(s)
  affective, 45
  approaches, 39–46
  philosophical, 60n3
  of suspicion, 45n26
Hirschman, Jo, 46–48, 189
historical criticism, xii, 10–11, 26, 30
historical reconstruction, 33–35
Holiness School, xiv
Holiness source (H), xiv, 17–18, 55
holiness, 49–50, 77, 118–19, 137–40, 151
homosexuality, 21–22, 75–77
horizon(s), 43–44, 50, 52, 77–79, 89
Horizonverschmelzung, 44n23
Houston, Walter J., 160n16, 180n63

INDEX

Hubert, Henri, 99*n*20, 101, 105
Hutton, Rodney R., 132*n*38, 133–35

identity, 94–97, 118–19, 125, 130
imagination, 5, 40, 44, 85, 88, 153
imago Dei, 4, 119, 142, 147
impurity, 65, 70, 72, 142, 146. *See also* dirt; pollution
indeterminacy, 5, 40, 83–87, 111, 114
instructions, 24–28, 56–57, 81–85, 98, 103
interpretation
   allegorical, 14
   anthropological, xii, 16, 26
   art of, 42, 60
   canonical, 23, 76*n*59
   defined, 44, 46, 189
   historical. *See* historical criticism
   literary, xii–xiii, 14–15, 25, 34–35, 52, 57
   object of, xii–xiii, 39–44, 57, 189
   process of, 4–5, 20, 42, 44, 90
   provisionality of, 4–5, 85, 90, 182–85
   rhetorical critical, xii, 30–36
   situational, 179–83
   spiritual, 14
   synchronic, xv, 16, 24*n*63, 25
   theological, 10–11, 79, 140–47, 161–62
immediacy, 4–5, 33, 41–42, 179
interpretive traditions, 5*n*2, 10, 23

Jackson, Wes, 48
Josephus, 180*n*63
jubilee, 21
justice, 116, 131, 140, 150–52. *See also* covenantal

Kamionkowski, Tamar S., 126, 134, 139, 158–59
Kaufmann, Yehezkel, xiv
Kearney, Richard, xi, 39*n*2, 42*n*19, 44
Keen, Karen R., 76*n*58
כפר / *kipper*, 63, 70–72
Kirschner, Robert, 157*n*4, 158*n*7
Klawans, Jonathan, 8–9, 13*n*24, 22, 23*n*59
Knohl, Israel, xiv–xv, 17–18, 64*n*17

knowledge, 42*n*17, 45*n*26, 60–62, 87, 186. *See also* understanding
Korah motif, 51, 160
Kugel, James L., 9, 53*n*58

Lam, Joseph, 69*n*29
language
   as discourse, 40
   generativity of, 106, 110–11, 114–17
   mediatory function of, 4–5, 39–40
   polysemy of, 40, 105–6
   power of, 89, 117, 119–20, 147, 188
   role of, 39–41, 95, 113, 118–19, 188
   symbolic, 4, 57, 94–95, 99–100, 106
langue, 40*n*6
Latour, Bruno, 45
law(s)
   conditional, 83
   dietary, 12–19 passim
   genre of, 25–28, 83–84
   and narrative, 26–30, 161–62, 179
   purity, 14–18, 139–40, 150. *See also* impurity
   vs. spirit, 7–9
Leach, Edmund Ronald, 95
leadership, 96, 155, 170, 179, 185
legal
   anthology, 19
   instructions, 27–28, 161, 182
   reasoning, 28
leitmotif, 54
Leuchter, Mark, 130*n*31, 159*n*12, 179*n*59
Levine, Baruch, 63, 108, 112, 148, 180
LGBTQ, 21–22, 75–77
liminality, 46, 102, 112–14, 139, 189–90
linguistic structuralism, 40*n*6
Liss, Hannah, 53
literary
   artistry, 24–30 passim, 130
   composition, 10, 24–25, 64, 163
   context, 14–15, 44–45, 76
   foil, 28*n*83, 158, 180–81
   interpretation, xii–xiii, 14–15, 25, 34–35, 52, 57
   portrayal, 80–87, 93, 164
   representation, 5, 26, 34
   structure, xiv, 10, 25–26, 55–56
   style, 4–5, 51–57

INDEX

literature, rabbinic 9, 157, 182*n*69
liturgy, xiv, 82
logic, 8, 14–20, 50, 74, 139, 150. *See also* priestly logic
love, 43, 77, 113, 186–90. *See also* desire

Macé, Marielle, 45
Magonet, Jonathan, 30*n*92
maim, 142
Maimonides, 8
Mann, Thomas W., 51
Mauss, Marcel, 99*n*20, 101, 105
meaning
    of being, 39–46
    construction of, 28–29
    density of, 57, 69–73
    discernment of, 20, 38, 48
    fluidity of, 85
    orientation to, xi, 5, 31–35, 183
    structures of, 13–16
memory aids, 27
מקלל / *meqallel*, 122–52, 164*n*31
metaphorical dialogue, 36–37
metzora, 47–48. *See also* צרעת / *tzaraat*
Meyer, Esias E., 159*n*15, 160*n*18
מחוץ למחנה / *michutz lamachaneh*, 47–48
microcosms, 138
midrashic exegesis, 182*n*69
Milgrom, Jacob, xii, 6–24 passim, 66–73, 78
Miller, Carolyn R., 33*n*103
Miller, Patrick D., 99*n*18
מנחה / *minha*, 53, 101, 104, 107, 167–69
מצוות / *mitsvot*, 84. *See also* law(s)
Moffitt, David M., 8*n*9
moral evolutionism, 8–9, 17–18
moral/ethical vision, 11–19 passim, 26, 49, 52. *See also* values
morality, 9, 18, 76. *See also* values
Moses, 3–5, 106, 155–83 passim
Muilenburg, James, 30*n*92, 32*n*99, 33*n*101
murder, 19, 133*n*43, 135, 142
Musser, Sarah Stokes, 82–83, 97*n*8, 99*n*17

Nadav and Avihu, 131, 150, 156–82 passim

name theology, 126, 131–40
names, significance of, 127–31
narrative(s)
    context, 94–97. *See also* literary context
    frame, 4–5, 81, 140, 143
    gaps, 162–63
    genre, 27–29, 52, 74
    screens, 56, 123, 137, 161–62
    time, 4, 81–86, 122
New Covenant, 8
Newsom, Carol A., 23*n*60, 28, 29*n*84
Nihan, Christophe, 25, 27, 126, 154*n*3, 163
Noth, Martin, 6*n*3, 128

oaths, 107–14, 116, 142–43
objectivity, 11, 43*n*23, 88, 108, 185
אהל מועד / *Ohel Moed*, 4, 47–48. *See also* Tent of Meeting
עלה / *olah*, 53, 63, 107, 181
ontology, 39–40, 44, 87
oral tradition, 23, 27
order
    vs. chaos, 121, 132, 138–52 passim
    created, 49–50, 76, 111, 114–17
    of difficulty, 73, 78
    of perception, 87, 152
    social, 105
    system, 13, 19
    word, 98, 128
Origen of Alexandria, 121*n*1, 149*n*90
Otto, Eckart, 159*n*15

parallelism, 24, 54–55
Paran, Meir, 53
parole, 40*n*6
particularity, 40–41, 61, 179–84
pathos, 179–80
Patrick, Dale, 27–28, 33*n*101
peace offering. *See* זבח שלמים / *zevach shelamim*
pelting, 125–26, 140–52
pentateuchal formation, 7, 11, 126
perspective, 43*n*23, 77–79, 84–86, 180–85
persuasion, 31–32
Peterson, David L., 53*n*58

phenomenology, 39–40, 43n23, 45, 60n3
piercing, 132–40 passim
Plato, 186
poetry, 53–57, 65, 70–74, 79–80, 88
polemic, 8, 143, 159n12
Polen, Nehemia, 8n9, 72
pollution, 13–14, 17, 137, 144–45.
　　　See also contamination; dirt;
　　　impurity; שקץ / sheqetz; טמא /
　　　tamei
polycropping, 49
portrayal, 80–88, 93
power
　　of language, 89, 117, 119–20, 147,
　　　188
　　priestly, 159–61, 170, 178–79
prescriptive, 7, 26, 16, 85
priestly
　　exegesis, 154–79, 182n69, 184–84
　　literature, 53–57, 63, 70, 80, 154
　　logic, 14–20, 78, 136, 148, 150
　　ordination, 159, 162, 171–78
　　power, 159–61, 170, 178–79
　　rationale, 15–16, 20, 142
　　rhetoric, 30–36, 160. See also rhetoric
　　values, 15–18, 20, 34, 50, 95, 151
　　vision of life, 18, 77, 81–90 passim,
　　　155
　　vocation, 178–85
Priestly Code, 7, 53
Priestly source (PT, P), xiv, 10, 17–18,
　　64–65, 111
primitivism, 9, 16–17
provisionality, 4, 85, 90, 182
puns, 130–31
purification offering, 19, 68–72, 102,
　　168–89
purity, 12–18, 26, 79

Qohelet, 5, 83
קול אלה / qol olah, 107–8
קרבן / qorban, 97–98

rabbinic literature, 9, 157, 182n69
רצה / ratsah, 63
reading, xiii, 5, 30, 40–46, 52, 59, 74
reciprocity, 41, 61n4, 94, 103, 140–41
redaction criticism, 10, 25, 154, 163

regestalting, 88, 179–84, 189–90
Rendsburg, Gary, 25n66, 123n7
Rendtorff, Rolf, 24n62, 25n66, 70n34
reorientation, 88, 179–84, 189–90
repentance, 114–15. See also confession
repetition, 30, 53–57 passim, 148,
　　157–58
representation, 5, 26, 34, 85
reproductive processes, 137
resonance, 45, 51–57, 61, 73–79
responsibility, 19, 80, 145–46, 176–77
restricted codes, 94
retaliation, 140–41, 148. See also talion
　　laws
retribution, 128–31, 147. See also
　　equivalence, talion laws
revelatory process, 20, 189
rhetoric, 31–36, 160–63. See also
　　priestly rhetoric
rhetorical analysis, xii, 12, 30–36, 163
Richards, Kent H., 53n58
Ricoeur, Paul, xiii, 38–46, 57–58, 60–61
ring composition, 24, 55–56
risk, 61n4, 88 103, 183–84, 186–90. See
　　also trust
ritual(s)
　　as communication, 94–95, 105–6
　　interpretation, 17–18, 30–36, 71–72,
　　　85
　　meaning of, 15–16, 26, 34, 85
　　narrativized, 30
　　portrayal, 26–27, 34, 85–86
　　purity, 12–18, 26, 70–72, 110, 146
　　reading, 5n2
　　studies, 26, 30, 34, 36, 94
ritualization, 30, 85–86

sabbath, 82
Sacks, Jonathan, 6, 95, 99, 118
sacrifice
　　bias against, 8
　　as communication, 94–106
　　formative function of, 118–19
　　restrictions on, 19
　　telos of, 83n77
sacrilege, 111–14, 123, 136–39, 142,
　　161–62
סמך / samakh, 63, 146–47

INDEX

sanctification, 138
sanctity of life, 18–20
Sawyer, John F., 4, 83–84
Schniedewind, William M., 23*n*60
Schwartz, Baruch J., 125*n*14
Scult, Allen, 33*n*101
Sedgewick, Eve K., 45*n*26
self-orientation, xi–xvi, 44–46, 59
semantic autonomy, 41
semantics, 40*n*6
semiotics, 40*n*6
separations, 104, 138. *See also* boundaries
Shelomith, 127–30
שקץ / *sheqetz*, 64–66. *See also* contamination; pollution; טמא / *tamei*
Sherwood, Stephen K., 127*n*19, 128*n*23
silence
    Aaron's, 173–78, 180
    of sacrifice, xiv–xv, 93–95, 100–106
    textual, 66–68. *See also* gaps
sin offering (*hattat*), 19, 68–72, 168–89
Sinai pericope, 81–83, 106
Ska, Jean-Louis, 23*n*61
Smith, Christopher R., 25*n*68, 161*n*22
Smith, William Robertson, 13
Socrates, 186–87
source-criticism, xiv–xv, 15–18, 55, 64
speech
    absence of, 93–94, 100–101
    divine, 25*n*68, 52
    function of, xiv–xv, 188
    human, 105–21, 133–37
    as literary device, 90, 155, 164–71
    power of, 133–52, 188
    See also discourse; language
spiritual
    decline, 7–9
    meaning, 14
    separation, 121*n*1
Steiner, George, xiii, 60–87, 150, 188
stoning, 122, 125–26, 140–52
strange fire, 131, 156–58, 171–74
strong drink, 172, 174, 176
style
    linguistic, 26, 36
    literary, 4–5, 51–58, 74

symbol(ic)
    action, 104–6, 146–47
    expression, 26, 78
    language, 4
    significance, 50, 57, 104–6
    system(s), 13–18, 50
    value, 9
    works of culture, 39
synchronic, xv, 16, 24*n*63, 25
system(s)
    classification, 12–17
    dietary, 12, 14–16, 18
    ethical, 15, 16, 19, 26
    purity, 12–18, 26, 79
    ritual, 15–20, 26, 34, 36
    sacrificial, 14–16, 18–19, 94–106, 117–19
    symbol, 13–18, 50
    of thought, 15–18, 78
structuralism, 14–15, 40*n*6
structure, literary, xiv, 10, 25–26, 55–56
supersessionism, 7–9
superstition, 16

tabernacle, 24–25, 55–56, 123, 137–38, 179. *See also* אהל מועד / *Ohel Moed*; Tent of Meeting
tabula rasa, 6
talion laws, 124–25, 140–48. *See also* equivalence; retaliation; retribution
טמא / *tamei*, 47, 64–66, 145. *See also* contamination; pollution; שקץ / *sheqetz*
taxonomy, animal, 15–16, 19
Taylor, Charles, 60*n*3, 86–88, 184
tense, verbal, 4–5, 84
Tent of Meeting, 3–5, 98. *See also* אהל מועד / *Ohel Moed*
theological equivalence, 68, 140–48. *See also* talion laws
Thompson, John B., 40*n*6
transferability, 50, 52, 188
transformation, 41, 179, 189–90
transgenic engineering, 49–50
translation, 61, 68–87
trespass, 122–50 passim, 162–64
Trevaskis, Leigh, 123*n*5, 125*n*14

Trible, Phyllis, 23n61, 32n97, 32n99, 33
trust, 19, 61n4, 96, 106, 114, 116. *See also* risk
צרעת / *tzaraat*, 46–51, 137–50 passim. See also *metzora*

Umwelt, 43
understanding, 42–43, 60–61, 74–78, 188. *See also* knowledge
unrelatability, 73–74

values, 15–20, 31–34 passim, 51, 95, 151. *See also* moral/ethical vision; morality
Vanhoozer, Kevin J., 39, 42n19
verbal
    aggression, 133, 136, 139, 142, 147
    conditional, 4, 83
    forms, 4, 83–84
    imperative, 27–28, 84
    imperfective, 4–5, 83–84
    perfective, 84
    structure, 36, 84
    tense, 4–5, 84
Verstehen, 42

voluntary offerings, 99, 101–3, 107
Vroom, Jonathan, 125n14

Warning, Wilfried, 25n68, 123n5
Watts, James W., 30–36, 160, 163
Wedderburn, A. J. M., 8n9
Weingreen, J., 132n38
Wellhausen, Julius, 7–9
Welt, 43
Wenham, Gordon J., 6n3, 123n4
Whitekettle, Richard, 30n92
Wiener, Nancy H., 46–48
wisdom, 21, 50, 155, 177–79, 184–85
Wittgenstein, Ludwig, 29n86
worship, 7–9, 19, 86, 175
wrath, 168–69, 173
Wright, David P., 146
writing, 23n60, 41–42, 187

Yom Kippur, 70–72

Zahn, Molly M., 29n84, 33n103
זבח / *zevach*, 53, 97–98
זבח שלמים / *zevach shelamim*, 53, 97–98, 104, 107

www.ingramcontent.com/pod-product-compliance
Lightning Source LLC
Chambersburg PA
CBHW062023220426
43662CB00010B/1451